Hell for Leather

A Modern Cricket Journey

ROBERT WINDER

INDIGO

To Hermione, Luke and Kit

An Indigo Paperback
First published in Great Britain by Victor Gollancz in 1996
This paperback edition published in 1999 by Indigo
An imprint of Orion Books Ltd
Orion House, 5 Upper St Martin's Lane, London WC2H 9EA

A CIP catalogue record for this book is available from the British Library

ISBN 0 575 40092 7

Typeset in Great Britain by Rowland Phototypesetting Ltd
Bury St Edmunds, Suffolk
Printed and bound in Great Britain by
The Guernsey Press Co. Ltd, Guernsey C.I.

Hell For Leather

Robert Winder is Deputy Editor of *Granta*. Formerly Literary Editor of the *Independent*, he reported on the World Cup for that newspaper. He is the author of two novels, *No Admission* and *The Marriage of Time and Convenience*, and lives in London.

CONTENTS

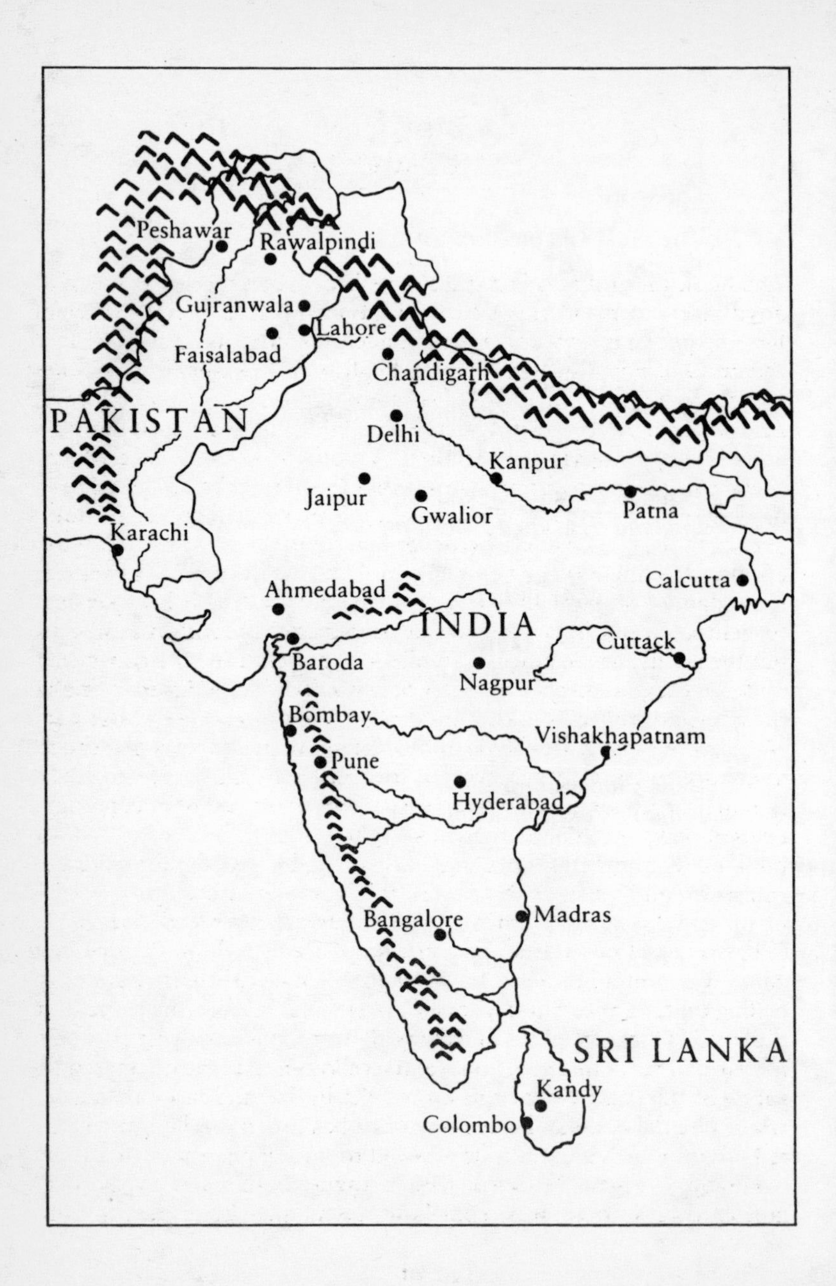
Peshawar
Rawalpindi
Gujranwala
Lahore
Faisalabad
Chandigarh
PAKISTAN
Delhi
Kanpur
Jaipur
Gwalior
Patna
Karachi
Calcutta
Ahmedabad
INDIA
Cuttack
Baroda
Nagpur
Bombay
Vishakhapatnam
Pune
Hyderabad
Bangalore
Madras
SRI LANKA
Kandy
Colombo

FOREWORD

The book that follows is a travelogue because cricket is, as much as anything, a form of travel. Even at the lowest level it is a matter of heaving gear into cars and nosing round unfamiliar roads in search of the ground. For a straightforward English professional, the summer months involve an exhaustive inspection of the country's motorways. And at the highest level it is a tense schedule of flights, coach journeys and overnight stops in airport hotels. A modern international cricketer spends more time in airport lounges than he does in the nets. If at times he plays as if he has a plane to catch, it is probably because he does.

I began the book as a cricket-lover for whom the game was a hobby. I finished feeling heavier-hearted, mainly because cricket has become, in England, a slightly dispirited affair. Many years of below-par performances by our international side have eroded the enthusiasm of all but the staunchest supporters, while so far as children are concerned cricket struggles – despite a variety of new initiatives designed to 'make the game attractive' – to capture the attention of anyone whose parents are not already wedded to it. Recently, I visited three sports shops in London in search of a cricket bat small enough for a five-year-old. In famous streets, where it is all too easy to buy any amount of cunningly devised ways for superheroes to slaughter aliens, the shops – full to bursting with training shoes, jogging gear, and baseball mitts – did not run to a child's bat. If these were the much-discussed 'grass roots' of the game, I thought, then they were already withered and thin.

I also began my journey as a cricket purist for whom the one-day game was a dumb, knockabout version of the real thing. I ended it feeling that, on the contrary, one-day cricket *is* cricket: the game as it is played in schools, parks and clubs all over the world. Test cricket is merely an elaborate extension – a marvellous and intricate one, to be sure – of the game most of us know. Yet in England more than anywhere else the one-day game is seen as a bastard, a grudgingly tolerated urchin which must not be allowed to undermine the main event.

Finally, I began the book with a vague attachment to the dim notion that cricket was somehow essentially English, that the manners and cutoms that grew up on our green pitches were still a decisive influence on the world game. Increasingly, I changed my mind. Of course I knew the line about how cricket was a West Indian game that happened to have been invented by the English, but I'd always thought this merely a charming pleasantry, a nice joke on our recent ineptness. Not until I stood in the raucous grandstands of the subcontinent and the Caribbean, or the hearty stadiums of South Africa, did I apprehend how thoroughly the balance of power – that is, the balance of enthusiasm – has swung. That Sri Lanka won the the 1996 World Cup was both illuminating and apt. The way they played gave a sunny boost to the idea of cricket as a vibrant and enticing spectacle.

There has been much talk, in the three years since the last World Cup, about the changes required to inject life into England's almost moribund domestic season. Some things have changed, thought not, perhaps, quite enough. Last summer, when England played South Africa in a half-empty Old Trafford, several thousand spectators who had gone to the trouble of buying tickets in advance failed to turn up. Watching England had, it seemed, become too glum and lacklustre an experience. And if these diehards were starting to think twice about going to Test matches, then what hope was there that they might ever by persuaded to take County cricket seriously again? This is something that only a decent run of international victories can heal. And since cricket, like any game, is playful and unpredictable, this might just happen.

It might not, however. Everyone involved in cricket knows that the 1999 World Cup is an important opportunity for English cricket to stake a vivid claim to national attention once again. Whether the game can seize the moment – or whether it will be left to television moguls to devise some new and more attention-grabbing cricket circus during the English summer – is another question. At the time of writing, it seems that the televising of England's Test matches will pass from the BBC over to satellite and cable television, and cease to be, in any obvious way, the kind of national event it once was. But blanket coverage of football on satellite channels does not seem to have damaged it; on the contrary, it has ignited an ever more avid following. Cricket has proved an infectious and durable game in the countries where it has taken root – countries imposed on by Britain's former empire, for the most part. Only a very confident pessimist would dare predict that its present confusions are anything other than a single chapter in a long and continuing story.

Robert Winder, London, 1998

— 1 —

THE FINAL CHAPTER

Lahore

It was half past ten on a damp and cloudy evening in Lahore. Streaks of drizzle fell from a black sky through dazzling floodlights, and the heavy, viscous roar of the crowd seemed to slop around in the concrete saucer of the Gaddafi Stadium. The 1996 World Cup Final was about to end. Out on the electric-green pitch the Australians, in their distinctive canary yellow plumage, waited hands-on-hip for the navy-blue Sri Lankans to knock off the winning runs. Columns of policemen, truncheons pockmarked by frequent use, circled the ground, and a gaggle of reinforcements with helmets and guns (five thousand of them) waited behind the concrete pavilion. It looked, if anything, like a video game: bowlers sprinted up in the centre of a shadowy X cast by the burning lights as if they were being shoved by a cursor. The Lahore crowd seemed to leap and writhe with pleasure. Apart from a handful of plucky Aussie backpackers and a few officials, everyone was shouting for Sri Lanka. Aravinda De Silva, on 103, cuffed yet another four across the shining outfield, and the crowd rose. The scores were level.

Down in the dark, windowless television control room, lit only by the banks of television screens relaying pictures from the cameras round the ground, they knew that victory was imminent; they had known it for an hour or more. 'Here we go,' murmured the (English) director, Gary Franses, into his mouthpiece. 'This could be it. Tight on the batsman, four. And get me some Sri Lankan flags. Greigy, can you give me a nice Sri Lanka win bite?' The South African born, neo-Australian, former England captain Tony Greig, in the commentary position three floors above, answered the call without a pause: 'One more run to win this World Cup!' he cried. 'This is a great moment for these Sri Lankans! What'll they be doing down in Colombo, I wonder!'

In the press room, sheltered from the vibrant atmosphere by thick glass (a spooky concession to peace and quiet: it was like watching the match on television, only with the sound down), reporters nodded and switched on their computers. In the hospitality boxes, government officers from Pakistan (and their relatives and friends) applauded the fact that, for the first time, a host nation had won the cup. Many of these seats had been commandeered at the last minute, leaving their rightful owners – about five hundred corporate guests – wandering the corridors, tickets in hand but with nowhere to go. Bishen Bedi, the former Indian left-arm spinner, was turned out of his seat, along with his wife; so was the legendary batsman Mansur Ali Pataudi. Several big names returned to their hotels in a huff. And there were a few of what the papers, next morning, described as 'unseemly exchanges' – meaning punches.

Some ticket holders could not even get into the ground. Mick Jagger took one look at the queue and went back to sit in his car while his hosts tried to wangle a special pass for him. Meanwhile, in the VIP enclosure, the Prime Minister, Benazir Bhutto, prepared to go down and hand over the antique silver (tempting to call it De Silver) trophy – bought from Garrards in London – to the winning captain. And only a few yards away stood the man her government had effectively blackballed from the competition, the man who had become a national hero when he brought Pakistan victory in the last World Cup and who was now an uncomfortably popular political opponent. Imran Khan was in a box sponsored by Pace, a Tesco-style supermarket chain, along with his wife and pals – Jagger, for instance. When Benazir arrived the stadium shrieked with whistles in a drastic burst of highly charged dislike. Imran stood on the balcony in his eye-catching white robe. 'The bureaucrats are trembling,' he said impassively. 'The Empress is about to arrive.' He turned to his friends and smiled. 'Shall I wave?'

Down in the control room there was no time for slacking. 'Tight on the batsmen, four,' the director repeated. 'It's still on here, no one's taking a break.' Glenn McGrath, Australia's tall opening bowler, turned at the end of his run-up, slipped the ball into his fingers and set off into his big, leggy sprint to the wicket. Sri Lanka's captain, Arjuna Ranatunga, stood with studied patience, unhurriedly watched the ball kick off the brick-coloured wicket for the last time, and slid it away fine on the off side. 'Six,' said the director, calling in the cameras he wanted. 'Six, six, six, five, and left, six – there it is! – three, seven, computer, computer, let's have it, GO!' The crowd went *Whoooaaaaaarr!* as it jumped up to clap and cheer: bottles, cards, hats and newspapers bounced into the sky. One eager group started to shove over the high railings that were supposed to keep them off the pitch. Soldiers trotted out towards the middle, holding a rope to fence off the presentation. The Sri Lankan players leapt into each other's arms, grinning and waving. And the television producer, Neil Harvey, made a rush for the door. 'Off to rescue my stump,' he said (the one with the camera in it, for those endearing shots of the batsmen's backside). There wasn't much chance of that, it seemed, not with Sri Lankans already fighting for souvenirs out there. 'Well, you have to try,' he said over his shoulder. 'They do cost ten thousand dollars.'

As denouements go, it wasn't exactly tense, not, at any rate, one of those toe-clenching anything-could-happen thrillers that aren't decided until the final ball. But it was, for everyone who was there – and for the half-billion or so watching on television – more gratifying than a mere nailbiter. Cricket can throw up hysterical climaxes as well as the next sport, but usually it produces a slower burn: the steady consolidation of a winning position, the gradual application of superior skill. The moving aspect of Sri Lanka's victory was not that they had somehow eked out an improbable win, but that they had played like favourites from the word go.

Here in the final they had won the toss and let Australia bat first, a bold gesture that cheekily flouted history (every World Cup final so far had been won by the team batting first) and an extravagant vote of confidence in their ability to overhaul whatever target Australia set. This was almost a taunt, and they had added a twist to it by keeping their slow bowlers on right through Australia's innings: a schoolboy error – everyone knows how easy it is to whack the spinners – that turned out to be inspired. So this wasn't like one of those football matches where the underdogs sneak a fluke goal and spend the next hour hoofing it off their own line. Sri Lanka looked a street or two ahead in every area: batting, bowling, fielding, thinking and cheek. Throughout the tournament they had brought dash and romance back into a game that had almost forgotten what those things looked like, and now it was paying off. They never looked rushed or hassled. They played as if they knew they were going to win.

That, at least, was how it looked in retrospect. At the time, well, anything could always have happened. Aravinda De Silva had scored a century that made everyone purr with appreciation; it had seemed faultless, predestined. But the watching spectators knew full well that each ball might be his last, and every batting side is familiar with the here-we-go-again feeling that falls upon the dressing room when wickets tumble. If he had been out, if Stuart Law had held on to an easy (by Australian standards) catch off Asanka Gurusinha, if, if, if. What Sri Lanka had to do in the closing moments was triumph over all the ifs and buts. They had to see it through. And that is exactly what they were doing.

How could anyone not be charmed? It was nice enough, in a sentimental sporting way, that a small, poor country like Sri Lanka, with no great resources to devote to cricket and no great record in previous World Cups (played twenty-six, won four), should be pulling off such an upset against the battle-hardened top dogs. No one had tipped them (apart from the New Zealander Richard Hadlee, who had made himself beloved in Colombo by suggesting that they were capable of winning) but neither did anyone doubt that they deserved it. For the last month they had batted with a calculated exuberance that cricket fans had never quite seen before: they had, in a way, changed the rules.

Most teams going into the World Cup felt that the key was a solid start, a steady acceleration and a hearty slog at the end. This didn't seem merely a wise tactic: it felt like a cricketing fact of life. But Sri Lanka upended this train of thought: against India they scored fifty off the first five overs; against England they smashed 100 off the first ten; against poor Kenya they racked up a world record: 399 runs in fifty overs. At a stroke – or in a flurry of strokes, perhaps – they were setting new standards for batting. And it was all very well for the wiseacres to say that this was a chancy way to play: it *was* chancy, that was the whole idea. Sri Lanka had re-examined the risk-to-runs ratio and decided that out-and-out aggression, on these good wickets, was not as risky as most people thought. And then they went ahead and proved it. Even the most jaded, seen-it-all-before cricket pundits, convinced that there was nothing new to discover about the way to play cricket (especially one-day cricket), felt the hairs move on the back of their necks. Sri Lanka threw caution to the warm winds. You could forget about the gentle thwock of willow on leather, one of cricket's sacred platitudes. These guys just went hell for leather from the word go.

And, of course, there was much more to it than that. Sport is drama – for winners and losers, read heroes and villains – and if Sri Lanka fitted the bill nicely as St George, then Australia made a great dragon. The glee that filled the soggy air above Lahore was inspired largely by an urgent desire to see the Aussies lose. For starters, they had thrown a hefty spanner into this World Cup by forfeiting their two games scheduled in Sri Lanka. A Colombo bank had been blown up by Tamil separatists two weeks before the tournament, killing ninety people; and Australia, citing confidential security advice, had refused to go.

This was seen as typical colonial pomposity: the whole of the subcontinent was insulted on Sri Lanka's behalf. Would Australia have refused to play in England, asked the head of Pakistan's cricket board, Arif Abbasi, now that the IRA had blasted the glass tower of Canary Wharf into the docks? Of course not. Shane Warne was unwise enough to mutter something about the issue not being the cricket, just that it wouldn't be safe to go shopping. Sri Lanka's foreign minister, Lakshman Kadirgamar, gave him short shrift. 'Shopping is for sissies,' he retorted. Australia seemed to have inherited England's mantle as the emblem of imperialist swagger. Poor England – when it comes to cricket, the rest of the world no longer takes us seriously enough to be resentful.

Australia had also given these same Sri Lankans a horrible time Down Under over the New Year. In that brief tour, Sri Lanka had been accused first of ball-tampering (not proved) and then of illegal bowling (not proved). One of Sri Lanka's key bowlers, the off-spinner Muttiah Muralitharan, was almost driven out of the game after being repeatedly no-balled by an umpire (Darrell Hair) who was assumed (not necessarily correctly) to be acting under orders ('Hair or No Hair,' read a banner at the final, 'Murali's Balls Are Fair'). The Australian players were plainly not to blame for any of this – the former captain, Allan Border, actually spoke out to say he thought it was a bit rough to put a guy's living on the line like that – but there were plenty of reports that they had given free rein to their famously foul mouths as the series progressed. Anyway, Muralitharan might not have been the right man to victimize: he was a fine bowler (his ten tight overs in the final swung the game Sri Lanka's way) but more to the point: he was the only Tamil in the team. The separatist Tigers, busy fighting a thirteen-year war against the Sinhalese majority for an independent Tamil state in the north (death toll: 40,000), were not amused. Several Australian players, notably McDermott and Warne, received death threats serious enough to make them think about withdrawing even before the bomb went off.

As if this weren't enough, it was Australia who had insulted Pakistan's national pride a year earlier by accusing their captain, Salim Malik, of offering bribes to his opponents as part of a betting scam. Shane Warne and Tim May asserted, in sworn statements, that Malik had visited their hotel room during a Test match in Karachi and offered him $200,000 to bowl badly. Warne thought they were supposed to split the money; May said he thought it was $200,000 each. Warne also alleged that Mark Waugh had been approached with a similar offer. The head of Australia's cricket board called it 'cricket's greatest crisis for twenty years'. But most Pakistanis thought it was a disgraceful slur; probably the Australians *took* the bribe, they said. Did you see that stumping Ian Healey missed? You couldn't put anything past those bastards. After a rather tortured process, during which Warne and May refused to go to Pakistan to testify, Malik was cleared, but the dust had far from settled. Most of Lahore had been hoping for an Australia–Pakistan final: they wanted to settle this in the ring.

All of which made for quite a wound-up atmosphere in Lahore. It was, in its way, a too-good-to-be-true final. And if anything it was the Australians who looked hotter under the collar. Fresh from an implausible last-ditch win in the semis, where the West Indies flung away their last five wickets for a dozen runs to let Australia off a hook that seemed to have its barb lodged firmly in their gullet, they arrived at their hotel with their eyes bulging and scores to settle. Sri Lanka had hinted, through Ranatunga, that the reason for Australia's withdrawal from the matches in Sri Lanka was simple nervousness. 'They have avoided us once,' he said as the final approached. 'But they can't avoid us now.' The Australians hadn't taken kindly to the suggestion that they were pansies. 'These fucking Sri Lankans are going to fucking get what's fucking coming to 'em,' Steve Waugh was heard to mutter on the eve of the match.

He turned out to be dead-on. Victory was what was coming, and they were getting it right enough.

In the stadium, a large military band started going thump-thump-

thump as soon as Ranatunga tickled away the winning run. The rain began to fall more sharply, and the police, reluctant to get wet, took shelter on the cement apron beneath the main grandstand. Security had been tight all day, as it had been throughout the tournament – even flags were banned, in case they became spears. Stewards ran out with a painted wooden podium for the presentation, and the police tried to rope off the area in front of the players' changing rooms. But it was too late. The crowd had managed to tip over the high green barricade-railings, and on it rushed. Hundreds of eager fans surrounded the players, pushing and shoving as they tried to clap a winning hand or shoulder. De Silva was run over and knelt on the turf, asking for water (he'd had a busy day – three wickets and two catches on top of his flamboyant century). The Australians mooched around looking into the stands with faraway expressions: no one wanted to talk to them. Dignitaries clambered on to the platform to have their picture taken with Benazir, and for a while it was hard to tell who was jostling more furiously, the photographers or the officials. The bigwigs up there in their suits had to hold on to each other to keep from falling off. Some of them stood on tiptoe so that their faces would appear in the photographs. A few fans seized the chance to shout slogans for Nawaz Sharif, leader of the opposition; during the match someone had launched a kite carrying his picture across the ground (a policeman intercepted it, carried it to the boundary, and ostentatiously stamped it to bits). The rain began to fall harder. One quick-witted public-relations type rushed up with a huge Fuji parasol to protect the top brass, but he was shouldered out of the way by the umbrella man from the official sponsor, Wills tobacco, which had, after all, paid ten million quid for the privilege of keeping the rain off Benazir's smart green outfit.

Mark Taylor, Australia's captain, climbed up to receive his loser's handshake, forced a polite smile, and stuck out his hand to the Prime Minister, who ignored it. He held out his hand again on his way out, but she ignored it again. No one had told him it was a treasonous breach of etiquette to shake hands with a woman prime minister. It was his second *faux pas* of the day, if you can call it a *faux pas* – maybe it was a gender-war protest. Before the match the teams had lined up in front of the pavilion for the national anthems. The Aussies kicked their heels during the first one, a martial-sounding dirge they hadn't heard before, and then kicked their heels through the second one too (their own). As soon as it was over they headed back to the changing room, and were about half-way there when the third national anthem started up. No one had told them they'd be starting off with Pakistan's. But hang on a minute, that sounded like . . . South Africa's national anthem. It was. After a quick burst it stopped, and technicians found the correct tape. For the Australians, there was nowhere to go. Sri Lanka stood out there on their own while the music played.

When Benazir handed over the cup to Ranatunga, there wasn't really room to lift it. He tried to climb down, but was elbowed by the throng and toppled to his knees, dropping the cup as he went. It was a serious jam: anyone who ended up on the ground would have a tough job getting on to his feet again. But Ranatunga has an impressively padded centre of gravity. Gurusinha grabbed his arm as he slipped, and saved the day. De Silva wasn't finding it any easier getting up on to the damn thing: there didn't seem to be any steps. He reached down and hauled up Jayasuriya, the man of the series. Eventually the pleasantries (completely inaudible in any case) were over, and Ranatunga tried to lead his team on a lap of honour. But it was impossible, they could hardly move. Pressing around them, the crowd danced and sang in the rain. Ranatunga was holding the cup high in the air, the only safe place, and when someone kept jumping up trying to touch it, one of the Sri Lankans gave him a thump to keep him at arm's length. A few policemen took advantage of their closeness to the players to grab their autographs.

In the end the Sri Lankans gave up and stumbled their way back to the dressing room. Ranatunga reached into his pocket to have a calmer look at the winner's cheque. Forty-five thousand dollars. Not much when you're spreading it among a dozen players, not when you think of what any middling golfer or tennis player takes home for being knocked out or missing the cut, and not when you consider that the tournament as a whole had generated revenues of almost $100 million. But the organizers had topped it up with a 'development grant' of $100,000, so it hadn't been a bad day's work.

And bloody hell – it wasn't there.

It was hard to believe – I mean, it had been in his hand a moment ago. But the truth was, someone had actually gone and bloody picked his pocket.

Unbelievable. All that money, phut, gone, just like that. Was nothing sacred?

* * *

Pinching the winners' cheque might not have been cricket, exactly, but in a way none of this was cricket. In England, especially, the folklore of the game likes to set its memorable moments on warm afternoons, with the sun slanting over trees and stretching shadows across the lush grass in some pastoral Never-never Land of luncheon intervals, cream teas and dozing vicars in bicycle-clips. But this wasn't anything like that. Where were the larks on the wing in the azure sky, the blossom on the bough, the trout plopping in the lazy river, the ripples of applause from old men in deck chairs? This smelt more like . . . money. This World Cup had been the biggest so far, by a long way: entrepreneurial Asia had taken the game enthusiastically and lucratively into the media age. The Indian newspapers kept calling it a 'mega-event', and the games had indeed been played in a blizzard of advertising contracts, big television deals, fat endorsement fees, legal wrangles and rights disputes. The event was thick with sponsors pouring money into the tournament to get their feet in the door of the subcontinent's vast audience of cricket-lovers. Fizzy drinks concerns, car and motorbike companies, camera and computer conglomerates, tobacco giants and fashion houses filled the television screens with eager spots proclaiming their love of the game. And behind this marketing frenzy lay a bracing political shift: cricket was being wrenched away from its spiritual home in St Johns Wood and urged in a new, distinctly Asian direction. The torch lit by Kerry Packer in Australia a generation before – the television-led attempt to turn a slow, arcane sport into a video-age spectacular – had been picked up and rekindled in Calcutta and Lahore. Cricket, for the first time in its life, was big business.

In this brave new world it made a perverse sort of sense for someone to swipe the prize money. Ranatunga stared out through the plate-glass windows, where the mob clambered and waved. Somewhere out there was a guy with a cheque – a unique souvenir. The police were trying to clear people away from the dressing-room area and even gave some of them a few whacks round the shins with their sticks. But who cared? It had been a long tournament: six weeks of solid cricket. And in Pakistan they hadn't had much to cheer about, except for victory over England, which these days wasn't such a big deal anyway. They clapped and shouted as if, for tonight at least, they were Sri Lankan.

While Ranatunga was hugging his coach and wondering what the four-X had happened to his money, Mark Taylor was being led a not-very-merry dance up and down the stairs of the members' block, looking for a place to hold a press conference. It was like an orienteering exercise: up the stairs, along the corridor, up another flight – no, sorry, back down again, along the corridor, turn *left* this time instead of right, up the stairs, open the door – whoops, sorry – down the stairs again . . . For one instant, Taylor's jaw tightened and it looked as if he was going to let loose a few choice Aussie idioms, but what the hell? He followed his leader without saying a word. Eventually they found the press room on the top deck and set up a little stand at the front. Taylor squatted down behind it and started catching cassette players thrown by journalists too far away to put them within range. 'Want me to turn it on for you?' He grinned as he put one down on the table. 'Doesn't make any difference, you'll make it up anyway.' The English reporters present, accustomed to a funereal, everything's-too-much-trouble atmosphere in their post-match interviews, weren't sure where to look.

Still, a quote is a quote, and these days newspapers are more anxious to report what is said than what is done – on the assumption, perhaps, that most readers have been watching the game on the box anyway. And Taylor brings a brisk chattiness to these conferences, which serves him, and his team, well. He didn't even wait for anyone to ask a question: he just launched into his summary. 'Well, we were a bit shy in the run department,' he said. 'We made 240 when we probably should have made 270 or 280. And then we dropped a couple of catches in the outfield which we never do. And Warney was maybe less effective than usual – there was a bit of dew out there and he couldn't get a real grip on the ball. But no excuses. We've won a lot of games, but we lost this one. That's cricket. But fair dos to Sri Lanka. They deserve to be world champions. They've improved a hell of a lot in one-day cricket. They have very positive batting and set good fields to the off-spin. I don't think they've bowled a side out in the World Cup, but that's the game . . .'

He could, you felt, have gone on like this all day: it was a fair, quick and sporting piece of public relations. But then he decided to drop his trousers just a little bit. 'One thing I will say,' he said. 'It's tremendous for the game that Sri Lanka have won. And the way Kenya played too. But we've got to stop sweeping things under the carpet. Whether it's the ICC or whoever, it doesn't really matter. But if we don't do something soon the game's going to break down. I'm talking about ball-tampering, throwing, everything. We had a captain's meeting here, and we need more of that. We've got to get off our chests whatever's on our chests – otherwise the game's going to break up . . .'

Well, that was some way to poop the party, wasn't it? Just when Sri Lanka had brought a cavalier lack of inhibition back to the game, here was the captain of Australia saying that the muck needed to be raked. But what muck? Throughout the World Cup there had been rumblings, most of them concerning the weight of gambling in the subcontinent and its possible effect on the matches. The ghost of the Malik affair was still pacing the corridors. In Pakistan, cynicism about cricket is so entrenched that hardly a match is above suspicion. When India had beaten Pakistan in a dramatic quarter final in Bangalore a week earlier, Pakistanis were quick to blame it on the bookies. Why were they offering two-to-one on a Pakistan win (ludicrously generous odds in a tight two-horse race) unless they were deliberately attracting money they knew they would not have to return? It was reminiscent of the time Pakistan lost a Test match against the forty-to-one no-hopers Zimbabwe, after which two players, Basit Ali and Rashid Latif, resigned from the team in disgust.

Was this what Taylor meant? If so, then he had a point. The consensus among cricket fans in Karachi and Lahore is that many – most – games are influenced by bookmakers, and not only those involving Pakistan. Four or five times I was told firmly that, sure, Lara was a great player, but of course that 501 he scored against Durham to set the new world record – obviously rigged. Rigged? I looked shocked. Oh, yes, the saying went: it was a fix-up devised to do down the Pakistani record-holder, Hanif Mohammad (whose 499 had stood for thirty years as the best-ever score). This seemed gaspingly paranoid. But it only partly matters whether there is fire behind all this smoke. The sheer fact that foul-play is so widely suspected is sufficient cause for alarm. Cricket – once a by-word for fair play, now a cliché usually served with a good dollop of sarcasm – was in danger of becoming not a sport, not an open contest, but just a piece of dishonest theatre, a more or less colourful spectacle, like wrestling. Was this how the game was going to end up?

It was a sombre end to a buoyant day.

— 2 —

WHERE WAS I?

Bombay

Literature was the first stop on my own World Cup itinerary. When I flew out from London I was worrying about (of all things) the future of the novel – the subject, chosen with foolish haste, of a talk I was scheduled to give at the PEN Club on the evening of my arrival. I had worked on the literary pages of the *Independent* for the last ten years, so this was, I suppose, something about which I could be expected to have a view. I had been invited by an eager cricket-and-literature buff who was also, incidentally, the finance director of a large Bombay automobile company, Mahindra and Mahindra. The firm was a keen cricket sponsor: its television adverts featured Kapil Dev in a Mahindra jeep, climbing every mountain and fording every stream slewing over mountain passes before checking in at a grand hotel in his dinner jacket. Anyway, it was a kind invitation and of course I said yes. But since agreeing to address the subject I had noticed only that it was the title of the speech given by Holly Martens in *The Third Man*, where it functions as a comic dig at the pompous innocence of the Englishman abroad. I did, perhaps, have something to say about the future of the book – I was happy to defend it against the doomy predictions of those who argued that computers would cut its throat – but the novel? Perhaps I could say that its future depended on who won the toss, and what the wicket was like.

I arrived at lunchtime. I had only been to India once before, but it seemed very familiar, even though it had been snowing in London when I left. If you took Southall High Street, bombed it a bit, took out the plumbing and the drains, dropped in thousands of people to camp along the road, starved them for a year or so, spread rubbish around, emptied a few lorry loads of cows and goats on to the streets, and turned the heat up to furnace-level, that would give you the drive into the city centre. They say there are more millionaires in India than there are in America; there's more of everything, so it sounds plausible. But you don't see too many of them on the highways surrounding the airport. Bombay is a narrow peninsula so every road is a bottleneck, and the drive in from the airport has become one of the classic routes in the encyclopedia of modern travel: the scrawny children sifting through piles of hot rubbish in front of hoardings promoting, for some reason, lingerie; the bony women clutching babies and tapping at the window of your car. It's all true. And, of course, it makes you feel awful, even if you risk the contempt of the taxi driver by sprinkling notes into the waiting hands (knowing, just to give an idea of the exchange rate, that a pound would keep you in a daily newspaper for two months). There can't be many more ugly sights than bloated, conscience-stricken Westerners parading their sensitivities *en route* to a club sandwich by the hotel swimming pool – though perhaps this is better than parading one's insensitivities. Either way, that, as they say in cricket, is India for you.

A quick word about Indian driving. Most English visitors find it a little on the hairy side, and sometimes make the mistake of thinking that Indians are lousy motorists. In fact, of course, the opposite is true. The traffic, a car-spotter's paradise of period saloons, clacking tri-shaws, oil trucks and vans that look as if they are held together only by the gaudy paintwork, really does flow, pushing, hesitating, checking and twisting in a busy swarm. Getting anywhere on these roads requires agility, timing and, above all, nerve, because no one can afford to stop. It's like a slow stampede: if you ever ground to a halt, you'd be trapped by the rest of the herd rolling round and past you. Anyone (like me) on the lookout for clues to the great subcontinental love affair with cricket could easily imagine that the quicksilver batting style in these parts has something to do with this highly refined road sense, which fosters such a slinky co-ordination between eye, hand and foot. Driving in India is like batting on a bad wicket: you have to be ready for sudden late swerve, subtle variations of pace, and the odd surprising bounce. The roads are alive with the sound of music: the rickshaws say, 'Horn Please!' on the back, and this is only partly because they do not have rear-view mirrors.

Probably it is silly to think that there is a grammar to this language of tooting and trilling: everyone I asked denied that there were any rules to it. But it does sound, as you veer and brake through the mass of chirping vehicles, like a swarm of birds or bats, whistling and chirruping to each other as they flick this way and that.

I was staying at the Taj Mahal, one of the world's great hotels, according to all the brochures. I'd been booked in by John Snow, the former England fast bowler turned travel agent who handles most of the travel arrangements for the press. I was going to be contributing articles and match reports to the *Independent*, so simply handed him a list of matches I wanted to go to and let his office take care of the how, where and when. The players, umpires, officials and media frequently share the same hotel, giving an overseas tour the feel of a travelling circus.

Anyway, it was true what they said about the Taj. There were spectacular views over the harbour from the upstairs seafront bar: if you craned your head you could see tiny boys leaping from the stone dock into the rancid water to please the tourists. Inside there were spacious tiled cloisters, luscious flowers, a roomy swimming pool surrounded by smooth lawns, great food, bars that plonked mounds of warm nuts in front of you the instant you sat down, roomboys who cleaned your shoes the moment you took them off – the works. The Taj chain was the 'official' hotelier to the World Cup, hosting teams, administrators, media people and the better-heeled sort of fan. For such a classy enterprise it was surprisingly willing to enter into the promotional spirit, to 'share the magic', as the sponsor urged.

'Yes,' said the food and beverage manager, holding up a wodge of memos and faxes from sister hotels in Calcutta, Delhi and Madras. 'We'll be putting large screens in the four bars, so we'll see if we can get people out of their rooms. The world these days is anti-crowd, it wants us to stay home and watch TV. And liquor is not allowed in the stadiums, so that's another reason. We're looking forward to it. We'll even have projections in the nightclub.'

This really was an eye-opener. The nightclub in the Taj was one of the hottest spots in Bombay, a dressy, dance-till-dawn Stringfellowsy kind of place full of slim girls in chic jeans and boys in black buttoned-up shirts. It was hard to imagine many countries where the in-crowd could get off on cricket, of all things, but in India the top players have a special status. They are glamorous, sexy, even – young, rich and handsome enough to be up there with film stars and musicians. One fashion show welcomed Tendulkar as its special guest, and the models sashayed up the catwalk holding miniature bats. Can anyone see Kate Moss dancing around with a poster of Graham Gooch? I don't think so.

The bar menus had been doctored to appeal to cricket fans. They were round, like cricket balls, and offered special cocktails – Kambli's Cooler, Sachin's Delight, Healey's Healer (a hangover cure) and so on. You could nibble away on a Taylored to Perfection (cheese chilli toast) or Michael's Mania (chick peas in spicy masala), or get stuck into Shane's Warning, Donald's Duck, Tendulkar's Thunder, whatever you fancied. Even the coasters looked like the white ball, with the seam and everything.

One thing was clear straight away. During the preliminaries to the World Cup the English newspapers had been full of remarks, by players, administrators and commentators, about the trials and tribulations of spending any time at all in the subcontinent. India, in these accounts, boiled down to a fearful pageant of poisonous food, violent illness, chronic delays and distressing squalor. What this turned out to mean, in practice, is that everyone stayed in some of the finest and most opulent hotels you have ever seen in your life, and that someone else – some patient, up-all-night travel wallah – made all the arrangements. Naturally, such criticisms of subcontinental habits did not go down well in India. None of these perils, they were quick to point out, had prevented Britain from sending an army to take possession of the place in much dirtier days; it was a bit rich to complain now that it spoiled the cricket.

This whole subject – the relationship between cricket and the British empire – was bound to be a major preoccupation in the coming weeks. Cricket is, almost exclusively, a Commonwealth game (though, ironically, it is about the only sport, in that blizzard of kayaking, frisbee-throwing, synchronized egg-and-spoon dancing and what have you, that is not actually in the Commonwealth Games), and the World Cup would in one sense be a gamesy parody of a Commonwealth summit. It was already evident, as the newspapers filled up with heated discussions of the Australian/West Indian decision to forfeit their games in Sri Lanka, that the old colonial reflexes remained in place. In a flash Australia had inherited England's traditional reputation as whingeing Poms, and if no one levelled the same kind of criticism at the West Indies (so who's calling

Ambrose a sissy, eh?) it was partly because they could not be made to fit the stereotype of the snooty (white) oppressor. Some commentators detected in Australia's safety-first stand a vague racism, a fear of dark places; no one tried to pin the same charge on the West Indians. As it happened, Australia's intransigence did seem a touch *de haut en bas* . . .

But all of this would have to wait: I had a speech to give. I paced my room, munched on a courtesy banana, tried to come up with something, and failed.

The PEN Club is in the library of Theosophy Hall, so I was surrounded by walls intimidatingly full of Eastern philosophy. The host, passing round the tea and biscuits, was Nissim Ezekiel, a noted poet whom we had, as it happened, interviewed in the *Independent* a year or so before. Everyone was extremely polite and hospitable, but I couldn't help feeling a bit strung out. Cricket fancies itself as a literary pursuit, but that means little more than that it encourages a polite form of speech sometimes thought of as literary. So it felt bizarre, having come here in search of willow and leather, to be speaking into a microphone about the status of fiction. I can hardly remember what I said. Almost certainly I hinted that novels were declining in schools because of the great sell-off of literature grounds; that the grind of the county library circuit in England was strangling the life out of letters; that what we needed was a Novel Academy where the most promising youngsters could be properly coached. Luckily, everyone was so polite and hospitable that they pretended not to be disappointed. On the whole, people were curious to know what I thought about Salman Rushdie, whose new book contained a lively satirical portrait of Bombay's folk-nationalist leader, Bal Thackeray. What can you say? He's a brilliant writer, unjustly hounded, and when was there ever a great author who didn't upset a few applecarts? Everyone was so polite and hospitable that they pretended to agree, although, as someone whispered to me afterwards, not everybody did. When I was asked which novelists I admired, I made sure I included some Indian authors in my list, such as R. K. Narayan and Gita Mehta, and when I returned the question to the audience I trembled, expecting to be confronted with some towering exotic genius of Indian letters, famous for novels of extraordinary philosophical richness and ecstatic sensuality of whom I had never heard. 'My favourite?' came the reply. 'Um . . . Well, I like Anita Brookner.' Oh, well.

I had been dangling over this gap between cricket and literature for most of my life, it seemed. I was thrilled to be here, partly because I knew that if I was back in London I'd only be watching all-night TV during the coming weeks. All sports spawn helpless adherents, but cricket, because of its tropical locations and extreme slowness, is the only one that encourages you to get jetlag in your own sitting room. For a decade I had been a novels-and-poetry man, and had even written two novels of my own in which cricket was mentioned (I think) once. But all the time the sound of bat on ball was drumming away in the background, both as something I did and something I followed. It was like something pressing down on summer days: the need to catch updates on the radio, slump in front of the television, and scan the daily papers. For years I, like thousands of others, trailed about at weekends with my kit in the boot and a map on the steering wheel, looking for the ground. I had even played cricket in India once, for a touring newspaper side.

But though cricket is a time-consuming habit of which I sometimes feel guilty, I do not have a special story to tell about it. It is not as if I grew up in a community of furious cricket lovers, people whose lives rose and fell according to the ebb and flow of the latest score. It is not as if my father had been a groundsman or anything; my childhood was not spent hiding among the gang mowers, inhaling the smell of stumps and nets and dreaming of grassy outfields. Occasionally I wish there were some enticing psycho-athletic disturbance in my formative years – a sudden glimpse of my parents playing cricket on the sofa, perhaps, that had seared itself on to my impressionable consciousness. If cricket had cured me of a lisp or dyslexia, if the game had been my way out of a suicidally intense failed love affair, if inswing bowling had turned me away from a life of crime, if cricket had been the only straw to cling to during my miraculous escape from drug-addiction, if I had been truly hopeless for thirty years, but that had never stopped me dreaming – any of these would have been just dandy.

But there isn't anything of this sort. I have no excuse. My cricketing education was well favoured and unexceptional: a matter of attentive schooling and a natural fondness for ball games. I was above average, but below par, good enough to get into teams, and sometimes be captain, but never special. Who knows, if I'd tried harder, really worked at it, truly dedicated myself, three games a week, say, plus long hours in the nets, then it is possible that maybe, just maybe, with the right encouragement and what sportsmen like to call 'that little bit of luck', I could have played a game or two as stand-in fourth seamer for Glamorgan or somewhere. Even that is probably a fantasy. One of the things we have to remember, when we carp and gripe about the players on television, is that they are all far, far better than the rest of us can even dream of being – however awful they look. Anyone can say they could have been better if they'd tried harder. Plenty do.

No doubt about it, though: liking cricket was a big help. All the schools I went to were keen on cricket, and they were keen too on people who liked cricket. It's a sad truth that sportsmen set the tone at these institutions: they tend to be brasher, stronger, noisier, more competitive and all-round nastier than the sensitive types they tease and humiliate. Salman Rushdie was telling the truth when he admitted that it was his lack of obvious sporting talent, more than his racial distinctiveness, that made Rugby seem hateful (there is always plenty of room for glamorous Imran Khan-types in the First XI). Intellectual life is lonelier: it offers none of the benefits of being part of a team; neither is it a very dramatic spectator event. You didn't catch big crowds heading down to the science lab to watch the brainboxes pull off an experiment, or up to the library to stamp their feet and cheer on the Chaucer buffs.

Still, I was in the theoretically lucky position of having a foot in both camps: scholarship material, but also a sporty jock. No one was horrible to me. Deep down, the bookish types thought I was a closet-yob, and this was true: I *was* sustained by elaborate cricket daydreams while the teacher acted out all the parts in *Othello*, clutching his forehead in the Desdemona scenes; and sure, I was more wrapped up in replaying (with slight revisions) my innings the previous day, adding a few boundaries, subtracting a few airshots, than I was in my exams. But perhaps it is one of the functions of sport to give you something unimportant to worry about, something to distract you from your real anxieties. Cricket – fantasy cricket, at least – seemed the quickest, neatest, most envisageable path to glory and acclaim, which I guess is what it was all about.

The sportsmen, meanwhile, knew that my head was in the clouds: that ghastly, tell-tale superior air I couldn't help adopting during the bawdy sing-song, the fact that I had been spotted accompanying the boys in glasses to non-compulsory T. S. Eliot nets. So while I was tolerated by both groups, I was a member of neither. The intelligentsia defined itself by sneering at people who liked pointless games, meaning me; while the athletes prided themselves on their rebellious attitude to academic work – only mugs read books. Me again.

At home – that is, during the holidays – it was a simpler matter. Mum and Dad were slipping apart, and my sister was busy running away: cricket kept you out of the house, away from the frightening crackle of domestic strife. It held out the promise of long, green afternoons with strict rules about behaviour and almost no shouting. Later, we moved into a small one-bedroom flat above a garage, so indoor life became a squash: anything to be outdoors. Best of all, cricket was approved of. Watching football highlights was heretical: you couldn't watch television during Sunday lunch (though *Gardener's Question Time* seemed to be OK). But cricket was different: you could watch for eight hours at a stretch and not be accused of laziness. It even had a definite article: you weren't just watching cricket, you were watching *the* cricket. It felt official, responsible, almost a duty. There were desirable side-effects, too: cricket teaches you how to use the washing machine, unless you want green splashes on your knees week after week and a red smudge in your groin; it also teaches you how to sew on buttons and repair rips – or used to, until the cricket world went nylon.

And, of course, if you watch the game for any length of time it starts to inveigle itself into your nervous system: the unending attention to technique, the subtle changes of initiative, the rolling drama as the spotlight falls on different players – players whose mannerisms you come to know well and can imitate on the playground or in the nets. All of us, back then, could speak Richie Benaud, prance up the wicket, show-pony style, like Tony Greig, or mimic the rounded, slow, chewing-the-cud approach of Raymond Illingworth.

That cricket was respectable meant that it was okay with parents and teachers. It struck them as civilized or, at any rate, polite. Even at public schools, footballers curse and yell, but cricketers tend to applaud each other and have lunch together and be generally sportsmanlike about everything. So although I was a keen literature student, cricket was all right. I could weaken at the thought of great heroines with dazzling names – Bathsheba, Natasha, Juliet, Tess – but also find room in my heart for John Edrich. I liked Yeats but was happy, too, to while away whole days bouncing a golf ball against the side of the garage with a stump. I once read that Don Bradman used to spend hours doing something like this; it was offered as one of the reasons for his supreme skill in later life. But this is just one of those rose-tinted failures of hindsight: Bradman wasn't a batting genius because he played stump-golf for hours on end; he must have revolutionized stump-golf, taken it to a new level.

One other thing about football: it inspires fierce, strange and now well-documented loyalties. Cricket doesn't, not in England at any rate. If you are Pakistani or Indian you might just commit suicide when the team is humiliated; if you're West Indian, you might feel the world has fallen apart when things go wrong at the Oval. But these are countries where cricket is one of the leading suppliers of national pride. In England you don't support cricket teams; you follow them. It's the game you support, not the team: cricket fans can be irritating drivers in the summer months – I know several who can't drive past a game-in-progress without slowing down and pulling over to watch a ball or two. Football fans have fantasies about their team winning the FA Cup, or the World Cup, or the inter-office five-a-side. Cricket fantasies – mine, at least – were more to do with playing: it was me scoring the winning runs at Lord's, not some remote star whose autograph I once nearly got. This might be because real duffers can't enjoy a game of football – it's too fast, too bruising, too humiliating. In cricket, well, anyone can hang around in the field for a few hours and wave a bat, when the time comes, at the ball. Even a non-starter can have one of those magical, dreamy, vicars-in-bicycle-clips days ('Loveliest of trees, the cherry now/Is hung with bloom along the bough') when everything clicks and he scores seven not out to save the match.

So although I followed the televised matches, and took my pocket scorebook along to the Oval when I could, the essential thing was to play. Thanks to my mother's emphatic faith in there being a right way to do things (and no other way) I had coaching. In the Easter holidays we would drive to indoor nets in Sunningdale – a big cobwebby canvas hutch behind a pub. I must have been quite young: to while away the journey we would count the lorries on the A30. And for half an hour I'd be drilled in the routine shots, and taught how to bowl. Back home in the garden, I'd set up the stumps and wheel away until it got dark. If there had been anyone to bowl back at me, then perhaps I'd have been a better batsman; but my brother was much younger, good for terrorizing when I was doing the bowling and very handy as a ball-fetcher, but not testing enough as a bowling machine. Relaxed in my older-brother superiority, it came as a shock, years later, when he turned out to be a better bowler than me. I wasn't jealous, though: he was welcome to his wickets (the bastard). I don't remember my father throwing balls at me (on the contrary I recall – blushing – being embarrassed that he didn't cut a racier, more six-hitting dash at the Fathers' Match) though I'm sure he did; so this is just the tragic amnesia of growing up. Probably he wheedled away for hours. I do remember cricket forming the main or only theme of letters home. 'Dear Dad, I took six for four against St Peter's. Also got 15 not out. Dropped a catch, though!!! Did you see Alan Knott in the Test? Sir let us watch it. Great, wasn't it? I think I need a new bat. Love Robert. P.S. And stamps.'

When I was a student I used to get holiday jobs coaching at that same cricket school. In the coaches' room were wonky photographs of Gary Sobers and Greg Chappell, the zing of an electric bar fire, steam from Thermoses of coffee and the smell of pipesmoke. The dusty changing room was impregnated with the rich raw odour of cricket: linseed, leather, canvas, chalk, smoke, sweaty socks and, on nice days, freshly mown grass. Out in the nets the ball made a loud crump when it hit the canvas walls, and you could hear manly bellows all around: 'Forward, boy! Yes! Yes! That's it. No! Not like that! Get that elbow up! Go on! Up! Yes, that's more like it! Again! Again! One more! Yes!' To a non-cricket fan, it might easily have sounded obscene.

Sometimes dads came and stood in the back of the net, to make sure they were getting their money's worth. I learned an interesting truth: boys always had more fun, and did better, when Dad wasn't there. Partly because the coach did better – you felt awkward teasing boys whose parents were within earshot. At lunch we would go to the pub, smiling at the sign outside that said Coaches Welcome, for hot soup (it was freezing in the cricket school) and beer. The afternoons always went more quickly than the mornings, somehow.

It was a fairly thorough apprenticeship. But after school I didn't play for a few years. I had got into Oxford a year ahead of myself, and had two summers abroad. The first was spent working as a waiter in France, where there wasn't often a game going on – the Mont Blanc massif makes the famous Lord's slope look a bit weedy – and then another in Iran. But I remained a slavish follower. In Chamonix, in the afternoon break, I would hover in bookshops reading the two-day-old cricket reports in the English newspapers.

A complete maths dunce, I could nevertheless be gripped for hours by the resonant algebra of cricket scorecards.

In Iran I was actually working on the sports page of an expatriate newspaper so would rip off the Reuters telexes and write my own juvenile commentaries on the English Test scene. And even when I came back to go to Oxford I hardly played. I still loved cricket in theory, but had lost the habit in practice. By this time I was keener on literature: cricket was a once-a-month dabble, not a way of life. I was also starting to hate the whole business of cricket – the long drives to matches, the struggle to find your kit, the crappy weather, the hanging around in post-match bars with cheery chaps in blazers with panatellas.

Part of this was just would-be bohemianism: it was unthinkable for someone who hoped people would fancy him an intellectual, perhaps even a writer (especially the gleaming historienne in the library downstairs), to be seen walking out of the Bodleian with a cricket bag. Some of it was real, though. Cricket gave me a bad temper: I hated having to apologize to my girlfriend as I plunged out of the house (late, of course) at half past nine on a Sunday morning. Cricket came to seem a weakness, an opponent, some sort of burden. Most of the people I liked didn't like it, and I was happy to see it their way. In fact, the other day I asked someone about those days and she confessed with a sigh that she had had no idea, back then, that I was interested in cricket at all. But one day, someone grabbed me out of the College bar at the eleventh hour when they were one short. And it turned out to be one of those blurry-balmy days straight out of Wodehouse. I said, well, I suppose I could give it a try, borrowed some kit, and said I was sort of a bowler. Then I went and got a helter-skelter ninety-six, caught in the deep trying to impress someone on the boundary. After that I did play for the college sometimes, but it was never that good again. They made me captain, for some reason – a bad move if you wanted a skipper who could be guaranteed to turn up at the right ground, on the right day.

But I was hooked again. I started turning out for my old schoolboys' team: the Old Bradfieldians, in a nice semi-serious competition for alumni: the Cricketer Cup, a limited overs knockout of a pretty testing sort (by my occasional standards). I never played enough to be anything more than a make-up-the-numbers bowler: the best I could hope for, as I steadily lost pace and accuracy, was to remain promising. It wasn't long, though, before I was the oldest person in the team, which tended to be refreshed each year by whichever good players had left the school. I just about kept my end up, and had the occasional good day; but I was also becoming the non-fielder, the one the others hoped the ball wouldn't go to. I started noticing they were clapping inordinately when I stopped the ball, as if it was an against-the-odds surprise. I could feel them holding their breath when I bowled, wishing I was faster, fearing the worst. For some reason the worst never happened. Playing for lesser teams I could sometimes get whacked all over the place by some village slogger who didn't recognize tidy bowling when he saw it; but these public-school batsmen were cautious and respectful. I didn't give them too much to hit, so they didn't hit it. And then we had a baby, and the whole idea of driving north to Shrewsbury on a Saturday night so you could eat curry with a lot of people you didn't really know and hang about in the rain on Sunday became ridiculous.

One of the nice things about the Cricketer Cup was that every now and then you came up against top players, though not as often as people hoped. Before every game, there was wild gossip that so-and-so would be playing. Apparently, Greg Chappell might be turning out for Charterhouse; apparently, Viv Richards spent a year at Repton. These rumours usually turned out to be false, but not always. Most teams had someone or other. We had a couple of our own: Graham Roope and Mark Nicholas, although they were usually not free to play.

Of course it was inspiring to play with real players. It was also enlightening: they tended to have bad tempers; they tended to hate cricket. One of them turned up one morning, squished his foot into the soggy grass and said: 'Hope you don't fucking expect me to fucking bowl in fucking this.' That's the other nice thing about cricket: it's so character-forming.

And it was understandable: I was the same myself, driving down the M4 with the rain lashing down, cursing and vowing never to play again. But cricket keeps sneaking up on you. The rain stops, the game gets going, you spend three hours sulking and brooding in the outfield, you drop a catch and crack your finger, and then . . . a miracle. The team finds itself on the brink of defeat, and you march out and slog a quick fifty to win with four balls to spare. Someone slaps you on the back and buys you a drink, and says they always knew you could bat. This happens.

Cricket? The best game on earth. Free next week? You bet – here, let me buy this one.

And so the trap springs shut again. If you can play at all, people ask you to. And at some early point an obedient worm creeps into your soul, making it hard to say no. The only excuse acceptable to cricketers for not playing is that you are playing already. The game knows how costly it is, so it can't afford to be punctured by the truth – if you say you'd rather be doing something else, you are shattering the illusory consensus, which is that there's nothing you'd rather do: only obligations can prevent you from playing, never pleasures. The camaraderie is built, to a certain extent, on shame: we are all deserters, we have all temporarily abandoned our lives, our families, our work, but it doesn't do to mention this. Cricket obliges you to pretend that you *have* to look after the children, never that you want to; that you *have* to go to Paris with your girlfriend, never that there's nothing you'd rather do. Some of the more old-fashioned cricketers even have a deadly phrase for days they can't play: Girlfriend Duty.

But cricket remains a hard game to leave, even when it's hard to take. These days I play for a team called the Gaieties. It's Harold Pinter's team, more or less, and it's good-humoured, competitive stuff – an ideal home for people who love the game but aren't so sure about the pink gin and cravats. Harold's matchless enthusiasm for cricket runs to weekly ring-rounds to make sure people are available, long stints of umpiring, careful record-keeping and generous, appreciative words for anyone who does well. It is good fun. We play all sorts: South Londoners with heavy bats and helmets and sponsored shirts who shout '*Waiting!*' every time they block the ball; genial actors who grin when they miss it; schoolboys who swear if you hit them for four – 'Fuckin' awful shot' – and ageing maestros who strive to repeat the feats of yesteryear. We're a fair team, especially keen on playing opponents who fancy themselves: the ones who have three bats and bold nicknames – Stonker, Winksie, Biffer – and need a drink every five minutes and are toughened by leagues and cry, 'Come on, Baz, let's 'ave it up 'im,' when their fast bowler comes on, and can't quite *believe* they're being humiliated by a guy in a dress shirt who was playing the trumpet till five in the morning. It is possible that clubs such as this are where the soul of cricket lives – loose gatherings of genuine cricket aesthetes – cricket for cricket's sake.

Of course, there are downs as well as ups. One day we went to Oxted – boring drive, an hour through South London – and the home side cancelled the game when we arrived. 'We tried to ring,' they said weakly. Harold was furious (not only on his own behalf: our ageless West Indian fast bowler had come down on the train from Newcastle). So off went an angry letter ('Never in all my years, etc.') to the president of Oxted. We all received a copy, except for one player who opened a package to find Harold's brand-new screenplay of *Lolita*. It was a nice surprise, the man was a noted novelist himself – gracious me, perhaps Harold wanted his opinion. He read it at once and dropped it round later that day.

'I think it's great,' he said.

'Oh, Christ,' said Harold. 'That was supposed to go to Universal.'

It took a moment for them to register what this meant. We can only guess at what Adrian (*Fatal Attraction*) Lyne thought when he opened the new Nabokov screenplay by Harold Pinter, and read instead an indignant letter to a cricket club just off the M25.

Perhaps he thought it brilliantly captured the tone of the book.

One of the grandest days in the club's recent history was the game against Roehampton. We declared on 264 for nought: the opening pair – let's call them Justin and Ian – both scoring centuries. To mark the occasion I wrote a rum-ti-tum John Betjeman rip-off, which included the following verse:

> Harold commandeers the bar
> (Justin's lager, Ian's wine)
> Recollects his finest hour:
> Caught midwicket, fifty-nine.

I sent it to Harold, and with scrupulous sweetness he wrote back to say he liked it very much, but that actually his top score ever was thirty-nine, and could I change it before he sent it on to everyone else.

And that's about it. I wish there was more, that I'd been better, or worse, madder, or sadder, but there isn't. I can't quite pretend that cricket is an insomniac obsession, or a pathetic mismatch, or the sustaining poetry of my life, though it is there all right, ticking away in some part of my consciousness – the desire to see great feats, the more fanciful wish to perform them, the permanent urge to know the Test score. When someone gave me a cricket book one Christmas

I realized with a flash of shame that I could name all the players depicted in the twenty-year-old jacket photograph, even the ones with their backs to the camera. When people say that cricket is a religion it is not just a silly exaggeration: the game creates in its disciples a little hole in the heart, roughly the shape of a bat and ball, and it turns out that this is a space that only cricket can fill.

These were the roads that had led me to Bombay. I had a job to do: I was news-gathering, filling in alongside Derek Pringle, the paper's main cricket writer, and one of my first tasks was to sit in my luxurious room at the Taj writing a preview of the tournament, cagily referring to Sri Lanka as 'many people's dark horses for the cup' (not daring to stick my neck out) and vaguely tipping the West Indies. My future-of-the-novel date meant that it was virtually impossible for me to attend the opening ceremony in Calcutta, which was fine: I'm not a fan of all that end-of-the-pier choreography, those awful we're-all-one-big-happy-family sentiments. So I had a day free to brood in Bombay before travelling up to Ahmedabad for the opening match: England against New Zealand. It was hard for anyone who had seen England's losing streak in South Africa just a few weeks earlier to imagine the team doing well, but you never knew. One-day cricket was, as they say, a funny old game, never over till the final wicket. It only needed a few of our best batsmen to click into form.

And England had been helped by the benign structure of the tournament. The twelve competing teams had been split into two leagues of six: the top four in each group would go on to the knockout stage. England were grouped with New Zealand, the United Arab Emirates, Holland, South Africa and Pakistan, and would be playing all of their games, bar this first one, in Pakistan. You didn't need to be a soothsayer to predict that the UAE and Holland would be going home after the league stage, so England had time to find their feet and form. The other group was stronger and more interesting: India, Australia, West Indies, Sri Lanka, Kenya and Zimbabwe. It was certainly possible that Kenya or Zimbabwe might spring an upset. But the real competition wasn't going to begin for three weeks.

If I had planned to go to Calcutta, I might well have cancelled the trip on reading the preview in the morning paper. The director, Gianfranco Lunetta, a Milan-based event-planner who had orchestrated the launch party of the 1990 football World Cup, issued a roomy statement about his plans. It did not bode well, speaking pompously about the fusion of Sport and Art by 'subliminal' messages featuring 500 dancers and a sound stage shaped like a cricket ball. 'It conveys,' promised the paper, '(and incorporates) the concept of man's challenge against himself and against his adversaries, but only of the noblest kind. Thus a challenge without dishonesty and above all in harmony with other people, whoever that may be.' Whoever, indeed. The *coup de grâce* would be provided by the arrival of the former Miss Universe, Sushmita Sen, who epitomized, Lunetta declared, 'true Indian beauty – with her dark hair and dark eyes'. It was hard to tell whether this was supposed to be Sport or Art, though only a pedant would point out that if it was merely a dark-hair, dark-eye combination he was looking for, he might as well have chosen Ravi Shastri.

I spent the day strolling the playing fields of Bombay, the fields where Sunil Gavaskar and Sachin Tendulkar grew up, watching hundreds of young boys playing cricket. These maidans of Bombay have an important place in the culture of world cricket. At weekends they fill up fast in the early morning; by nine o'clock there are scores of games going on, with any old bits of wood or steel cable for stumps. The boundaries overlap, like the Olympic rings. Forget the playing fields of Eton, they have long since been supplanted by the smart suburbs of Australia, the expensive groomed school pitches of South Africa, the beaches of Barbados, and these dry grounds in Bombay. They have been much written about as emblems for the undimmable love of cricket that holds sway in the subcontinent. Certainly, the sight of all these rough-and-ready matches would be enough to bring tears to the already misty eyes of those nostalgic in-my-day Yorkshiremen who get jobs as commentators. The not-quite-green acres are like a valve, a hot breathing space in the heart of the city; huge roads clatter alongside the big red-brick turrets of the Raj architects, and bounce the roar of traffic across the overlapping outfields. Perhaps this simple physical fact helped explain cricket's huge attraction: in these crowded cities, it offered a breathing space, the boundaries pushed back the population for a few hours, and gave people what in this part of the world they most lacked: fresh air, elbow room – room to swing a bat.

The next morning I woke up with a start when the phone rang at three o'clock. It was the travel rep, who had come, with unsolicited zeal, to take me to the airport. I shouldn't have been startled – I'd been booked on the flight for months. But I had it in my head that I was leaving at six o'clock in the evening, not the morning. I had even arranged to meet someone for breakfast at the Gymkhana club. But hell – I zipped up my suitcase and ran downstairs.

The roads were empty; my man scudded through red lights without touching the brake. Bursting with gratitude, I gave him a huge tip, about what a taxi would have cost in London.

About a week's salary, in other words.

On the plane I fell asleep. The World Cup hadn't even started, and I was already whacked.

— 3 —

CAPTAIN CALAMITY

England vs New Zealand, Ahmedabad

Over 30,000 people filed into the Gujarat Stadium in Ahmedabad to watch Dominic Cork, the success story of recent English cricket, running across the dewy grass, at nine o'clock in the morning, to bowl the first ball of the competition to Craig Spearman, the New Zealand opening batsman. The size of the crowd was a tribute to the local thirst for cricket. You wouldn't catch that many people turning out to watch England in England – there isn't a ground big enough. So it did feel like a grand occasion. Still, it was an oddly early start, and what with the rival pairs of kit (England wore blue, the Kiwis wore grey) the white ball, the black sightscreens and the featureless desert around the stadium, it didn't really feel like cricket at all. Ahmedabad is a historic and busy place, a noisy, dusty (one Moghul emperor christened it Gardabad, the City of Dust) and prosperous textile centre as well as the spiritual home of Gandhi, but the cricket ground is out on the northern edge of the city, ringed by dusty tracts of dead ground. The roads leading to it offer a glimpse of rural life: neat stacks of cowpats dry in the sun, and small breakfast fires fill the air with an acrid earth-dung scent. Nothing is visible from the stands except for the huts, plastered with adverts for Pepsi and Coke, that surround the entrance where women carve tiny wooden bats for tourists. The atmosphere of the ground itself – a bare brown concrete dish – adds to the feeling that you are in the middle of nowhere. In the semi-distance, two women steered a flock of goats through the empty landscape.

But the first ball was perfectly okay: it swung away outside the off stump, the batsman left it, and the crowd (what's all this about Indian crowds being patient?) booed. Cork walked back, broke into his rushed, straining-at-the-leash run-up, and had another go: this time the ball slipped harmlessly down the leg side. You could see he was trying to get the ball closer to Spearman, force him to play a shot, but he overdid it. The third ball was another regulation delivery, curving away towards the two slips. Spearman took a step forward, lifted his bat, and let it go. This was suiting him fine: at the start of a match, especially a match like this, you could ask for nothing more than a ball you didn't have to play. I once went to some schoolboy nets at the Oval, in London, and when I aimed a swipe and missed, John Edrich (an England player!) called from the end of the net: 'Leave it, son! Best shot in the book, leaving it!' At the time it seemed like an insight; now it seems like an emblem of what is wrong with English coaching. Players are taught to ape the mannerisms of the experts before they can even play. There's not much point learning how to leave the damn thing before you have learned how to hit it.

But Spearman was happy to feel his way into the morning; already he was shaping himself to the trajectory of the ball, the way it slanted away from the bat; already he could begin to gauge the steady, lowish bounce – it didn't look like anything was going to spit up into his gloves on this thick, terracotta-coloured wicket. Here came the bowler again, sprinting in, twisting into his action and – no worries – Spearman watched it sail by. Another one came down, then another. Spearman left them both alone. Edrich would have fainted with pleasure. Cork stamped on the marks his feet were making at the bowler's end, which might simply have been the gesture of a man anxious to signal to the crowd, the television cameras, his teammates and the opposition that it wasn't his fault: he was skidding a bit. But in fact you could already see the scars in the ground. It really was wet out there.

Here came the last ball: straighter this time. Spearman leaned forward and squirted it with a dull thonk out to cover point. No run, but it was the first shot of the match, and the competition. There was an ironic rumble from the stands. Cork took his cap from the umpire and the fielders jogged, obeying the time-honoured choreography of the change of ends, to their new positions. Two men jumped over the hoardings and ran out with a bucket of saw-dust, which they tipped on Cork's footmarks.

So there it was: a maiden over. On paper, not a bad start for England. But there are maidens and maidens, and this wasn't one of those where the batsman is in trouble, but somehow hangs on. It was, if anything, a victory to New Zealand. Michael Atherton had won the toss and decided to field, a risky tactic for which he would, of course, be ridiculed by the wise (after-the-event) men in the media. But at the time it seemed like a positive move. The only help England's bowlers were going to get all day would be in the first hour, when the ground was damp and the air was cool. Cork, Martin, Gough and White all swing the ball a bit, on their good days, but none of them is especially fast. Helpful conditions in the first few overs might just give Atherton – or Michel Artherton, as the scoreboard put it – a head start.

Still, it was a risk. England had recently revealed themselves, in South Africa, to be faint-hearted when it came to batting second and chasing totals, however low. The dismal low-point in a string of crushing defeats came in East London, where they set off in pursuit of 129, made it to 75 for three, and then bellyflopped to 115 all out. This was only one of the reasons why many of the so-called sages who follow England were adamant that they should bat first. The last three one-day matches here in Ahmedabad had all been low-scoring affairs won by the side batting first, and someone had even run the rule over the last World Cup held in India and Pakistan, in 1987, and found that very few games (a quarter) were won by sides chasing. There was, on the other hand – in cricket, there is always an other hand – plenty of local scuttlebutt to the effect that the first hour really was the only time to bowl: after that, the sun would take the zap out of the wicket entirely. And perhaps it didn't matter what had happened here in the past. The groundsman had prepared a brand-new wicket, never used before, and confidently predicted plenty of runs. The whole strategy depended on attacking these New Zealand batsmen from the word go: in effect, Atherton was trusting his opening bowlers to win the match. Cork hadn't given away any runs, so it looked okay in the book, but he hadn't threatened the bat either. England had eight or nine overs in which to make their mark and, well, that was one gone.

It had taken England sixteen hours to get from Calcutta to Ahmedabad. They rose at five o'clock in the morning after the opening ceremony, changed planes in Delhi, and finally staggered into the hotel at nine in the evening. 'If I were a football manager,' said Illingworth, 'and you asked me to do the travel we've just done, you'd be laughed out of court. I mean, we travelled all day yesterday, and the day before that we had a day doing nothing really [a nice way to describe the opening ceremony]. It's the same for both sides, but that doesn't make it right.' A few days earlier Mike Atherton had declared that he was not going to whinge about travel. In the *Sunday Telegraph* he wrote: 'The need to be upbeat has been stressed by the management. Schedule changes can sap the patience of the hardiest traveller. We must take all setbacks in our stride, open our hearts to the subcontinent.' Obviously the management hadn't told Illingworth about this sensible policy. But the *Sun* sympathized, describing the journey as a 'hell trip . . . a gruelling journey . . . a nightmare jaunt', and warning Athers about the pressure of playing in 'vindaloo heat'. This only goes to show how much depends on how you put things. Of course, if you say that the players were turfed blearily out of their beds in the middle of the night, ferried to the airport and obliged to hang around waiting for the plane to leave, before stopping in Delhi for eight hours of purposeless time-killing, and then queuing their way back through the hot, crowded airport for another dreary flight and another sapping bus ride, then sure, it doesn't sound much fun.

But you could just as easily say that the players rose early, helped themselves to an orange juice from the well-stocked minibar or a sweet ripe banana from the dish on top of the television, and headed out into the deliciously cool Calcutta dawn. They didn't have to carry any luggage, apart from their personal stereos. Someone else would heave the coffins full of cricket gear and suitcases on to the bus. Then there was the thrilling ride through the empty streets of this great city, streets where British soldiers had once subdued vast crowds (and choked to death in the famous Black Hole), streets where Gandhi had lain on a mat starving himself almost to death, begging his countrymen to stop killing one another. Just over there were the great buildings of the Raj, shadowy architectural reminders of a glorious and inglorious past; that way was the mission where Mother Teresa, a Catholic amongst these millions of Hindus, had brought a tear to the eye of the West; over there lay the scars left by the Maoist cadres in the 1970s, who wrenched the city to their will in a rash of bank robberies, riots and factory closures. Just that way was where the wife of the French consul was hacked to death in her bed by the new zealots.

Calcutta: even the name has a fierce bite to it, a hot, sharp edge, and even empty (or relatively empty – perhaps a million people sleep on the streets, no one knows the number) it feels vast and slightly terrifying, a bit like the worst the world has to offer, and a bit like the best. Always there are the weird alignments of the familiar, the exotic and the squalid: an English church tower, a temple edged with palm trees and a bullock snouting along the line of rubbish. At this early hour the streets were already alive with bakers and beggars, carts piled high with vegetables, cows and goats and dogs and little cooking fires. And out by the airport is Dum-Dum, home of the exploding bullet. All the guidebooks mention it, not because it is anything to be proud of, only because it seems symbolic. It is hard to feel sanguine on a drive such as this. If you don't feel exhilarated, you probably feel sick.

Well, then there'd be a quick flight to Delhi, head deep in the colourful local newspapers, and from there it wasn't far to the palatial Taj hotel for a morning by the pool. A few lengths to get the flight out of your system, a nice lounge in the sun, and then a lazy lunch, with a couple of beers, maybe. There'd be time to finish off your book, chat to the South African and New Zealand players who were making the same trip, a game of chess if you felt like it, or perhaps a cab ride to look at the sights. If you were feeling energetic, there'd be time for a set or two of tennis before the coach left for the airport. The short flight to Ahmedabad would get you there just in time for dinner, afterwards you could take a cup of coffee out into the cool garden behind the hotel to look at the view over the river, where a few lights flashed, bats looped over the rooftops and late birds sang beneath the oriental stars. Listen – you could just hear late trains chugging into the railway station, by the celebrated shaking minarets on the Sidi Bashir Mosque (if one shakes, the other sways as well). It might cross your mind, as you waved at the waiter for a refill, that in England it was pissing down. And all day long, from dawn till dusk, you wouldn't have had to open your wallet.

An absolute belter of a day, in most people's book.

As it happens, it isn't as if the players complain. They do mutter about touring being 'boring' and there being nothing to do. It was on a tour of India that Phil Tufnell had famously commented, 'Done the elephants, done the poverty,' a nice enough laddish joke, which caused him only to be depicted as an ignorant clown. That remark is much-remembered in the subcontinent (with relish, in Pakistan), just as Ian Botham's clumsier line about Pakistan not even being a place you'd send your mother-in-law is recalled with fury in Lahore (and delight in Bombay). These remarks have contributed much to the perception of English cricketers abroad as dim Philistines. It is true that they travel without zest or enthusiasm, and true too that this probably affects the way they perform on the pitch. But it is not wholly the players' fault. They only rarely have days off as such. They are either playing, having nets, or travelling. And it isn't, in truth, all that easy to think what to do when you suddenly have a few hours free in a strange city. You can wander around sightseeing, sure, but that is not as straightforward as it sounds (and, let's face it, sightseeing has its own moronic aspects) because if you are an England cricketer you would immediately be surrounded by a large crowd of extremely chirpy and enthusiastic cricket fans and autograph bandits. And they *grab* you, here. You couldn't ignore them even if you wanted to.

And it isn't that you mind, exactly, but on the other hand I think I'll just head back to the relative safety of the hotel, if that's okay with you. One of the reasons why the players like hitting the golf course is because out there on the fairways is about the most private place there is. Of course, if the management organized things properly, so the players knew when they had days off coming up and could plan outings, that would be different. Or the management could plan outings for them, trips to the cinema, to historic sites, to spectacular scenery, to golf courses, whatever. This, of course, does not happen. The players never know if they are having a free day until the evening before, when the team meeting decides they need a break. Not enough time to arrange to meet a friend, say, not enough time to hire a car and book a hotel somewhere on the coast and go exploring – these things take a bit of planning. And, anyway, the players are so whacked from all the cricket, and from all these five o'clock starts at the airport, that a day off means, first and foremost, a lie-in. And so it goes.

This World Cup was not going to present the players in a very edifying light: they were in a dry country, and were going to stay close to the beer supply in their own rooms, But much of this is imposed on them. The game has not given them time to turn themselves into amateur historians or keen students of architecture. A few have portable hobbies: Jack Russell was always nipping out with his sketch pad and painting the local market; he even sat back on the planes and knocked out portraits of his fellow passengers (posing for a photo by way of a modelling fee). But not many. Most don't even use the gleaming hotel swimming pools. They have been institutionalized by cricket; for most the only thing they've really had to worry about, ever since they emerged as eager teenage cricketers, is what time the coach leaves.

If you ask them, they'll say that the airports are 'okay, not too bad'. They do know better than to moan in public, even though they also know that nearly everyone moans when they are hanging about in airports: it is the *lingua franca* of travel to swap delay-stories, just as dullness is built into airport design – it is one of the ways we moderns seek to obliterate the surreal riskiness of flying. But the papers are more than happy to moan on their behalf. And it is true that the travel is a bit more tedious for the reporters than it is for the players: they don't get whisked through the VIP lounges, they have to lug their own bags, they have to sit with laptops on their knees thinking of something to write for tomorrow. On days such as this, when there's no cricket, the best they can hope for is to grab a word with Illingworth and hope he'll say something like 'If I were a football manager I'd be laughed out of court.' Actually, it is one of the charming things about him that he talks with this absolute lack of side or tact. He chats away as if he's grumbling to his cronies in the Ray Illingworth bar at Farsley cricket club; he doesn't modulate his speech at all if it happens to be the bloke from the *Mirror*. Again, one has to appreciate the way these quotations are generated. It isn't as if Illingworth, barely able to conceal his disgust at the travel arrangements, has summoned the press and given them a piece of his mind. What happens is that the reporters nudge up to him and ask for a word, he sighs, shrugs and says, all right, then, and they ask him a few non-questions about how the preparation's going, and then at some point someone says: 'Anyway, bet you enjoyed the journey'; and he says, 'Well, it's not ideal is that, but what can you do?' and *bang*, the next thing you know it's 'Illy Raps India!' Quite why he keeps falling for it is a mystery. It's a bit like those archetypal scenes in films about escaped British prisoners of war: they tunnel under the barbed wire, grope through forests at night, steal chickens, climb mountains, borrow wobbly bikes, and speak fluent German all the way. And then finally they bump into a Gestapo man at the station who says, 'Cigarette?' And they say, 'Thanks, old boy, don't mind if I do . . .' Whoops.

* * *

All of this travel sickness was completely beside the point so far as the match went because New Zealand were on the same plane. Peter Martin took the ball from the other end, and did the same as Cork. If he bowled at off stump, the ball swung away; but if he started it down the line of leg stump, it kept on going. Nathan Astle, who had recently been converted into an opening batsman, pushed his third ball away on the leg side for a single; then Spearman did the same, for two. Off the final ball of the over, he threw the bat and skied the ball high over mid-off for another couple. It looked lucky, but actually it was a calculated risk: the fielding regulations mean that there can be only two men on the boundary for the first fifteen overs, so even a lofted mis-hit is a safe shot. Two overs for five runs.

Cork came rushing in again. A week ago, in a practice match in Lahore, he had broken down with a dodgy knee, giving the papers something to groan about. In truth, there was a story here: Cork hadn't stopped bowling for a year, and his knee was crying out for a rest. To anxious England-watchers, he did seem to be fighting to get to the wicket. But now he was getting the line bang-on: the ball veered away from Astle's bat, caught the edge, raced low to second slip, and OWAAZZZEEEEE ... Graham Thorpe dropped it. Okay: not easy, fast and low. But what are slips for? Even at the time, it felt like an important moment. The whole English game plan was to snaffle a few quick wickets: if they failed to do that, they might as well have batted. 'I don't believe it,' said Tony Greig. Damn, damn, damn.

But at least the wasted chance had got the crowd excited. They were still streaming in – thousands of policemen had set up elaborate bottlenecks to make sure loads of people missed the start – and in India it is never too early to be raucous. And if the cricket is dull, well, there are plenty of reasons to be cheering: whenever a television camera points in their direction, for instance, or whenever a woman walks past. When Kapil Dev appeared in the press box, the place went wild as word spread. So Cork was dashing up to the wicket with a fair roar in his ears, and he got it bang-on again and WHHOOOOoooohhh, the ball skimmed past the bat and slapped into the wicket-keeper's gloves. This was more like it. He bowled out the over, another maiden, the right sort this time; and the field swung over again.

Martin didn't look happy. He had done well enough in South Africa, but he looked big and top-heavy here, teetering up to the wicket and spraying the ball towards the batsman as if it was slippery – maybe it was. But wonder of wonders he, too, found the edge. It was a shortish ball, Spearman aimed to slash it away, and it sliced straight to second slip again. This was much easier – shoulder-high – and it smacked into Thorpe's hands and spun to the ground. It isn't easy for crowds to laugh in unison, but this one tried: HA-HAARRGGGHHH! Poor Thorpe. He knelt on the ground, looked at his hands, squinted up at the sky – no, couldn't really blame the sun – stared at his hands again, tried not to catch anyone's eye, and slowly forced himself back to his feet. 'I don't believe it,' said Tony Greig.

What happened next was predictable. Martin strained for a bit of extra speed, overpitched, and Spearman slammed it through the covers for four. The next ball was the same story: it went rifling away towards the boundary, but this time Craig White plunged and saved it. And after four overs, New Zealand were ten for nought, when they should have been five for two. After the match, Atherton and Illingworth were mocked for suggesting that if only they'd held on to their catches then everything might have been different – but it was true. Cricket is full of fine lines, and England had spurned the chance to swing the game's momentum their way.

Having said that, it isn't bad luck when catches are dropped: it's bad catching. I was up in the press box, where scores of reporters haggled over the single telephone (a couple gave up and went back to the hotel to watch the game on telly). After a while, an Indian writer turned and asked: 'England's fielding? Is it always this bad?' If only one could have said no. As it was, the painful memories of their awful sequence of defeats in South Africa came back to the surface. When Martin toppled heavily to the ground, the ball squirming under his body for four extremely stoppable runs, he was ignominiously demoted to deep mid-on. Off he trudged, petulantly kicking the white fielding circle, spraying a cloud of chalk into the air. Oh, Christ, you thought, looking at the stiff shoulders out there. Here we go again.

Poor England. They had been looking all right a couple of months earlier. In the English summer they had drawn a Test series against the West Indies – no mean feat, even if the opposition was in the middle of an acrimonious bust-up – and played with plenty of backbone in South Africa for a while. They had a strong World Cup record, and were regarded by the rest of the World with the kind of gloomy, unenthusiastic, you-have-to-hand-it-to-'em respect accorded, in football, to Germany: England never looked like much, the story went, but they were solid meat-and-potato professionals, always hard to beat. In five World Cups they had reached the final three times. But something bad had happened down in South Africa over the New Year, something that couldn't simply be magicked away by saying that it was all in the past. The wounds were too fresh.

Remember the final Test in Cape Town? England hadn't had a very dynamic series, but they hadn't lost a match. Atherton (twice) and Stewart (once) had saved them in tight corners with a resolution that was, by English standards, heroic. So the series was gridlocked: this was the decider. On the first day, England fell apart, scoring only 150-odd. But on the second day they fought back impressively: South Africa, like England, looked too anxious to bat properly. The highlight was the session between lunch and tea: two hours in which South Africa scored just thirty-five runs for the loss of two wickets. By any standards this was dry stuff, but it was absolutely compelling. Inch by inch, over by over, Angus Fraser and Peter Martin clawed England back into the game. It was hard to look away because, while every maiden over was another small twist of the noose from England's point of view, it would have taken only a couple of wild balls, a clout or two for four, to have unravelled the tension and let South Africa spin away to freedom and safety. Neither of these things happened. The batsmen, terrified of making a silly mistake, risked nothing; the bowlers, for once, didn't attempt anything fancy either, just kept the pressure on. There was nothing in this quiet afternoon you'd want to put on the television highlights – no leaping catches, swooping saves on the boundary, colossal whacks for six or scattering stumps. And the crowd was almost silent, tense with the desire for something to happen out there. For two hours, no one moved.

This is one of cricket's improbable virtues: it does not need to be exciting to be unputdownable. And this, in turn, is one of the reasons why enthusiasts respond with such light hearts to that moment, early in the English summer, when Richie Benaud says, 'Morning, everyone, and welcome to Lord's.' It isn't that they feel they are being welcomed back into some infantile nursery where order prevails and everyone knows his place and the modern world doesn't exist and there is, indeed, choccy cake still for tea. Nor is it simply a pleasant ritual noise, like a cockerel's cry, bells, or the opening chord of some favourite symphony. And it isn't merely that they know, hearing Richie's voice, that they are in safe, knowledgeable and good-natured hands. The words also carry something of the resonance of 'Once upon a time'. They signal the beginning of a story, and we can relax in the certainty that it will be a story of an innocuous, childish sort, a fairy tale or folk myth, because whatever happens it will end in handshakes all round. There'll be a bit of Beauty and the Beast (Lara against Merv Hughes, say), a trace of David and Goliath (India versus West Indies, Lord's, 1983), a little touch, as Richie might say, of Tortoise versus Hare (Boycott facing Botham), and many others.

Anyway, this was Tortoise versus Tortoise, and South Africa were in a flat panic: they had the game at their feet, but couldn't score a run, and kept losing wickets. They seemed paralysed. The new ball came due and Atherton, in a shrewd move for which he received no credit, decided not to take it. 'We'd seen Pollock against the new ball before,' he said. 'And we felt he liked it coming on to him that bit quicker. So we kept the old one.' It worked. Pollock was out, and that brought to the crease the number eleven. No ordinary number eleven, either. Paul Adams was an eighteen-year-old coloured kid, with a certain cocky assurance, who had been the star of the South African season. He had only played a couple of first-class games when he was picked to play against England in a provincial match and – would you believe it? – bamboozled them. There was a noisy popular campaign to pick him for the national team, but it was hard to believe this could happen. What this lad needed, according to traditional English cricket wisdom, was a few hard years in the counties – that would sort him out, show whether he had staying power or not. But maybe, in the new land-of-opportunity South Africa, it was possible. Anyway, here he was. He had bowled well, but he was hardly a batsman – how could he be, with a bowling action like that? So Atherton brought back Malcolm, another sensible move. Adams had never faced anyone this fast in his life, and Dave Richardson, up at the other end, was famous for being a bit cowed by real speed.

Quite a lot of strong feelings were bubbling away at this point. Devon Malcolm had become a symbol of the perplexity surrounding English cricket. He was by far our fastest bowler, and somehow you knew that if he played for any other team he'd be a feared and dangerous opponent. But he had never really been trusted by the

England set-up, which winced every time he was hit for four. He had come out here to South Africa with a big wind in his sails: the last time the two sides had met, at the Oval in London, he had blasted them out of the match with nine wickets and a lot of bruises. Australians and Indians looked on with envy: here was the kind of out-and-out quickie all teams would give their right arm for. But England, hmmm. Managers and pundits alike fussed and worried that he was too wild. Illingworth chose to wind him up a bit. He and his entourage publicly pilloried his action and his attitude. He was, they said, a 'nonentity'. Malcolm wouldn't listen to advice, he wouldn't work, he wouldn't learn. He could bowl fast, they said, but that was it. He didn't have a 'cricket brain'.

There might or might not have been a few grains of truth in this. Malcolm might not have been very pliable. But he was thirty-three, a bit old to change a bowling style that had served him pretty well – well enough to take Test wickets at roughly twice the rate of Illingworth himself (in the average Test, Illingworth took two for sixty-two; Malcolm four for seventy). But even if the coaches were right about Malcolm, did they really think that a public dressing-down would do any good? I suppose there are some people who, like racehorses, react well to a stinging slap across the neck. Most, though, go a bit wonky and desperate. Everyone knows that in cricket, as in any sport, the decisive issue is confidence. Instead of making their strike bowler feel strong, they were making him feel anxious and petulant. Malcolm was picked, then dropped. Then picked again, then dropped again.

He was in an especially invidious position on this tour as England's only black player – the only black player on either side come to that: in the much-vaunted new South Africa, the black population (90 per cent of the national total) was still not represented in the team. Anyone with an ounce of wit or imagination would have made Malcolm the promotional focal point of the tour. Early on, Nelson Mandela came helicoptering in to Soweto, shook hands with Malcolm and said, 'I know you. You're the destroyer.' Illingworth, meanwhile, was swearing at him in the nets (Malcolm said he was told to 'fuck off'; Illy insisted that he only said 'piss off', so that's fine, then) and throwing up his hands in horror. The story ended up running on into the summer, when Illingworth's ghosted autobiography raised the subject again and led to his being fined by the powers-that-be. It was all very stupid.

So here we were: Malcolm, who despite Illingworth's very public reservations was still picked for this crucial last Test, had the chance to polish things off. Who knows what would have happened if he'd been feeling happy and sure of himself? At any rate, it all went horribly wrong. Dominic Cork started it. Adams plopped forward, got his bat to the ball somehow, and blocked the ball out to short gully. Cork grabbed the ball, turned and hurled it past the stumps for four overthrows. And it wasn't the runs so much as the change of atmosphere. It was the first boundary South Africa had scored for about four hours. All that bated-breath tension, all that agonized worrying as the home side crept into their shell, erupted. Newlands, an exceptionally pretty stadium in a lush western suburb of Cape Town, all bougainvillaea and orchids over the barbed-wire fences, burst into life. There was even more to it than that: Paul Adams was, like Malcolm, a symbolic figure – he was the first black (well, coloured) man to make the team, and was also a novice, with an utterly unorthodox bowling action. In England, you could be sure, he would not have been allowed near the Test side. One wag said he looked, when he bowled, like a frog in a blender – a tag that stuck. His head disappeared in a whirl of arms and legs: he looked as if he was about to spring into a cartwheel. His chin ducked down into his stomach (breaking every single rule in the MCC manual to do with still heads and level eyes) and for a moment you feared that he had broken his neck. And from somewhere in this spinning tangle of limbs came the ball, looping gently up the wicket towards the batsman. He looked like a joke; but, so far, the joke had been on the batsmen.

So on the one hand you had England's only black player, a troubled trier who was neither welcome nor believed in. And then you had South Africa's: youthful, original and cute. You didn't have to be a sociologist to appreciate the significance of this: you could feel it in the atmosphere. Adams made South Africans happy: he was just what they wanted and needed. Everything he achieved on the actual pitch was a bonus. Malcolm, though, made Englishmen frown: if there was any point to him at all, he was supposed to be our answer to Curtly Ambrose. It was almost as though, if he kept getting thumped for four, we might as well pick a white guy. Anyway, the crowd shouted and hooted with extra zest. A day's worth of beer and barbecue fuelled the cheering: it was like the lid blowing off a pressure cooker.

Malcolm hurtled in, leapt into the crease and blazed down, well, a perfect ball – a straight yorker. Adams jumped in the air, jammed his bat near it, got a tiny nick on the ball and sent it flying to fine leg for four. Malcolm tried to repeat the trick. This time it nudged the pad and ran away for four more. One last effort: the ball arrowed in again, missed the bat, and YESSS! – but no. It hit a footmark, jumped up over the stumps, cleared the wicket-keeper, and went for another boundary. You could feel the disapproval radiating out from the slips: one of the worst feelings, for a bowler, is the paranoid sense that your teammates are saying, 'Huh, told you so,' behind their hands. You want to explain that it wasn't your fault, that it's bloody hard to come back when you haven't bowled much for the last two months because you were dropped, and rotten luck to leak all those runs off the edge. Plus why wasn't there a fine leg – or a leg slip – eh? Indignation and shame quickly curdle into anger and hurt pride. Malcolm was a terrible sight as he walked away stiff-legged, like a drunk, or someone with broken legs; he tried thrusting his cap on to his head in a jaunty way, as if nothing had happened. Not long ago he was being called Malcolm Devon by the previous chairman of selectors, and now this. It looked as if one thought was flashing across his mind – the thought that flashes across the mind of everyone who plays cricket even occasionally: God, I hate cricket.

Afterwards, everyone had lots to say about this over: Illingworth and Atherton both blamed Malcolm for failing to rise to the occasion. Illingworth went so far as to chastise him for not peppering Adams with bouncers, as instructed, and if this is true, it is greatly to Malcolm's credit that he rebelled. Really, it just felt like a sudden intrusion of village cricket into the edgy, tense mood of an important Test match. Any club bowler knows the feeling – you've sorted out all the proper batsmen, and then some know-nothing muggins starts slogging it all over the place. Either way, South Africa started batting with the merry abandon that, until now, they'd been too crippled by nerves to attempt. Richardson scored fifty; Adams thirty. Cork came back to replace Malcolm, and fell into the same trap, trying to bowl wonder balls instead of aiming for a steady, unsettling line. All the bowlers had a try. Peter Martin eventually cracked it, finding the edge of Richardson's bat. The ball flew straight to second slip, and . . . and no one was there. Such was the disarray in the field that Atherton had dropped the fielders out to save runs. Inevitably, one fine glance went scudding down to Malcolm at third man: he knelt down to pick it up in the textbook manner, but the ball darted through his shaking hands for four. The crowd shrieked and rocked with amused glee. It took less than an hour, and South Africa, improbably, were back in charge.

Before the South African innings, if you'd offered Mike Atherton a South African total of 240 he'd have bitten your hand off – it was better than England could have hoped for. But such is the role that context plays in cricket: having been so close to a strong position, they were now in a skid. However, if they could keep things steady tonight, then they could start again tomorrow, eighty or so behind, and they wouldn't be out of it. The task now was to set South Africa a nerve-racking target in the fourth innings. The way they had batted in this one, there was a good chance they wouldn't get 200. But cricket teams are like medieval armies: once they are retreating, they lose their shape – enemy horsemen scatter them to the four corners of the field. It was up to the early batsmen to form a square, to soak up the charge and take the spring out of the South African stride.

For spectators, there was one bit of good news. The game had developed so quickly that there was no question of a draw. There were still three and a bit days to go – even Atherton couldn't bat for three days. As it turned out, he barely lasted three balls. Donald came at him like a hot wind, and he jabbed at a rising delivery and sliced it into the wicket-keeper's hands. It seemed inevitable, for reasons not really apparent on television where, framed by the neat conventions of the box, every ball looks the same. But out there in real life, the mood of the stadium is a big player.

It was late afternoon in Cape Town: the tail end of a hot day. The locals had arrived early to set up deckchairs and barbecues on the grassy slopes; eggs and steaks and tomatoes fried and burnt, and so did noses and shoulders. Now the sun was beginning to sag towards Table Mountain, whose giant silhouette reared over the ground like some enormous grandstand, and the dustbins overflowed with empty beer cans. And as Allan Donald sped towards the wicket, his face streaked with zinc war paint, blond hair lighting his path like a tracer bullet, the crowd got, as they say, behind him. CLAP, clap, clap, clap, CLAP, clap, clap, clap, CLAP clap clap clap – it started slowly, then gathered pace and volume as it spread round the stands. CLAP-clap-clap-clap, CLAP-clap-clap-clap, CLAPaclapaclapaclapclap, CLAPPACLAPPA CLAPPAOOOOHHHH!! English cricket crowds are famously, comically sedate, and every time they show any signs of exuberance (usually it's the West Indians and Asians who are responsible, with their horns, conch shells and drumming beer cans) they are held to be 'spoiling it for the others', and told to zip it. But this was quite something: from the boundary it felt as if a huge wind had sprung up. It takes a fair amount of nerve to survive in these conditions – it is a lonely feeling having 20,000 or so people willing you to fail. The players themselves are sanguine about it. Ask Atherton whether he's bothered by the noise and he says, 'Not really. If anything it's good, helps you concentrate.' Donald admits only that 'Yeah, it gets the adrenaline pumping.' So maybe this is just one of the thousands of points at which the idle imagination of the spectator floats free of events on the field. But in this heated atmosphere the bowling looked unplayable – you felt there'd be a wicket every ball. England looked dead.

The next morning Allan Donald was waiting for them, marking out his run like some vicious albino bullock snorting and pawing the ground. Stewart didn't last long (about six minutes). Nor did anyone else. For an hour or two Hick and Thorpe looked as if they could haul England into calmer water, but when they were out, the rest just came and went. South Africa were left with a few runs to knock off, which they did with nonchalant ease, and that was that. A crushing ten-wicket defeat inside three days. The wheels had well and truly come off. England reluctantly played a hastily agreed one-day match against Western Province – a good idea: thousands of English fans had flown out to watch five days of cricket, and they'd been swizzed out of two of them – and lost. Then they played seven one-day matches against South Africa, and were thoroughly walloped. They tried to pretend that it didn't matter; they even muttered that these matches were not 'important' – a fatal bit of reasoning, since it suggests that games aren't worth winning unless they are 'important', which raises in turn the uncomfortable truth that no games are 'important', they are just there to be won or lost, and you might as well win and be cheerful as lose and be miserable.

And England did look miserable as they stumbled from defeat to defeat. Devon Malcolm was flown home and promptly blew the whistle on Illingworth, foolishly suggesting, in the *Daily Express*, that the chairman might not have been so tough on a white bowler (he didn't know, evidently, that Illy was once awarded an honorary degree by Hull University for his contribution to racial harmony). The powers-that-be tried to keep a lid on it; even Mark Ramprakash's 'tour diary' was vetted by the management, who drew a red pencil through the bits about his roommate (Malcolm) phoning home to moan about the way he was being treated. And there was a rumour going round that Illingworth had actually told Ramprakash himself, on the way out to bat, 'Good luck, son. Get some runs. It's your last chance.' This couldn't have been true; no one could be that dense. But the counties, the real powers in the game, were restless and pushed for an explanation. It ended up with Illingworth resigning as team manager, making way for David Lloyd, and being obliged to recognize that his days as chairman of selectors were numbered too.

Atherton caught some flak as well. A month or so before the tabloids had dressed him up in robes and plastered 'Arise, Sir Mike' all over the back page, after his epic innings in Johannesburg (185 not out). Athers was presented as a military hero, a redcoat seeing off the Zulu hordes at Rorke's Drift, just down the road, in a grand rearguard action. Now there were dark hints that he should be replaced as captain, perhaps by Dermot Reeve. Reeve himself had flown out to South Africa for the one-day series, been picked for only three games, bowled only a handful of overs, and then been dropped from the World Cup party. None of this was surprising, because the team looked like a shambles. They used the games to 'experiment', but it looked more like casting around for straws. In one match they sent Craig White and Jack Russell out to open the batting. They didn't seem to know how bad it all looked. They were tired, fed up with being away from home, up to here with cricket, frankly, but that wasn't much use to the fans back home, the ones who pay for the game in television ratings. It is hard for these people, hanging on to straps in the London Underground twice a day, or stuck in lousy traffic for two hours on their daily commute, to sympathize with all this shite about how hard touring is. All the what's-wrong-with-English-cricket feelings, never far from the top of people's minds (because everyone knows that there is lots wrong) came hissing to the surface.

And now, after just ten minutes of their first World Cup match, those same feelings were fizzing up all over the place. It is one of the pleasures of cricket that, slow and long as it is, several stories converge on any one moment: Illingworth and Atherton had been saying until they were blue in the face that South Africa was all in the past now. And it did seem, when the players converged on an airport hotel at Heathrow to embark on their World Cup adventure, that they were in a chipper mood. A room had been set aside for media interviews, and the players wandered in and out, stepping over cables, blinking in the brilliant white television lights, and chatting by the pot plants.

'Say something for sound, would you, Mike?' said the cameraman. 'One two three four five six seven eight nine ten – is that all right?' said Atherton.

'It's warm in here,' said Illingworth, sitting beside him. 'Hope you're as warm as we are.'

Dominic Cork was over in the corner, putting up with jibes about his new crewcut. 'Don't worry,' he said. 'I'm having it finished off in Lahore tomorrow.'

Alec Stewart was talking away to camera. Most of the interviews lasted about three minutes, but he seemed to be chatting for hours.

'So, who are the key players for England?' he was asked.

He glanced around. 'Well, obviously Thorpy.' He smiled. Thorpe stood behind the camera and stuck out his tongue.

'And Dominic Cork, of course,' said Stewart, as Cork leaned in and gave an ironic handclap.

An Indian television crew was trying to get Robin Smith to agree that he was no good any more. 'Oh, but really,' they insisted, 'your technique was found wanting.' Smith politely disagreed. 'Well, I'm not sure I'd say that . . .' he said patiently.

'Well,' said Illingworth, 'we had a lot of comings and goings at the end of the South African trip. It'll be more settled this time.'

Stewart was still going strong, blue eyes staring at the camera. 'Christ,' said Cork. 'He'll be telling them the birthweight of his babies next.'

They seemed merry enough. But the past can't quite be wished away: sometimes it is like standing on a rake which jumps up and bops you on the head. That's how it was now, here and in Ahmedabad. The crowd was delighted: it was all for New Zealand, if only because they were playing England. And why shouldn't these people want England to lose? Just a couple of miles away was Gandhi's ashram, a tranquil acreage of dry ground and bungalows shaded by trees and with a long, cool view across the Sabamarti river. It was here that the great man had sat, spinning and thinking, for fifteen years before embarking on the marches and fasts about textiles and salt that shook the imperial grandees in Delhi and London. This was still the heart of the burning resentment against the British impositions on India, and you only had to be sixty now to remember those servile days of colonial rule. The Ahmedabad crowd was notorious in English cricket circles: it had once thrown stones at the English women's team when they played India here, as if to show the memsahibs who was the boss. It didn't feel the least bit hostile now, although there were thousands of armed police in the stands, just in case. The people just jeered.

New Zealand, though. To English eyes, they have always seemed like a poor man's Australia – slightly less talented, slightly less professional, slightly less bolshy, and slightly easier to beat. Of course, it is characteristic of the English approach to all sports that we cherish this sort of inflated, or perhaps just dated, faith in our teams' standing. In football, we persist in believing that we are a top nation, although we do not always even qualify for the World Cup, let alone win it (out of the last six tournaments, England have failed to qualify three times). Most English cricket fans would instinctively see New Zealand as easy meat, but in one-day cricket they have beaten England almost as many times as they have lost (seventeen wins, twenty-one defeats). And in the last World Cup they came top of the group section, edging out England on the way, before narrowly losing the semi-final to a resurgent Pakistan. But they had not had the best of times lately. Their star player, Martin Crowe, had retired hurt for good this time. They had a new side of which it would be unfair to expect great things. For them, the match was a chance to stake a claim on the world's attention, and already they looked busy and purposeful.

Whereas England . . . I don't know, I suppose we shouldn't have been surprised. Anyone who has watched our chaps in recent years knows the feeling: a heaving sense of puzzled national embarrassment. Why do our players seem so stodgy and uncertain, while theirs seem so vigorous and composed? Some of this is an illusion: we do not watch overseas teams very often, only when they are playing England. So we only have a hazy idea of how they are doing, and rarely look closely enough to perceive any shortcomings. But you couldn't help noticing, looking around the impressive cast list at this World Cup, that other countries seemed to produce bold athletes like Donald, Ambrose and Waqar Younis, attacking daredevils like Lara, Tendulkar and De Silva, relaxed naturals like Mark Waugh and Inzaman-ul-Haq, or subtle maestros like Warne, Kumble and Mushtaq Ahmed. It couldn't be just that they were foreign: over the years we had included plenty of foreign-born players in our team too. But their foreigners seemed to be better than our foreigners. There was clearly something wrong with English cricket: for a couple of decades now it had produced bad-tempered cheese-and-pickle types who played too much, ate too much, drank too much, travelled too much and complained too much. Goodness knows, we had plenty of money, plenty of grounds, plenty of players, plenty of everything. But all these other countries just seemed to have more zip. It didn't seem fair. Boo-hoo.

Thus runs the aggrieved fan's lament. But maybe we shouldn't be too hasty, after just ten minutes of the first match. The idea that our game is in decline has been a common threnody since the last century; cricket is perversely nostalgic. In 1901, the Surrey captain wrote in *Wisden*: 'The energy, the life, the ever-watchfulness of ten years ago are gone, and in their place are lethargy, laziness, and a wonderful yearning for rest.' And even further back, in 1882, the publication *Lillywhite's* mourned the demise of the fast bowler in terms that are still heard now: 'The practice of fast bowling in our schools and colleges is, sadly, neglected.' Cricket was going down the drain even then. But there is no serious reason to suppose that while every other sport in the world has increased in pace and skill, cricket has gone backwards. Everyone knows, in their hearts, that Jim Laker wouldn't have taken all those wickets against a modern Australian team. Even in the trembling black-and-white footage of his ten-wicket masterpiece, you can see how chronic the batting was. Ian Botham put it rather well when he pointed out that Fred Trueman, the unrivalled leader of the in-my-day school of cricket criticism, might be perfectly successful bowling today, but sure as heck wouldn't be called Fiery Fred.

There is an additional, imperial reason for England's seeming weakness in international competitions. We were all high and mighty in the 1950s, but this was a bad decade for most of the countries we were playing. We used to beat the West Indies when, thanks to our own social engineers, they fielded teams exclusively made up of white men. Only now were they emerging as a real force. In the subcontinent, the empire had only recently withdrawn (1947) and the subsequent massacres left the newly independent nations both drained and hardly in the mood to concentrate on bats and balls.

All that has changed. It isn't that we have declined; it is merely that history has levelled the playing field. We are no longer playing, and beating, and congratulating ourselves for beating, nations we half maimed and confused.

So it was silly to be too gloomy too soon. Cork was bowling with bristling menace. A nice away swinger beat the bat; another rapped the batsman's pads. Since his dashing introduction to Test cricket – seven wickets, followed by a hat-trick against the West Indies – he had been an invigorating addition to England's bowling attack. But already the effort was taking its toll. Out in South Africa, during the final Test match, Allan Donald was talking about the physical and mental burden on fast bowlers in this age of non-stop cricket, and he broke off to gesture out to the middle, where Cork was bowling. 'I mean, take Cork,' he said. 'He's a young guy and he wants to bowl, so fair enough. But how long can he go on like this? It's only a question of time before something breaks down.' It seemed to be coming true. Corky's knee was becoming one of the mantras in the England entourage. Every time the pressmen got a chance to talk to Illingworth or Atherton they would ask, 'What about Dominic? How's the knee?' It is strange: sport is all about youth and dynamic fitness, but during this World Cup there was a geriatric tone to many of the conversations surrounding England.

'How's the back, Athers?'

'Oh, mustn't grumble. It's okay when I'm playing.'

'Corky's knee?'

'It'll be okay by Sunday. He's resting it.'

'Hicky's thigh?'

'He strained it fielding. We'll know better how it is in the morning.'

'Robin's groin?'

'The best advice we have is a week. He might be available for the second match.'

Later in the tournament I asked Dermot Reeve whether there was ever a day, maybe the first game of the new season, when a cricketer felt absolutely tip-top and raring to go. He just grinned. It was such a stupid question. There was always a bruised finger, a splattered toe, sore shins, wrenched shoulders, stiff backs, a twisted ankle, pulled ligaments, strained tendons, tiny stress fractures that would get worse if you didn't do something about them – always something. 'Never,' he said, trying to imagine what such a day would feel like. 'There's never a day like that.'

But Cork was battling through with his usual fierce-eyed vim. He jagged one back into Spearman and swung into his extravagant appealing routine – a leaning-back, arms-raised plea, which he thoughtfully holds for the photographers. It wasn't out, but Spearman, miffed, tried to wipe the next one back past the bowler's shoulder. Cork stuck out a hand and, by some miracle, the ball stuck. The breakthrough! Maybe it wasn't too late; maybe England could pour through the breach and regroup.

Maybe not. Peter Martin was bowling like a net machine, dropping the ball straight into the batsman's stroke. The new man, Fleming, drove him straight back to the pavilion for four, then jogged an easy single. Nathan Astle, perhaps feeling he'd been in long enough now, took a step down the wicket and lifted the ball high over midwicket for six. The next one was driven through the covers for three. The crucial opening phase, the hoped-for dawn raid by England, seemed to be over. New Zealand looked as if they had wriggled free. It was going to be a long day, after all. When Cork dropped short, Astle leaned back and cracked him past cover for four. Cork slapped his thigh, and you could tell that the next ball was damn well not going to be short. It wasn't, and Astle was ready for it: he moved forward smartly and drilled it firmly for three more runs. Illingworth came on to see whether finger-spin would grip on this wicket, and his first ball was sliced away to third man for a boundary. Gough came bounding in, a parody of the bowler he had seemed a year or so ago, and Astle clumped him skywards over mid-on for six. Then he slashed him square for four. The guy was running amok. English fans hadn't seen him before, except for a few weatherbeaten souls in Yorkshire where Astle had played two seasons for Farsley (Ray Illingworth's club) in the Bradford league. And in England it is hard to get around the idea that if we haven't heard of someone, then he can't be any good. The instinctive tabloid reflex, out in Ahmedabad, was to conclude that England were being taken apart by some nobody. But the truth was, Astle looked like a class act: brisk but unhurried, aggressive without being wild. His fifty came up in the seventeenth over, with the score on seventy-five. Afterwards, the New Zealand manager Glenn Turner was asked by English reporters what he thought about Astle (the manager's comment being thought far more newsworthy than the man's score). 'Well, that's his fifth century this summer,' he said. 'He's a good player.'

The hundred came up in the twenty-first over: at this rate New

Zealand were going to get a huge total. A swirl of vultures drifted in the blue sky, attracted by the scent of easy pickings.

Somehow, without doing anything especially brilliant, England hung on. Two New Zealanders got carried away by their excellent start and were caught at deep square leg going for big hits off Graeme Hick. Thorpe was the man who held both catches – proof, perhaps, that this was where he should have been fielding all along, but also a sign that his nerve hadn't entirely gone. There were still plenty of misfields, and Atherton dropped an absolute sitter at mid-off, but the New Zealand innings was stalling. Astle was losing the strike: his first fifty had come in an hour; his second took nearly two hours. To the naked eye, it looked very much as if he had struck out boldly early on, and then calmed down. Some experienced cricket writers jumped to this conclusion. 'After the initial flurry,' the *Telegraph* reported, 'he settled into the anchor role.' In fact, his scoring rate increased: his second fifty took fewer balls than his first, even though there weren't so many eye-catching fours. This was a nice example of how misleading mere observation can be. A computer, with its cool, analytical head, would not have been fooled. It is one of the axioms of one-day cricket that you need to spread your fielders around and protect the boundary; but sometimes this merely allows batsmen to score even more freely. It might have been better to have kept a tight ring of fielders and put up with the odd four: it is one of the unfairnesses of cricket that a fast bowler who is clonked for two boundaries is held to have bowled badly, while a spinner who is stroked around for four singles and a couple of twos is felt to have kept the brakes on.

England, it goes without saying, have been slow to exploit the resources available to the modern game. Out in South Africa, there had been much interest in Bob Woolmer's laptop, which contained a ball-by-ball analysis of all the games South Africa were playing under his management. Here was a case in point: only statistics could tell the truth about Astle's innings, and help people plan a response. Illingworth, of course, had pooh-poohed all such modern mumbo-jumbo. 'My laptop's in here,' he declared, with bizarre self-assurance, tapping his head. 'I've seen every single international game since I retired in 1983. There's no way anyone can tell me something I don't know about cricket.' You have, I suppose, to admire the man's bravado; perhaps he even believes this. He would probably regard it as some sort of southerner insult to be called 'modern', and has been famously unenthusiastic about any of the more subtle psychological approaches available to sportsmen these days. One of his first gestures as England's supremo was to sack the team's counsellor (the Reverend Andrew Wingfield-Digby) on the grounds that only softies needed that sort of help – 'a shoulder to cry on', as Illingworth called it. 'If you start bringing shrinks and spin doctors into the dressing room,' he said, 'it probably means you haven't got the right people in the side.' Could he be serious? Did it do the players any harm to have a friendly supporter close by, someone they could confide in without fearing they'd be dropped? Did Illingworth want them to do better, or did he only want the 'right people' in his team? Convictions such as these can look good when you win, but they don't half seem pig-headed when you lose.

Still, when Astle hit an easy-peasy full toss straight to Hick at midwicket it seemed that England's luck had held. The Kiwis were sitting very pretty on 196 for three with ten overs left, and would have expected to get 260, at the very least – just as the groundsman had predicted. But the last ten overs yielded just forty-three runs. In his newspaper column the next day. Sunil Gavaskar mysteriously attributed New Zealand's total to a 'late flourish from Thomson and Germon', but only Gavaskar could think that forty-three off the last ten was a 'flourish'. Richard Illingworth came back and bowled three overs for four, and England bowled four for just eight at a telling time. It wasn't a bad total, but it wasn't a good one either. New Zealand were not a renowned bowling side, so the odds, if anything, were slightly with England. On the down side, Cork had dropped another easy catch towards the end, which wasn't costly in itself but added further weight to England's image as complete no-hopers, and Hick had pulled a muscle in his leg. And while one sympathizes with injured players, it isn't always easy to feel sorry for such an injury-prone team. After a while, it doesn't seem like an accident. Atherton's bad back was famous: the poor guy could hardly get out of bed in the mornings, and he shuffled around the hotel like an old man wearing broken-down slippers. Alec Stewart had a finger that seemed to break if he picked his nose with it. Cork, Smith and Fairbrother were all struggling. And now Hick looked like a goner as well. This whole show had only been on the road for a week, but it already felt rickety as hell. And it was no use complaining about it, because everyone knew what was causing it: all of these players had been playing, practising or travelling non-stop for the last few years. It was permatour, and on the rare occasions when they weren't playing for England they were schlepping round the country playing county games in front of a few pensioners and children.

Oh, well, lunch at last: a nice piece of tandoori chicken and a cold squashed samosa. Spicy smells filled the warm air. Indian cricket grounds used to be tea and biscuits; now they have been replaced by their modern equivalents, Coke and crisps. It makes quite a change from the beer, pork pie and salad-cream flavour of English grounds, or the burned-fat barbecue smoke of Australia and South Africa. No one gets drunk at cricket grounds in Ahmedabad, because Gujarat is an alcohol-free state. In fact there was only one place to get a beer in this city – the bar of the hotel where, as coincidence would have it, the teams were staying. Even there you were served only if you produced a permit, and to get the permit you had to take your passport off to the excise office and fill out a form claiming to be an alcoholic – hardly perjury, in many cases, but still something requiring great dedication. Actually, the drinking habits in this low-alcohol part of the world were having a noticeable off-the-field effect on this competition already. Coca-Cola and Pepsi had both been banned from India for two decades by a government that did not want American multinationals to hoover profits out of its thirsty, teetotal millions. But in the last year or so the ban had been lifted, and the fizzy-drink giants were now allowed a free run at this vast market. Coca-Cola had become one of the official sponsors of the tournament: it paid $3.7 million to Pilcom for the privilege. In return, it got big advertising displays at the grounds (and hence on television) and also won control of the drinks intervals during the game. They had designed a red trolley in the shape of a Coke bottle, and it would rumble out, towed by a tractor, on to the field every hour or so.

Pepsi seemed to have lost a key battle in this new cola war, but they fought back fiercely, signing up the top players in a witty advertising campaign that dominated the commercial breaks on television and the giant billboards in the city streets. Sachin Tendulkar would be playing cricket with small boys, and smashing the ball through people's windows. Then he'd reach for a Pepsi, flip his cap round like a disc jockey, and say: 'Pepsi: Nothing Official About It.' Mohammad Azharuddin would wink down from every roundabout: 'Pepsi: Unofficially Yours.' It was an unusual sight to see cricket presented as a form of rebellion, but it worked. Coke was implicitly made the chosen drink of the 'officials' – the corrupt administrators, the tedious old-timers, all those boring old has-beens who said the game was going to the dogs. Who wanted to drink with those guys, anyway? It was a good gimmick.

Just outside the entrance to the stadium in Ahmedabad, in fact, there was a huge wall painted with the Pepsi logo – a wall, it turned out, that had been purpose-built to hold the advert. There was also a Pepsi blimp floating in the blue sky. Coke had grabbed the in-ground rights, but Pepsi were taking to the skies. After about half an hour you could see policemen arguing with the balloon handlers, and forcing them to take it down: Coke throwing its weight around, by the look of things. And you had to be high up in the stadium to see it, but a while later Pepsi's rebellious labourers tried to set the blimp going again on a piece of dead ground about 400 yards away. There it hovered, unofficially yours.

Later, there would be court cases about all of this. Coke were furious to find that sponsoring the tournament didn't stop the players from going off and doing deals with Pepsi. Some of the players, in turn, protested when Coke started using footage in television spots of their own great moments in cricket, arguing correctly that they were under contract to a rival sugar-and-water combo.

Coca-Cola was only one of several 'official' sponsors. The chief one, of course, was Wills tobacco, which had paid $12 million for this to be called the Wills World Cup. During the opening ceremony Saeed Jaffrey, in one of his more endearing gaffes, had forgotten to credit the tournament's leading patron. 'I'm sorry,' he said. 'I've been calling it the World Cup. It is, of course, the Wills World Cup.' Of course! The other benefactors included a textile company ('Vimal salutes the spirit of cricket!'), an airline (Cathay Pacific), an automobile concern (Hero-Honda) and a shipping company (Gargill-Western) – quite an interesting group, not at all the traditional cast list of cricket sponsors. This tournament had been devised as a moneyspinner, and there were plenty of takers willing to pay huge sums to have their name attached to the carnival. Whether this could have happened anywhere else but in the subcontinent, with its booming population of cricket lovers, was not clear.

Talking of cricket lovers, it was Valentine's Day, and the papers were full of strange messages. Some of them were direct: 'Jyoti, Meet me near Dairy Pen at 5.30 p.m.'; some of them were heartfelt: 'My dearest Sanjukta, I am really grateful to you for standing by my side whenever I am in a soup'; and one or two, to be honest, seemed ill-judged: 'Love is like playing bridge in which grand slam depends both on cards and players.' Love is like bridge? Love is like four people sitting silently round a table staring at their hands, and calculating odds? Two hearts, anyone? But there were a few genuinely frantic messages. 'Rasna,' moaned Vasu, 'your beautiful eyes makes me wise like mango ripe. Your gorgeous hair makes me blair like nibbu pani. You little ery makes me try Sahara dry. Your pleasant smile makes me think a while like a orange wine. Please do visit or bullet pierces my head like mint with the hole.' I'm afraid I do not know what an 'ery' is, though it sounds enticing; nor do I know what orange wine thinks like. But that's love for you.

Lunch was over: here came Atherton and Stewart. The game hadn't gone well so far, but it was still there to be won. Atherton took guard, crouched into his watchful stance, and glided the first ball down to fine leg for one. The crowd mooed gently, and cheered heartily when a good throw came thumping back from the boundary. Stewart played out the over, and round it went. Then: disaster. Dion Nash loosed off a weird ball that looped high like a full toss, then wobbled and dipped into Atherton's toes. He played all round it and was bowled. England were one for one, and on the run.

Hick and Stewart batted solidly for an hour or so without ever quite looking on top of the bowling, which was steady. Stewart showed a few signs of form. He'd spent his week back in England in the nets at East Molesey with his father, trying to get his feet moving a bit more, and was striking the ball cleanly. He didn't even seem to be feeling the ill-effects of his crack on the skull during fielding practice the day before, when a big hit from the New Zealand nets bounced once and thumped into the back of his head. Indecision got him in the end – he played a palsied, plopping sort of half jab at a slow ball and looped it back to the bowler. But the hundred was up, and Hick was threatening to take command. He was batting with a runner (Atherton) and it suited him: he just had to stand there cuffing the ball and pottering disdainfully off to square leg. Every now and then, apropos of nothing, he let fly: Chris Cairns was lobbed for four on the leg side, then patted for four more on the off. It was all a bit slow – with fifteen overs to go England needed another 100 – but they did have seven wickets in hand (Thorpe had come and gone) so the chase was on. And then, another farce: Fairbrother clipped the ball and set off for a sharp run. Atherton, seeing that

Roger Twose had pulled off a fine diving stop, hesitated, then went for it. Too late. Twose sat up, threw the ball in, and Atherton sprawled in the dust some way short of the crease. It was a shame: Hick was going along smoothly enough to have won the match. He and the skipper headed for the pavilion, and out came Jack Russell.

Whether Russell should even have been playing was one of those moot, selectorial talking points that dominate conversations about English cricket. As it happened, there was no choice today. The only other batsman in the tour party, Robin Smith, was injured. But given that Alec Stewart was a thoroughly good wicket-keeper, and given that England were short of a top all-rounder, didn't it make sense to hand Stewart the gloves and pick another batsman? Opinions vary. The MCC coaching manual regards it as 'an absolute' that you should always pick your best wicket-keeper, but this was formulated long before the modern style of one-day batting. Instead of Russell coming in at six, it could have been Mark Ramprakash (or Maynard or Hussein or Brown or Gooch), some out-and-out attacking batsman. All of this was magnificently beside the point right now, but it is the kind of thing everyone talks about at cricket matches – there were 30,000 selectors inside the ground, and millions more watching on television. Cricket is relentlessly, exhaustingly subjunctive, permanently occupied with what could have been, what might have happened. Russell had batted well in South Africa, but was he a comforting sight coming in at a point such as this? Not really: the situation didn't call for terrier-like defiance. He scored two runs from nine balls, sensed he needed to get a move on, and spooned the slow–medium pace of Gavin Larsen straight to mid-on.

England were falling behind now: there were only twelve overs to go and they still needed ninety runs. Neil Fairbrother was hoicking and flailing wildly: one top edge spiralled just out of reach of the keeper, another fell just in front of a fielder who seemed to have lost it in the sun. But at least he was pressing – there had been something a bit sedate and unpurposeful about the innings so far. England entered the last ten overs needing eighty-three, a tall order but not beyond the bounds of possibility. Craig White struck a six, and the crowd hummed: they would be quite happy to love England, you realized, if we had more people who hit sixes and played with a bit of derring-do. Part of their lack of enthusiasm for our team was aesthetic. And almost at once White went for another one and was caught in the deep. Fairbrother took a big heave and was bowled – not his fault: he had to chance his arm. And suddenly England were running out of batsmen. Six overs to go, fifty-two to win – no chance. But hang on: Cork slogged Thomson over long-on for six, then took two fours in a row off Danny Morrison, one of them a cracker, the other a sneaky inside edge that only just missed the stumps. Thirty-two off four. Don't say anything, but this wasn't over. A couple more big blows . . . There was an awful lot of stamping and clapping now, an almost permanent ooh-aah from the stands. Indians love boundaries, and they love cheering. Now, at the beginning of the over, they drummed their feet on the concrete and clattered their empty water bottles on the railings. It might just go right down to the wire.

This sort of will-they-won't-they see-saw is at the heart of one-day cricket's popularity. It had been a long day, and now it was all coming down to these last few overs. If you closed your eyes, you could imagine the bowler dropping short, and Cork clouting it high into the stands to the left. Then leaping down the wicket to carve another one high over the deep man at cover. A couple of pushed singles, a fine nick through the empty slip area for another four, and England would need only – what would it be? – fourteen off the last three. Practically routine.

This is not what happened. Cork was caught behind, Peter Martin came out, and people started to leave. As it happens, he can bat okay, but these people had seen him field so you couldn't blame them for giving up. Sure enough, he dollied one to midwicket, and that was that. Darren Gough and Richard Illingworth were never going to get twenty-three off the last two overs, or fifteen off the last one. So although it finished up looking close – England fell short by twelve – they were always a couple of overs off the pace. There was never a moment, except in fantasy, when you could truly believe they were going to do it, only that they might, that they still could, that it wasn't completely out of the question . . .

And it hadn't been a bad game – if you were a New Zealander it must have looked pretty good – but it hadn't exactly been a snorter, either. Afterwards, the captains and managers filed into a small room in the pavilion to address the press. 'Shall I stand or sit?' said Illingworth. 'Be easier to stand, wouldn't it?' someone said. 'Well, it would be easier to sit,' said Illingworth. 'But I'll stand for you if you like.' He's so damn *obliging*, Illingworth, it's almost touching. Or is it the obligingness of a man who is so inured to the ways of the media that he no longer cares what people say?

Most of the questioning was about the decision to bowl first. Had there been much discussion about that? 'Not a great deal,' said Illingworth. 'The easiest time to bat may have been early on. The wicket got lower and slower all day and made it difficult to play shots. With the nine o'clock start the ball may swing early on, but you are never sure for how long, or whether the ball will be wet or not. Whether we got it right or wrong I don't know. It was Mike's decision. You'll have to ask him about that.'

This was a rotten thing to say, even if it was true. Perhaps the most telling admission was that there hadn't even been much discussion about it. Why the hell not? What else did they have to talk about the day before the game, if not how they planned to play it?

Ask Mike? The press couldn't wait. 'Well, you couldn't really fault our batting,' he said. 'Two thirty wasn't a bad score. But we dropped our catches, and fielded poorly. That cost us the match.'

Yes, but what about winning the toss and putting New Zealand in? Did he regret doing that?

'What did Illy say?'

He said to ask you.

'Oh.' Atherton grinned, then toughed it out. 'The balance of the side was right,' he said. 'The decision to insert was right. I'd do it again.'

But the damage had been done. The reporters scooted back to the hotel, a smartish concrete novelty out by the airport, with an army of eager gardeners deployed to paint the poolside flowerpots a nice bright rust colour, to write about the rift between the captain and the manager. 'Atherton At Odds With Manager Illy,' cried the *Express*. The *Sun* had Illy accusing the skipper of 'cocking up'. And the *Mirror* didn't mince words either, attributing the defeat to 'Captain Calamity'. In a story titled 'De-Ath Wish 4' it declared, in underlined headlines: 'He put Kiwis in . . . He missed big catch . . . He failed with bat . . . He ran out Hick.' The *Mail* went for 'Captain Calamity' as well. None of them mentioned the remark made by the New Zealand captain, Lee Germon, who sat down, flushed with victory, and said, 'Actually, we were looking to bowl first. There was a bit of moisture out there early on.'

The Indian papers had a hard job restraining their pleasure. 'British

Lion,' said one headline. 'Weak In the Paw, Long In the Tail.' The *Indian Express* was speechless at the dropped catches: 'It left one wondering if Michael Atherton's men were handling a cricket ball or a grenade with its pin released.' The editor of the *Asian Age* wrote: 'The good news is that things can't get worse. The bad news is that they may not get better.' This, he concluded, was a 'typical' England performance: 'England at normal form: dropping catches as swiftly as they come.' The *Pioneer* noted with grim pleasure that 'For a change, the English chose not to blame the defeat on the dust.'

So there it was. England had only played one match, and already the pack was circling. The rest of the cricket world looks on with amazement and sympathy at the way cricket is written about in Britain's big-selling papers. The game itself only ever seems to be the minor surface aspect of the deeper drama – the personality clashes and disputes that might or might not rumble on behind the scenes. It is not made up: you only had to watch Atherton and Illingworth at these press conferences to see that they were hardly bosom pals. Sometimes Athers would lean back in his seat while the Chairman was talking and raise his eyebrows in mock surprise, as if to signal his incredulity. But was this the main story of the day – the speculative suggestion that the two of them hadn't agreed whether to bat or bowl? Newspapers have an uncannily conventional feel for what 'the story' is, even if there isn't one. Today, the story was that England had lost and played poorly – but that was nothing new. The press insists on wanting to know *why*.

One of the reasons why English cricket has such an appalling record of pathetic excuses – the smog, the food, the pitch, the weather, the travel, the fatigue, the ball, the crowd, whatever – is that they are always asked why. Why, why, why? As if there's a reason. If you lose a game like cricket, it is usually because the other team has played better; sometimes it is because the other team *is* better. But in the face of this dogged questioning a generation of managers and players has grown used to saying something, anything, by way of an answer. And you are not allowed to be light-hearted. If, as Ted Dexter did, you ironically suggest that maybe it was because the stars were out of synch, then that is regarded as an unforgivable rudeness, a refusal to take the question seriously. And out come the Loony Lord Ted headlines.

There are many problems with English cricket, and one of the biggest is right here, in the deadly quagmire of the press conference. As the World Cup progressed, England's deficiencies in the public-relations field would become more and more obvious, as would the unfriendly judgemental tack of the papers themselves. None of the individuals involved want England to do badly, exactly, but the reflexes of the industry are alert only to England's failures. Poor performances encourage people to write leaders about how our decline in cricket is a symptom of our political confusion and so on; good performances have never encouraged those same leader writers to relate success on the field to England's powerful cultural and economic advance, an only slightly more ludicrous inference.

In any case, the really extraordinary thing about this result, in terms of the competition itself, was that it didn't matter. England had to win only two games to be sure of reaching the quarter finals, and there was only a freakish chance that they could lose to either the United Emirates or Holland, their next two opponents. For the sake of morale and publicity they would much rather have won, but Pakistan had been humiliated in the early games of the previous World Cup, and still went on to beat England in the final. And this time the competitiveness of the cricket had been even more willingly sacrificed to the cause of commercial prosperity, so the early games meant little.

In planning the tournament, Pilcom had admitted three more countries than last time – three non-Test nations. In one way it was a progressive move: part of an admirable attempt to spread the cricket gospel to new parts of the world, places like Holland and the United Arab Emirates. In another way, it was merely two more television markets to develop. Either way, the extra teams made it twelve altogether, which rendered it all but impossible for everyone to play everyone, especially in a huge country like this. In the last World Cup, in Australia, nine teams played in a single league, and the top four went through to the semi-finals. No one could afford to lose too many matches: if they did, they might not get through to the knock-out round; and this meant, in turn, that every match was important. But a nine-team league involved only thirty-six matches, just about feasible in a month-long tournament; while a league with twelve countries would take sixty-six fixtures to sort itself out. Even if you based the competition on half a dozen centres – Calcutta, Lahore, Bombay, Bangalore, Madras and Colombo, say – it would be an impossibly crowded schedule. So now we had two groups of six, with the top four in each group going through. Some of this was driven by a benign, demotic impulse to give the Indian public at least a glimpse of the action; partly it was to do with politicians wanting lucrative fixtures in their own backyard. Either way, it meant that this World Cup was an extraordinary travelling circus and a great spectacle – but also that the early games were almost entirely pointless, except as exhibitions: warm-ups before the real event.

A year before the tournament, it was obvious that the top eight teams – Australia, England, India, New Zealand, Pakistan, South Africa, Sri Lanka and the West Indies – would qualify for the quarter-finals. And from there on it would be sudden death. We were facing three weeks of less-than-urgent fixtures, followed by a week of scintillating drama. Come to think of it, it might have been this structure that inspired Australia and the West Indies to forfeit their games in Sri Lanka: they knew they would still qualify. In Ahmedabad, after just one match, it was possible to envisage an intriguing possibility. England could go into the quarter-finals as the fourth-placed team to face Sri Lanka, probable winners of the other group (with their two-game head start). If they won, they might go on to play New Zealand in the semi-final and avenge this early disappointment. They could thus get to the World Cup final without even playing Australia, India and the West Indies – and what kind of a contest was that? Or say they lost in the quarter-final against Sri Lanka? In that case they'd be out of the tournament, again, before they'd played those three big guns – and what kind of a contest was *that*? International cricket is a pretty small world, and for England to take part in the so-called World Championship and not face up to three of their historic rivals was dismaying from the sporting point of view, and foolish even from the commercial point of view – these were the games the television audience would have paid to see.

Still, England had to behave as if it mattered. The next day there they were, back in the nets. What choice did they have? If they lazed around the pool or played golf there'd be pictures in the papers proving how idle and pampered they were, and letters would pour into newspapers banging on about how the youth of today didn't understand the work ethic. But one of the disastrous failings of the England set-up on this and previous tours abroad is that nets are regarded mainly as a chore, or even a punishment. Other teams practise; we just have nets. The players jog a couple of laps of the ground, then form a semi-circle around the trainer for a few exercises:

touching their toes, hopping up and down with one leg in the air, and so on. A couple of years ago, in the West Indies under Keith Fletcher, England performed by all accounts the same warm-up routine every day for ninety-nine days, and it didn't seem to have changed much since then. The players went through the motions – well, a job's a job, isn't it?

Batting: the players take it in turns, just like at school. It doesn't look very purposeful: they block the first few, then attempt a shot or two, and finish by clomping the ball as hard as they can. Out in South Africa, when the Test series was over, both teams turned up at Newlands for nets. England did the usual, but South Africa, under the stewardship of the vaunted (English) coach Bob Woolmer, seemed to change gear noticeably. Gary Kirsten had batted like a sticking plaster in the Test matches, rarely attempting a shot in anger. Now, he was slogging every ball, picking his bat up high and swinging into everything Donald and Pollock could throw at him. He was bowled about four times and snicked many more than that, but no one was minding. If he'd been English, you felt, there'd have been furrowed brows. He'd have been told to get his head down and concentrate. But he was deliberately changing his rhythm for the upcoming one-day games, adjusting to a more aggressive tempo. 'Yes, it's something we do,' said Woolmer. 'Sometimes we get the boys to try and hit every ball for six. You don't hit sixes by accident, you have to practise it. Plus it's good fun.'

It didn't look much fun in Ahmedabad. The nets were low at the side, so the ball kept flying out. Even the journalists and photographers hanging around had to keep their eyes peeled while they chatted.

'How'd it go yesterday? Look out!'

'Thanks. Christ, I was up till midnight trying to file. Had to phone it over in the end.'

'That's nothing. We couldn't get a line at all. Had to get reception to send a telex.'

Atherton leaned on the railings behind while Hick batted, pads on, waiting for his turn, not even flinching when the ball whacked into the fence about six inches from his head. Alec Stewart plonked himself into a chair in the pavilion and talked reporters through the contents of his suitcase: twelve tins of baked beans, a dozen of tuna, forty tea bags, loads of Mars Bars, Cup-a-Soup, muesli bars. Was that what he'd had for lunch? Yep: tuna, baked beans and pitta bread. He hated Indian food: for dinner he would have chicken and broccoli. 'If we get to the final,' he said, 'I'll have eaten forty-two consecutive chicken breasts.' Oh, and fruit. 'Bananas, yeah. I'll eat anything with skin on.'

It isn't just England who bring their own. Australia had videos, a portable casino, music, games – a whole toyshop. They didn't plan to go out much while they were here.

It was quiet in the stadium today: a post-match torpor had descended on the ground. The drinks stands, the tea and samosa outlets, the tables piled high with crisps and biscuits had all been taken away and workmen were slowly dismantling the furniture. At one point the players had to take cover when a swarm of bees ignored the warnings and staged a pitch invasion. The day before the match was different: there was a scrum out in the middle while both teams practised in the nets and loads of journalists and officials wandered around the outfield. Everyone was having a look at the reddish-brown wicket, wondering how it would play (no one knew). Labourers were installing a cable in a trench leading from the pavilion to the wicket to connect up the StumpVision camera, which would allow viewers the occasional blurred glimpse of a batsman's inner thigh. Local reporters quizzed visitors about their views. Derek Pringle, who had opened the bowling for England in the last World Cup but was all baggy shorts in the press box this time, said that he thought the New Zealander Cairns was a fine all-rounder, especially as a batsman, and winced the next morning when he read that he had accused Cairns of being past it as a bowler. You did have to be careful what you said.

I had been a bit nervous going in because my accreditation pass, neatly printed with a photograph on a laminated card, permitted me to attend just two matches, neither of which I was going to. But no one did more than glance at the red Wills World Cup logo on the top. Inside, I went into the club office and explained the problem. The man had a look and told me not to worry. So I didn't. But it was clear that a double standard was operating here, conveniently in my favour. The Indian newspapers were already full of complaints about the ease with which Western writers were able to move around. 'Accredited journalists were being prevented entry at certain points,' reported the *Indian Express*, 'while any white Caucasian could gain unchecked access – including tourists.'

It was true. Perhaps the security people had read about the famous episode when Sunil Gavaskar turned up to play in the bicentenary Rest-of-the-World match at Lord's, and was turned away ('I don't care who you are, if you haven't got a pass . . .') by some unbearably officious bouncer. Perhaps they feared that they might bar entrance to someone who would turn out to be David Gower or Ian Botham – these English players all looked the same, didn't they? As it was, anyone who looked like a player was semi-permanently signing notebooks and programmes. Anyone following the cricket was asked, just in case. I frequently explained to the young (and not-so-young) boys and girls that they didn't really want my signature, I wasn't a player or anything, but they persisted, delicately feeling it would be rude to withdraw. But when you've signed they look down at your scribble and ask: 'Who are you?' The Gowers of this world can dine out on a story like that – it is pleasantly self-deprecating. For the rest of us it is a harder question to answer. During the match, up in the press box in Ahmedabad, someone had spread word that the man sitting next to me, the correspondent from the *Manchester Evening News*, was the New Zealand bowler Dion Nash. Scores of boys and girls came up with scraps of paper for him to immortalise.

Up on the concrete seats the hand-painted advertising hoardings were drying in the sun, ready for the big day, while the players went through their drills. A small horde of policemen stood and watched them bat. Afterwards, the senior figures toddled over to the press to lob them quotes, with the weary air of people throwing crumbs to pigeons, knowing that they'd gobble them up and still be hanging around for more tomorrow. 'Well, I was pretty low three days ago,' said Robin Smith, talking to the assembled reporters. 'But I've had a lot of physiotherapy, and it's responded well to treatment. I've even been running up and down the stairs – that's me, dedicated.'

The press withdrew, happy, and the Sky cameraman came in for a one-on-one. Smith waited while he twiddled the lens, and listened carefully to the question. How was his injury? 'Well,' he said, giving it a lot of thought, 'I was pretty low a couple of days ago, but I've had plenty of physiotherapy, and it's really responded well to treatment.'

Illingworth and Atherton stood in the centre of a knot of men with notebooks. A few Indian reporters tried to edge within earshot. 'I'll talk to you later,' said Illy. 'After I've done the English boys.' He didn't. Neither did Atherton. Both men walked past the Indian writers and headed for the changing room. The result was predictable. Atherton, not for the first time, found himself being called 'Captain Grumpy'. 'Isn't the Raj over, Mr Illingworth?' asked the paper the next morning. 'The press,' it conceded with endearing candour, 'was a harassed lot trying to get access to the team's brains trust.'

Brains trust? They weren't missing much. What kind of tactics would we see tomorrow? Wait and see. How do you rate New Zealand? I think it'll be a tough game. How do you like your kit? Fine – trousers are a bit small.

One question brought an alarming answer, though. Who was going to open with Atherton?

'As of now,' said Illingworth, 'we'll open with Stewart.'

As of now? There was only a day to go. Did that mean that things might change between now and then? Could it really be true that this team had managed to play eight one-day games in South Africa, and then to spend a week practising and planning in Lahore, and *still* hadn't decided what to do? Dear oh dear.

But maybe he was just hedging his bets. Neither member of the brains trust sounded bullish or enthusiastic, or even hopeful; that wasn't their aim. Both knew that if they made any rash promises, if they sounded anything but a cautiously optimistic note, they could look like idiots if things went wrong. So they tried, as always, to be neutral and platitudinous. They succeeded, too. There was nothing to say, after all.

It was off to Pakistan now on another 'hell trip' involving an overnight stop in Delhi, a nothing morning, a flight to Karachi, and then a connection to Peshawar. This was an ingenious route: Ahmedabad to Karachi is only a couple of hundred miles as the crow flies, and it really shouldn't take a whole day to get there. But even the crows don't fly that way. The India–Pakistan border is a tense one, and there weren't many ways through. Still, it gave everyone time to read up on Peshawar, if they had a mind to. There was lots worth reading. Amidst all the excitement about Sri Lanka, it hadn't been much noticed that only a month ago a bomb in Peshawar had killed sixty people. It was a famously dangerous place, the gun-running trading post for drugs and, they said, nuclear smuggling to and from Afghanistan, a risky drive away up the Khyber pass. Thanks to Gandhi, Ahmedabad was one of the shrines of pacifism. Peshawar was the opposite: feudal, violent, warrior country. Fundamentalist, too. Up here, during the holy fasting month of Ramadan, a wounded fighter might not even be permitted an intravenous drip.

The press corps sat around in the airports recalling their own previous visits to the North-west Frontier. Most of them had been shown how to fire Kalashnikovs into the air like tough rebels. Once, they had been ushered into a back room and shown a high pile of what looked like leather, all stamped and embossed ready for export. It was hashish.

'Bloody hell,' said someone. 'Good job Beefy wasn't there.'

Graham Gooch's memory lingered on. 'This nan,' he had said once, arriving in the mountainous, blood-soaked, history-swamped city and chomping on some warm new bread, 'is fucking world class.'

Which reminded someone else of the time Keith Fletcher, with his R-less Essex drawl, had struggled to make himself understood to an Australian waitress.

'Can I have some siwerp, please,' he had requested at breakfast one morning.

Siwerp? The waitress looked nonplussed.

'Siwerp,' repeated Fletcher. 'Fer me powwidge.'

Still no sign of anything like comprehension.

'Siwerp!' cried Fletcher. 'Wuddy tweacle!'

Oh, well. When you're watching England, you've got to laugh, haven't you?

— 4 —

HOME THOUGHTS IN DELHI

Night fell like a rock as we flew into Delhi for a stopover in an airport hotel, gasping in the hot, smoky air as we climbed off the plane. And I was thinking: Why cricket? What is it about this damned game that has so seized the imagination of Britain's colonies?

Browsing in a Bombay bookshop, I had leafed through a copy of a new work, a set of essays by historians and sociologists called *Bombay: the City as Metaphor*. It was three hundred pages or so, and as I scanned the book, and then the index, and then the book again, it became apparent that there was not a single mention of Bombay's most famous citizen: Sachin Tendulkar. And he might have been only twenty-two, but he had also been making headlines for nearly a decade. When he was thirteen, one Bombay newspaper devoted a whole page to him, following a remarkable series of batting exploits in various school cricket competitions. He was the youngest player ever to do practically everything: the absolute archetype of a batting genius. He played for India when he was sixteen, and scored his first century (against England – does that count?) when he was seventeen. A few months before the World Cup he had signed a marketing deal with WorldTel, the sports management company that had scooped the television rights to the World Cup, which would guarantee him $5 million. His merry face glimmered down from advertising hoardings all over Bombay, promoting Pepsi, Visa and the national cause, and his name was on everybody's lips. Yet he didn't rate a mention in a supposedly serious work on urban psychology. It wouldn't be odd for a collection of essays about London to ignore, say, Mark Ramprakash, because only a small percentage of the population would know who he was. But Sachin Tendulkar plays a big part in the emotional life of Bombay's people: they follow every swing of his bat, and invest in every glance of his eye. It would be patronizing to assume that everyone loves Sachin – Bombay is a big place, and has a city-sized population of non-fans, not to mention a city-sized population of people who can't read and don't have free weekends. But surely he rated a mention.

In a way it was typical. Sport, though it consumes vast amounts of money, energy and time, is rarely seen as anything more than an innocuous pastime, and does not carry much weight in the hierarchy of human endeavour. It is pored over at extravagant length by newspapers and television, yet does not feature much in history books, mainly because its effects are hard to weigh and measure. It is many years since C. L. R. James pointed out, with something like indignation, that none of the histories of *fin-de-siècle* England that he had read took account of the most famous man of that period, the man whose deeds charmed the nation: W. G. Grace. The signs outside cricket grounds back then announced an entrance fee of threepence, or sixpence if Grace was playing. Tendulkar was a similar phenomenon, and not just in the boy-genius sporting sense. He was hardly a noble savage: his father was a literature professor and his brother a prize-winning poet. His immense talent and appetite for the game had been discovered and released by thorough coaching. It was the same with Brian Lara: tempting though it was to presume that he had swung, fully formed, from some magical Caribbean palm, the truth was plainer. He was one of eleven children and had been enthusiastically trained at the well-appointed Harvard club in Trinidad from the age of six. He went to Fatima College, one of Trinidad's top grammar schools, and swiftly made his mark. They used to play a special brand of junior cricket there – no stumps, but you were out if you missed the ball. 'He would be in there all day,' the school principal recalls. Bradman might have practised with a golf ball and a stump, and Tendulkar played with a bouncy rubber ball; but Lara used a ruler and a marble.

Why couldn't England produce players like these? It was one thing to suggest, as James and his followers had, that cricket was an agency of cultural liberation in the West Indies (and elsewhere), a popular theatre for the playing out of larger social tensions. But why cricket? Why not some cheaper sport like football, or athletics? The cultural motive was obvious to the point of being trite: clearly, in mastering cricket, the colonies were taking possession of an emblem as well as a game. Beating England at cricket was an especially satisfying way of beating the bastards at their own game, one that had spawned all those resonant colonial platitudes to do with fair play, respecting the umpire's decision, and decorous conduct; to win at football (or small-bore shooting, or ice dancing, or the triple jump) wouldn't have carried anything like the same charge. Besides, football was the game of industrialized urban labourers, fellow victims of the capitalist-imperialist plot, whereas cricket was the chosen pastime of the officer class and the civil service. So it had to be cricket.

But even this didn't explain the sheer vigour of the enthusiasm for the game in the West Indies or the subcontinent, the boys playing in the roads and patches of wasteground at all hours. There must be something about cricket itself, some quirk of sporting aesthetics that makes this long, convoluted game especially appealing to those exposed to it (apart from the fact that it is a good game for hot countries – try playing football on a sweltering afternoon in Madras or Jamaica). Cricket romantics have often liked to believe that there was something culturally specific about cricket, that it was as suited to the British character and temper as it was alien to, say, the French or Italian. But this is obviously hokum. Lord Harris, the one-time Governor of Bombay, pompously reckoned that 'the Indian' would never have the patience truly to master the game, and this is as idiotic as his belief in cricket as a calm redoubt against Bolshevism. Cricket is still used, in films and by stand-up comedians, as an image of all that is typically English – that is, poncy, arcane, stuffy and remote. But this won't really wash any more, not now that the game is, if anything, typically Asian or typically Caribbean. Who knows? Perhaps France, Germany and Italy would love cricket too if England had colonized them for a century or so. Perhaps if our missionaries had been as fierce and zealous as the Portuguese, we would be playing Test matches against Brazil.

One could go on about this for ever. Sometimes it seems that people do. But the truth is that cricket fans rarely talk about why they love the game; its claim on us is assumed, like membership of a cult. The social intercourse of England, among men, at least, is shot through with crafty masonic verbal tics by which fellow fans seek one another out: cricket is, above all, something to talk about. These days the fashion is to put down any enthusiasm for sport as an incomprehensible laddish mystery. But this makes it all seem like a winsome folly, a sheepish addiction rather than a simple indulgence. In the end we watch sport because it's fun, and like all the best sorts of fun the high points are paid for by a long apprenticeship of dull moments. To pretend that this pursuit of fine escapist pleasure is actually some sort of vaguely endearing neurosis takes a bit of nerve. In this interpretation, wives and girlfriends are supposed not just to tolerate their partner's exclusive hobby but to find it charming as well.

That seems a bit steep. Football fans may win hands down when it comes to punching-the-air hysteria or sour fury, but cricketers, and their legendary widows, can't be taught anything about the longer, sadder symptoms of obsession. They are the ones who, in winter, get red eyes from watching cricket through the night (one more over – all right, until the next wicket, then). They are the ones who, during Test matches, entrust their emotional sense of direction to the progress of the game, picking up the score by peering at the television sets in shop windows, craning to catch the latest on someone else's car radio, or ringing up a friend. The Australian Prime Minister Gough Whitlam had it about right when he was asked, during a break in an economic summit, what he thought was Australia's gravest need. 'Two quick wickets before lunch,' he replied – a joke, but also the truth.

There are shelves full of cod-psychological interpretations, most of which put it down to the arrested development of your average (English) man – again, no one dares suggest that this applies to West Indians. Certainly it is one of cricket's appealing features, to young boys, that it requires them to behave like little grown-ups, wearing miniature versions of the same clothes, using cut-down versions of the same equipment, and mouthing the same vocabulary as adult players. There is a substantial collection of gestures: how to appeal, how to act when you are out (throw the bat through the pavilion window, etc.), and hundreds of rules, which to a young mind seem extremely serious and proper. The flip side of this, naturally, is that to adults the game is, indeed, impregnated with many of the simpler aromas of boyhood. Some grown-up cricketers do, to be sure, spend thirty years trying once – just once – to re-enact some stirring high point of their youth, which is indeed pretty fond and foolish.

But this isn't the reason why people like the game. Many more men hate cricket than love it: it is hardly a built-in, biologically wired affection. And although some boys like cricket because it's fun to whack the ball and hog the limelight, or entertaining to bowl cleverly and ruin someone else's day, most have a more awkward relationship with the game, half-hating the thing they love. This seems not so much 'male' behaviour as the dumb inheritance of traditional roles.

There is no obvious reason why women wouldn't like cricket *en masse* if more of them played it in their youth, but for the last couple of hundred years they have not been encouraged to play it (or any games), for all the obvious social-political reasons: someone had to stay home and look after the kids while Dad spent his weekends at the club. And cricket, more than any other game, is one you probably need to have played in order to acquire the taste, or the habit. It is so crammed with variation – the different ways to grip the ball, or bat; the elasticity of the field placings; the tactical shifts and sudden alterations to the balance between bat and ball – all the things that go without saying for anyone who has played a bit but which are not really visible to a casual onlooker. There isn't any doubt that women can and do play and adore cricket; the fact that it is relatively rare is a tribute only to the cultural pressure against it. Actually, given that sheer physical power plays a smaller role in cricket, except for fast bowling, than in almost any other game, one might expect the gap between women and men to be modest. If a slim, frail-looking fifteen-year-old Indian boy like Tendulkar can score first-class centuries, then there's no remote reason why women can't. In 1994 England's women won their own World Cup final at Lord's, and were rewarded for their unpaid pains by receiving the trophy out on the pitch, not on the balcony where women are banned. In 1996, women were allowed into the holy places for the first time, and the fuss the old codgers made only emphasized what a remarkable and generous concession they thought it was. The 1996 *Wisden*, despite a well-aimed blow at the men-only world of the Long Room in the introduction, devoted just two pages – out of 1440 – to women's cricket.

Socially, in England at least, the game has been the unlucky recipient of many of the worst aspects of the Victorian gentleman's-club culture: exclusive, masculine and full of ghastly Rotarian mannerisms. Public schools are often blamed for this; although, these days, even the best players from public schools struggle to make good in county cricket, the game is often seen as an extension of the fagging system. Of course, there is something in this: cricket is an English institution. Cricket, public schools, the Empire: there's no need to labour the point, really. Part of the original Victorian purpose of public schools was to create an élite cadre of imperial bureaucrats and soldiers by the simple expedient of destroying in their charges, at a stroke, any sense of home, of belonging to a place. Generations of boys went to school far from where they lived, which meant that they knew hardly anyone in their home towns. To replace this disrupted sense of community, the schools offered instead membership of a class, an intangible but infinitely recognizable matter of habits, accents, assumptions and shared references. Cricket became one of the few bridges – heavily patrolled, with barbed-wire perimeter fencing, but still a bridge – to the rest of the world.

This educational culture – élite schools for the propagation of muscular Christian values – was one of the most far-reaching methods by which Britain extended its influence through the Empire. In the build-up to the World Cup England had practised at Aitcheson College in Lahore, Imran Khan's *alma mater* and a rust-coloured version of Charterhouse. In Barbados it was schools like Harrison's College and the Lodge which perpetuated the Victorian ideals of obedient sportsmanship long after these things had begun to dissolve in Britain. It was the influence of schools such as this which ensured that cricket, far from being overthrown and uprooted by the independence movement, became the emblem of the new social order as effectively as it had been the emblem of the old one.

Trevelyan's celebrated notion that if the French aristocracy had been able to play cricket with the sans-culottes they would not have lost their châteaux might sound sentimental and glib; but it is not a complete joke. Cricket in England did and does introduce earls to orphans, millionaires to paupers, barristers to barrow boys. It gives people something to talk about other than the huge unmentionable tracts of good fortune that separate them. And, of course, cricket has seeped into the general language: not long ago I heard a radio presenter quizzing his African correspondent about the latest developments in Rwanda. 'So what,' he asked, 'is the state of play?' It was a *faux pas*, but only a slight one. We all knew what he meant, just as we know what it means to be stumped, or caught out, or on a sticky wicket. It all helped the average Etonian to feel much more at home in the officer's mess in Calcutta, with a game against the Bengal Lancers coming up, than he ever could at home.

This was the tradition I seemed to be heir to. Not, on the face of it, a happy one: how could you not have mixed feelings about it? It is one of the reasons why cricket is so clubby and defensive and obsessed with social graces. It is why cricket has been anxious to preserve social distinctions – between gentlemen and players, between seniors and juniors, between men and women. Only in 1996 did Surrey remove the wall between capped players – the seasoned pros – and the rest. But this love of tradition also helps explain why cricket feels, to many of its followers, a legacy or a burden, something we're stuck with. The game's chapbooks are full of sad quotations about how cricket is like a mistress, but this is just wishful thinking, and very insulting to mistresses. Cricket is like a cantankerous elderly relative: it is slow, complicated, demanding, and involves a lot of driving about on Sundays.

But it is quite possible both to love cricket and to hate the things it is usually taken to stand for. Back in the middle of the eighteenth century, when it all started, cricket was popular as a women's game. In those days, it was widely regarded as far too effeminate for chaps, who would much rather be sticking pigs or baiting bears. It was a woman who invented over-arm bowling, the stays in her skirt proving awkward for the underarm lobs that were then the order of the day, and this was perhaps the key breakthrough in the development of the sport, introducing at a stroke the variations open to a bowler, and forcing a corresponding refinement of the rustic swipes that would have formed the batting orthodoxy of the underarm era. Back then, the men were mere spectators, standing around in top hats, keeping the score by carving notches on a stick, laying (large) bets on the damsels, getting drunk (gambling, too, was in there at the dawn), and cracking bawdy jokes; a maiden over, they decided, was so-called because nobody scored. The embarrassing snottiness of Lord's, with its footling ban on women from the sacred rooms, is only the surface expression of a widespread sense in the game that women are the enemy, the ones who want to stop you playing, obstacles to a good time. Ask any coach about the state of cricket these days and he'll say that there are still plenty of talented youngsters, but at a certain point they go and discover – here the eyes roll to the ceiling, half contemptuous, half jealous – *girls*. Much of the flowery Edwardian writing on cricket, even the impish satires of P. G. Wodehouse, assumes that prowess at cricket might be the way to a girl's heart: there are endless blushing débutantes trembling with hope and desire as Harry takes the field against the mighty Australians. Talk about fantasy: many a hopeful teenage cricketer has been left staring at his feet as the girl of his hopes decided, in the middle of his best cricket anecdote, that maybe it was time she went to the loo.

Still, you can't blame the game for the social culture that in

England, at least, has grown up around it. Many cricket apologists go along with the idea that it is just a loopy male rite, or admit that it can be deadly dull, but it's the camaraderie, don't you know. Why don't they just come right out and admit that cricket is a ferociously absorbing game? It has something of the dizzy vertiginous joy spoken of by chess freaks. It offers an enclosed space, that lovely green bowl, which somehow contains limitless possibilities for different outcomes. It is both very simple – you throw it, I'll hit – and immensely detailed, with a two-hundred-year accretion of rules to govern the progress of play. It is slow, dragging on for days, and very, very fast: it has been calculated that against the quickest bowlers a batsman has about a third of a second to see and hit the ball – faster than the ordinary human-reaction speed. It is at once tame – all that loitering in the outfield making daisy chains – and very dangerous: the roll-call of smashed noses, ruined teeth and black eyes is impressive, and broken fingers, fractured shins and ripped shoulders are routine. It is a team game, offering a sense of belonging, and is democratic, in that everyone gets a turn. It is also fiercely individualistic: at any one time there is only one bowler, and only one batsman, and it is up to the batsman how long his turn lasts. Most cricketers, if they are honest, would rather score a century and lose than score nought in a victory.

Nor are these individual contests crudely gladiatorial: they are sly, and always framed by the larger context of the match. For the batsman on strike, it is not one against one, it is one against eleven – quite an uncomfortable feeling, which in turn introduces an element cricketers don't talk about much: the presence of keen competition between teammates. They are all in it together, but they are also rivals for the spotlight. You only have to listen to the way cricketers talk about one of their teammates, when the man in question is out there batting, for instance, to hear the undercurrent of rivalry that hums into the supposedly good-natured joshing. In any cricket match, be it a village green knockabout or an international, you can see disgruntled bowlers scowling on the boundary having been taken off just when they were getting into the groove, or batsmen chuntering about being dropped down the order. And when it comes to professional cricket, this selfish streak is even wider. Each of the players is, in a way, a small business: his prime concern is to hang on to his job by staying in the team. He is dependent on the collaboration of his teammates, but not so heavily as a footballer or rugby player. Cricket is quick to recognize individual efforts: even opponents are applauded when they reach a century or break some record. Indeed, the whole game sometimes seems designed merely as a platform for virtuoso performances. Winning just makes the job more fun.

Some of the individual tussles are almost invisible. I remember once hearing Richie Benaud describe a one-day international between India and the West Indies; the West Indian opening bowler, Malcolm Marshall, was bowling with ferocious speed and zip. 'We're in the tenth over,' Richie said calmly, 'and Sunil Gavaskar is about to receive his first ball from Malcolm Marshall.' He paused, letting the implications sink in that Gavaskar was a shrewd old maestro, or perhaps just a scaredycat avoiding the bowling. 'A little touch of experience there,' he added, the vague Shakespearian echo lending a mock-epic tone to the sneaky truth. Even teammates compete. In his days as captain of Leicester, Ray Illingworth was notorious for giving one of the other spinners a quick bowl before lunch to see if the wicket was turning before deciding whether to bowl himself. And in the anecdotes that course through professional cricket, Geoff Boycott was famous for his jokes about accidentally running out his teammates.

So although cricket is all about camaraderie, it is also a solitary pursuit, holding out the promise both of loneliness – the long, humiliating walk back to the pavilion – and glory: witness Lara's procession through a tunnel of raised bats after his record score in Antigua. It is repetitive, yet fluid; elaborately choreographed, yet full of improvisation. It requires big strong men (fast bowlers) and little cunning types as well: sheer size is not an advantage. Indeed, it is a commonplace that most of the greatest-ever batsmen – Bradman, Hanif Mohammad, Gavaskar, Border, Lara, Tendulkar *et al* – were or are midgets. Cricket gives brain a better than even chance against brawn, and this makes the game attractive to swots. Most engaging of all, perhaps, is the pervading tug-of-war between hope and expectation: cricket fans do not watch what the players are doing; they witness, with pleasure, or horror, what the players are *attempting*. And the tiniest incident – a ball that keeps a bit low, the sudden hint of swing in the air, signs of frustration in the batsmen – obliges us to revise these hopes and expectations constantly. It is all influenced by nice things like grass, air and soil: the weather and the ground conditions play a large role in deciding what kind of a game it will be. And the whole teetering structure sways on the caprices of fortune. In every great innings there were moments early on (a close shout for lbw, a lofted drive that was only a yard away from the fielder) when it could have ended in tears. The average duck is only a century cruelly sawn off before it had a chance to bloom.

All of which allows cricket to be not just a spectacle, with winners and losers to gratify our competitive desires, but also a story. No other game can create such a long and crowded narrative: the ending is always up in the air, and the script is in a process of constant revision, which is one of the reasons why cricket 'highlights' are so unsatisfactory on television: robbed of the open-ended mood that surrounds each ball of a live match, they seem drained of tension. When Test matches are on, it's a five-day soap opera, with characters enduring melodramatic ups and downs as the game ebbs and flows. And each match is only one episode in the larger drama: the series. People who find cricket unexciting, and write caustic polemics about how tedious it is, miss the point completely. Cricket rations its thrills, preferring to toy with our expectations, hopes and dreads. The dynamic of the game, for those who play as well as for spectators, is one in which an eternity of inglorious moments is made bearable by the possibility of one redeeming glory.

Most club cricketers have had days where they drive for two or three hours, get out for nought, don't get a bowl, and skulk around in the outfield on a freezing May afternoon for three hours. Oh, well, you can hear them say afterwards, at least I didn't drop a catch. These days have to be endured, though, if the sunnier times – the big score, the five-wicket haul – are going to come. I don't go along with the Victorian myth that cricket is character-building: cricket doesn't seem to have built all that many great characters, tending if anything to the opposite, to produce petty, pedantic, officious types. But it does confront its followers with a wide range of everyday emotions – dejection, fury, self-loathing and so on – and serves them up in easily digestible, fun-sized portions. It isn't an accident that so many cricketers are nail-biters: the game chews at your heart. Patience has as large a role to play as audacity, and there is room for passages of excruciating, agonizing boredom. But even these can be exhilarating. When India bowled well against England in the first Test match at Edgbaston in 1996, Richie Benaud found himself murmuring, after the first few overs, 'We've been going for forty minutes, and there have been five runs.' He hesitated, wondering how best to summarize this spectacular burst of inaction. 'Thrilling stuff,' he said. To a cricket fan, all other sports, all those games which clamour for high jinks, seem a bit flat and one-paced.

As a topic of conversation the whole artfulness of cricket is that it feeds so many different interpretations: it satisfies national pride (vexed, in England's case), speaks to those who love dashing exploits (Laker's Test, Botham's Ashes) as well as to those who prefer stoic resistance (Atherton in Johannesburg); it can also be appreciated merely as a remote branch of numerology: statisticians love cricket, and with reason. The cricket scorecard is a masterpiece of concise arithmetic, a small-print grid of names and numbers which somehow, refined by centuries of zealous effort, manages to be entirely legible as the coded story of the game. It is perfectly possible to take the scorecard of a game you have not seen and re-create, in detail, not just the sequence of events but the peaks and troughs of excitement too. Plenty of ageing fans snuggle up with *Wisden* in the cold months, dreaming their way through whole matches, whole seasons.

All of this would sound fairly nancy to most of the players and reporters converging on this World Cup because, to them, cricket is . . . a job. And, Jesus, business trips aren't all they're cracked up to be, you know. Also, these notably English musings were not very relevant on these dusty streets. It was becoming increasingly clear that the home of cricket had moved. England was no longer the rightful deed-holder, up on its landlordly, Lordsy perch: it was just one of many countries that played the game, and not even one of the best. Someone had once remarked that cricket was a West Indian game invented by Englishmen, and the sport that had spread through the empire was now – no doubt about it – burning more brightly in the former colonies than it was at home. We ranked seventh or eighth, depending on how we had fared lately against New Zealand. Cricket, perhaps, was rather like the English language: as V. S. Naipaul has asserted, languages flourish and enrich themselves on the buzzing edges of the linguistic empire, not in the stale centre (a rather mechanical view – as if there is a 'centre' in any but a historical sense). But the buoyant enthusiasm for the game in Bombay alerts you to the fact that sport, not just cricket, but football, rugby, golf and tennis too, is one of the great lasting gifts of Britain's global adventuring.

The build-up to this World Cup had shown that the subcontinent, with its eager cricket public, had become not just the commercial and emotional muscle of the game, but its political leader as well. The second wave of cricket's journey through the world is being pushed along by expatriates from India, Pakistan and Sri Lanka: it is they who are taking the game through Asia and the Middle East; they, perhaps, who will keep the flame alight in England. Check out the stars of the team (Headfield Junior School, Dewsbury) that won the Wrigley Under-Eleven trophy in 1995: Zahir Asmal, Nabeel Hafez, Zafaria Hughes, Murtaza Hussein, Nasir Hussain, Suhail Ibrahim, Zubair Ibrahim, Zuber Patel and Fida Zafir. Here, perhaps, is the future of English cricket. Who knows? Perhaps the game will creep through Europe under their influence. It has a foothold in Holland, Denmark, Italy and Spain. Imagine: a European Cup for top-class cricketers. Perhaps, one day, some future Dominic Cork will come running in from the Casino end in Monaco (if you can't see the mountains it's raining, Ray Illingworth will chortle, and if you can see them, then it's about to). Perhaps, one day, we will turn on our televisions and hear Richie Benaud saying, 'Morning, everyone, and welcome to Lourdes.'

The mere fact that it was being held here was proof of the way the balance of power had shifted to a new time zone. When the World Cup began, in the summer of 1975, it was held in England, which at that time seemed emphatically to be the home of cricket: Lord's made up the rules, and our team had not yet become a bit of a joke. More to the point, England was the home of the one-day game. While other, lesser, we presumed, nations clung to the idea of cricket as an elaborate five-day enterprise, we had pioneered the limited-overs version. It was extremely popular, and an international one-day contest seemed like a natural way to have a carnival of world cricket. One-day cricket was a novelty, so the atmosphere was light-hearted. It didn't occur to anyone to think of the winners as 'world champions', because this obviously wasn't real cricket. Not everyone treated it as mere fun: Australia's fast bowler put two Sri Lankans in hospital ('I kept smiling at Thomson,' said the tiny Sri Lankan batsman Ranjit Fernando with sweet naïveté, 'hoping to keep him in a good mood'). Nor did everyone think it was such a great idea in the first place: Sunil Gavaskar staged a puny one-man protest by opening the batting and staying there for the entire sixty overs for a pompous, work-to-rule thirty-six not out. You wouldn't catch anyone pulling a stunt like that today: the one-day game has become the moneyspinner, the golden goose, and batsmen are expected to get a move on. Ironically, it is England, having started the craze, that is now dragging its feet and adopting sniffy airs about the biff-baff version of the game.

The first couple of World Cups weren't much of a contest. The West Indies were so good back then that no one else stood a serious chance. They won easily, and again in 1979. But in 1983, against all the odds, they lost in the final to India. It was a memorable game: India stuttered to 170 in their fifty overs – not really a serious target for Greenidge, Haynes, Richards and the rest. They set off as if they wanted to catch an early flight, and promptly collapsed. India won a famous victory – one that inspired the huge audience in the subcontinent. And so the idea was born, in Calcutta and Lahore, of hosting the 1987 World Cup in India and Pakistan. It was a surprise to the game's rulers at Lord's, who had assumed that the tournament was a natural part of the English summer pageant (Ascot, Henley, Wimbledon, Lord's). And at the time it seemed like a hijack. The India–Pakistan combination studied the International Cricket Council's voting rules and discovered that if they wooed the smaller nations (especially the Asian ones, such as Malaysia, Bangladesh, Singapore) then they could squeeze their bid through even though the nine Test-playing nations have two votes, the sixteen asociates only one. England were caught on the hop. Their bid for the 1987 World Cup was the 1983 proposal plus inflation: £54,000 guaranteed to each full member, £12,000 to each associate member, and £62,000 prize money. The Indo–Pak presentation trumped this easily, pledging £75,000 to the full members, £20,000 to the associates, and an expanded prize kitty of £93,000. They also threw in details such as paying for laundry and medical expenses. The deal went through. The chairman of the Indo–Pak management committee, N. K. P. Salve, wrote a book about the deal, referring modestly to his own 'Himalayan fortitudinous struggle' and claiming that it 'shook the very foundation of England's century old supremacy in the administration of international cricket'. He wasn't far wrong. It was partly the seizing of the high political ground by the Asian countries that led to the strict ban on cricketing ties with South Africa, a ban about which the old axis powers, England and Australia, had mixed feelings.

But it seemed fair enough. And when Australia put in to host the 1992 version, no one complained. The assumption was that next time, in 1996, it would be England's turn again. The West Indies had waived their right to hold the tournament in the Caribbean (too few grounds, too few hotels, too few aeroplanes and too much sea) and brave new South Africa had only just been readmitted to cricket's top table: they were still on probation. So it was, without question, England's turn. A meeting of the ICC agreed that England would host the next World Cup. And exactly the same thing happened. Pakistan refused to accept the minutes of this meeting and demanded a new one. It took place in the famous old Long Room at Lord's in February 1993, and swiftly turned into another acrimonious tussle.

England's bid was supported by Australia, New Zealand, South Africa and the West Indies – the big boys, or so they thought. But India, Pakistan and Sri Lanka had come up with an aggressive rival bid, and, more to the point, had secured the backing of Zimbabwe, the only other test-playing nation. (There was a bit of history to this: when Zimbabwe applied for first-class status back in 1990, England abstained. So there!) England still held a five–four advantage, but this in itself was not enough: the rules insisted on a two-thirds majority. Once again, the destiny of the next World Cup was in the hands of sixteen 'associate members'. England had guaranteed them £60,000 each as a profit-share in the World Cup, which by now had become a more than plausible commercial venture. India, Pakistan and Sri Lanka pledged almost double that: £100,000 each. Money talked. The votes poured in for the subcontinent: Bangladesh, Malaysia, Namibia (where hardly anyone played cricket) and Gibraltar. Gibraltar! The cheek of it! Ten cricket clubs, all tinpot little expat English homes-from-home!

The debate began at ten o'clock in the morning, and ended at nearly midnight. 'It was,' recalled John Stephenson, then the MCC Secretary, 'the longest and most awful meting I've ever attended. I'm afraid our chaps from the TCCB were a bit wet. They just sat there with their mouths closed while the chappies from India and Pakistan – particularly Pakistan – did all the shouting.'

Chappies? That wasn't the only phrase of Stephenson's to expose the bewildered, old-fashioned reflexes of the Lord's top brass. Either way, England's cricket chiefs were thoroughly outwitted. They withdrew their bid, with the proviso that they were guaranteed the right to host the following World Cup. And that was that. The 1996 World Cup was going to Asia.

And so here we were, in the land whose money had carried the day, a land of visible squalor and poverty. I had walked up to Bombay's Wankhede Stadium to have a look at the preparations: I would be returning here for the match between India and Australia in two weeks' time, and there had been lots of talk about how the ground might not be ready. A couple of years ago it had been dug up by Shiv Sena activists as a protest against the possibility of Pakistan playing on it, but Bombay was one of the spiritual hearts of Indian cricket so matches here had a special magic. The forthcoming one was supposed to be a day-night affair, but only one of the floodlights had been built. There certainly wasn't going to be time for the mandatory hundred hours of tests. 'There is a sixty per cent possibility that the game will be a day affair,' said Ravi Mandrekar, marketing officer for the Bombay Cricket Association.

I also had a practical worry: accreditation. At this stage, I still didn't have a pass. I had filled in the forms, months ago, stating which games I wished to attend but, since then, it hadn't been easy to find out what had become of them. I wasn't especially worried, as everyone was in the same boat. But we had all been issued with strict warnings about security: no one without the correct identification tag would be allowed within miles of the cricket, we were promised. One of the things I was hoping to do at the stadium was to find a friendly official who might be able to lend a hand.

In the event, it didn't matter. I wore a jacket and tie, and the policemen made no effort to stop me as I walked in. But it didn't look like the most tactful day to bother anyone with stupid questions about accreditation. A hydraulic crane had fallen on to the pitch, and sent oil spilling over the grass in the outfield. The crane itself was an emergency measure, designed to speed up the erection of the floodlights, and it crashed over when one of its wheels slipped in the mud. It didn't look good: the great steel rig had thumped a big crater in the grass. The curator was handling things with fantastic sangfroid. 'The situation is well under control,' he said, staring at the brown, wrenched turf. 'Horticulturalists have been summoned.' In one way this was a pity. It could have been a historic first: crane stopped play.

But for sheer last-minute chaos nothing could match the opening ceremony. Calcutta was certainly in a state of feverish excitement. There was a procession through the jammed streets of the City of Joy, or the City of Dreadful Night (take your pick): 200 motorcycles, twenty floats and hundreds of cricket stars. Calcutta's famous beggar population was thoughtfully shoved out of sight. The cavalcade was supposed to take three hours. It took six.

The ceremony itself was on two channels: Star Television, Rupert Murdoch's satellite network in Asia, and Doordashan, India's equivalent of the BBC. Quite a few lawyers must have been watching the opening credits with damp eyes (or a smirk, who knows?), because the wrangling over the television rights had been a bruising saga in itself. Way back in 1993, in an initiative that barely raised an eyebrow in the papers, a Bangalore-born Harvard man called Mark Mascarenhas bid £10 million for the world television rights to the World Cup, and succeeded in securing them from the joint Pakistan, India, Sri Lankan Cricket Commission (Pilcom). Pilcom rubbed its hands in glee. In the previous World Cup the rights had gone (to Rupert Murdoch's Sky) for just $1 million; so this was a heady increase. This World Cup was a gold mine.

How were they to know that Mascarenhas, with his persuasive bullish charm, would go on to sell subsidiary rights for over £20 million – a remarkable turn on a deal many thought was bound to go sour? 'Everyone thought the bid was ludicrous,' he said. 'But I could see that the situation had changed since 1992. There was competition from cable and satellite in nearly every market. Cricket just hadn't been commercially measured before.' The British rights were sold for £7.5 million to an American cable consortium called CPP, who were just trying to set up a network in the UK (Wire TV) and looking for programmes to run on it. The London papers hardly noticed that any of this was going on, but they should have (and could have: Mascarenhas wasn't remotely seeking to hide his light under a bushel). Not that he'd done anything wrong: why should he sell the rights to a low bidder (like the BBC)? But the deal did raise some pretty uncomfortable questions about the state of broadcasting in this country. If big sports events, such as the World Cup, were going to be priced as loss leaders for cable operators looking for a marketing gimmick, then what was to stop them from being sold to a different company every time? Just when you'd got yourself a Sky satellite dish, you'd have to get a Wire wire. Next time, you'd have to get something else – a Breeze TV windsock, a Yes! TV nodding donkey. The frailties of the British regulatory system were put on clear display when Wire TV imploded. The rights to broadcast the cricket were now held by a company that had no network in Britain. Great.

In the end, a BBC–Sky deal was cobbled together a few weeks before the World Cup. Even this provoked plenty of sour comment. For cricket the satellite channels were lucrative sponsors, but they still played to small audiences. Shoving the World Cup on to Sky, with its tireless upbeat salesmen blagging us into watching a game we already loved, meant that in England the tournament would be something of a sideshow. But the real broadcasting drama was in India itself. Mascarenhas had originally sold the rights to Doordashan, the state-run TV giant that had, like the BBC in England, been covering cricket for years and felt divinely sanctioned to continue doing so. Since Doordashan controlled various important engineering aspects of television production, such as satellite uplinks and so on, they pretty much had to be included in any deal. But Mascarenhas took them to the brink. When they failed to come up with one of the rolling payments on time, he went off and sold the Asia–Pacific satellite transmission rights to Star Television. Doordashan at once threatened to down tools and sabotage the entire event, leaving India – not only one of the host nations, with several hundred million avid cricket fans, but well over half the entire world audience into the bargain – with the unthinkable prospect of a cricket black-out. The matter wasn't resolved until just four days before the opening ceremony. The disputing parties agreed to submit to the soothing arbitration of the aptly named Mr Salve, now minister for power. The high court in Delhi directed Doordashan to pay (in rupees) the outstanding $4.75 million of its rights fee into an escrow account, a ninety-day deposit which would be frozen while the negotiations proceeded. Doordashan had to give up their ambitious demand for TV rights to the matches 'in perpetuity', and also had to swallow a clause they had tried to spit out, which barred them from carrying advertising for any tobacco products except those of Wills, the 'title sponsor' of the World Cup. Coverage, it was agreed, would continue on both channels: effectively, war was undeclared. Mascarenhas was able to walk on to the pitch in Ahmedabad and have his photo taken with the crack team of commentators he had assembled. 'We've made our peace with the government,' he smiled. The British production company Grandslam had been awarded the contract to provide the actual coverage: in recent days eight units had been jetting into the subcontinent in chartered Ukrainian airliners, with tons of equipment, miles of cables, and various camera crews from all over the cricket-speaking world.

And now, at last, the show was on the road. But what kind of a show was it? As Eden Gardens filled up with dancers, the loudspeakers belted out one of the great classics of Indian music: the waltz from the Symphonie Fantastique by Berlioz. Hundreds of women and children dressed in the colours of the competing nations linked arms to symbolize . . . well, what? Was cricket really trying to sloganize itself into an apostle for world peace – on the assumption, perhaps, that Waugh-Waugh was better than war-war? Sport is good at provoking the sentimental passions – many a flinty upper lip has trembled during those slow-motion tributes to victory and defeat – but this was ridiculous.

The teams started wandering out, in alphabetical order, more or less. The announcer, Saeed Jaffrey, began with a bizarre burst of self-congratulation, claiming that he 'needed no introduction' before embarking on a magnificent piece of improvised burlesque. 'And here come the West Indies,' he mumbled, as the crowd applauded the entrance of the United Arab Emirates. 'Let's have a big hand for South Africa,' he said, as Zimbabwe pottered out on to the grass. Shane Warne came out chewing gum like a blond koala. After the final, the World Cup's official gum-provider announced that Australia were the most avid chompers in the competition, and Warne got them off to a flyer here. Maybe he was nervous. One of the letters he had received, after all, swore that he and his teammates would be blown up in the baggage hall if they dared set foot in Colombo airport. Here came England, sunglasses on to protect them from the harsh glare of the Calcutta night sky. There went the real South Africa, cheerfully introduced by Jaffrey as 'the team from the UAE', Someone obviously jabbed him in the ribs here, because he fell silent for a moment. 'You see,' he confided – the wrong tone to attempt in a stadium that big – 'the problem is we seem to have lost South Africa . . .' You could hear him looking around for some straw, anything, to grasp at. 'Ah!' he cried suddenly. 'I recognize them. That is the West Indies! Ah! Led by captain Richie Richardson. Ah!' Tony Greig, commentating, was having a tough job keeping up. 'There's a great all-rounder,' he said, and you could almost hear him rustling through his notes. 'Er, Brian McMillan,' he said eventually. There was a special roar when the Pakistanis walked out: it was the first time they had set foot on an Indian cricket pitch for nine years, and there were plenty of vociferous Hindu nationalists who were keen to keep them out for another nine at least. Greig tried to catch the special drama of their appearance. 'Wasim Akram, one of the great . . . er, Waqar Younis,' he said. There was a bit of Dire Straits, then a Schubert impromptu, a burst of Vangelis or something, and then – hold on, this sounded almost like . . . Indian music! It was. Indian music. In India! An uncanny fusion of art and geography. Actually, the repertoire sounded very like the answering Muzak on the Pilcom switchboard, which I had called several times that day. What happened was that someone said, 'Hello!' and then you spent five minutes listening to great subcontinental chartbusters such as Beethoven's Ode to Joy and, improbably, 'London Bridge is Falling Down'.

The teams were led out by models who had been chosen for the way they symbolized India – dark hair, dark eyes, er, blue jeans, white T-shirts. It turned out that the special dresses they had been supposed to wear hadn't arrived so they went on in civvies, except for the Indian escort (Miss India, naturally) who escorted Mohammad Azharuddin out to the middle in a bright blue sari. The teams formed straggly lines radiating out from the ball-shaped central stage, somewhere on the Art–Sport cusp. Then the Governor of Bengal said a few words ('I feel deeply honoured, etc.'), the girls formed floral patterns around the podium, and the lights went off. On television, shot from high-up, you could see the floral pattern clearly, and it was quite nice. It would have been better if they had been able to film the event from a blimp, as planned, but there had been a bundle of last-minute glitches to do with air-traffic clearance and, what with one thing and another, the blimp was still in Birmingham.

Miss Universe, Sushmita Sen, emerged on to the platform, her dark hair and dark eyes symbolizing India. There had been a lot of raucous talk about her part in the extravaganza. Indeed, there were rumours that she was planning an exotic striptease as she was winched down from a helicopter wearing nothing but the twelve national flags, which she would unpeel and hand out to the huge delight of the 100,000 men in the stands (who knew a gesture of universal harmony when they saw one). There were complaints about this, not surprisingly. So in the end she came up from below on a dumb-waiter and tamely handed out flags to each captain in turn. Mike Atherton held on to his Union Jack and you could see him struggling to keep a straight face. Whoever it was, in the famous story, who had scrawled FEC on his locker – Future England Captain, or Fucking Educated Cunt, take your pick – couldn't have guessed, surely, that Atherton would one day spend fourteen hours flying from Lahore, on two short flights that didn't connect, so he could stand here accepting a silk banner from a beautiful Indian girl who had somehow beaten down stiff challenges from Miss Pluto and Miss Saturn to scoop the coveted Universe honours.

The lights went off, and here came the lasers. They flickered around wildly for a few moments, then stopped. 'Just a little delay,' said the man who needed no introduction. 'Quite a strong wind blowing up.' The lasers were attempting to project a cartoon on to huge net curtains that had been hung in the centre of the stadium, but the breeze was flapping them about like, well, exactly like net curtains. It was hard to tell whether that was a truck driving through a mountain range, or a skiff on an angry ocean. Every now and then the image whirled, splintered and formed itself into a map, but it was no easy task to tell which country was which. There was some kind of story – a small boy growing up dreaming of cricket, and then becoming a star himself. Mother Teresa (symbolizing Calcutta) flashed up before the curtains rolled up and tipped her off. A bowler sprinted up, arched his back, and then the wind came up again and he collapsed in a heap. Stumps appeared and disappeared. It was a shambles.

A helicopter appeared overhead and dropped flowers, like confetti, on the harmonious scene. Fireworks burst all over the sky. A singer climbed on to the central stage and sang a traditional cricket ballad – 'May all creatures of the world be happy . . . may there be peace' – and her performance was only slightly spoiled by the man with a camera who followed her around, crouching like a lion-tamer whenever she veered in his direction. The whole thing had cost $2 million, apparently, and 110,000 people had turned up to cheer the teams and give the World Cup a big send-off. The dancers were quite nice, and the fireworks were colourful; but not many of the 110,000 went home happy.

At any rate the Indian papers went – to put it mildly – bananas. It was a 'big flop . . . an unmitigated disaster'. The captain of the Indian football team went along and concluded: 'It was like a village festival.' The much-vaunted laser effects, said one critic, only succeeded in making the stadium look like a 'poorly lit aquarium'. One had to sympathize with Lunetta: staging an event of this size in Calcutta, of all places, is no one's idea of a picnic. But the director did not escape criticism. 'Lunetta,' wrote one paper, 'should be tied with a rope and detained in Calcutta.' Nearly everyone was offended by the expense, perplexed by the naff pseudo-cosmopolitan aesthetic, and dismayed by the sheer ineptitude of the thing. Given the modest size of the winner's purse, it was indeed an extravagant waste. There were letters and leaders, columns and cartoons. An effigy of the Pilcom secretary, Jagmohan Dalmiya, was burned outside Eden Gardens. A member of the state assembly demanded legal action against him; another called for his arrest on the unusual grounds, not often cited in court, of 'cheating the people'. Pakistanis were offended when the laser show blithely included the disputed state of Kashmir in the map of India. The final sting came when the ground staff at Calcutta announced that the pitch had been all but ruined by the opening ceremony. The central stage was thirty feet high, and rested on four iron pillars dug eighteen feet into the lush grass. If nothing else, that fact ought to have been noted by the players: the semi-final in Calcutta looked, even at this early stage, like a match in which you'd want to bat first.

A few days later, in a long letter to the *Asian Age*, which the newspaper mischievously printed in full, Lunetta drew himself up to his full, absurd height. Cricket fans, especially English cricket fans, are used to bad excuses, but Lunetta's frantic, windy apologia was something else. He was, he declared, replying to the 'enormous quantity of lies and slanderous reports' that were written by 'misinformed papers and journalists and by all kinds of scoundrels often covered by cowardly anonymity'. A splendid start. 'Neither I nor my company were responsible as regards the technical and engineering aspects,' he said, of the wind-blown curtains. 'Half Moon neither created nor assembled nor manoeuvred this construction and therefore could not and cannot be held responsible for anything by anyone.' He just went on and on. Of the models' clothes he said: 'We only had two choices: to exit, as we did, or to take the microphone and say, in world vision, that the show had to be interrupted because the models' sarees were missing as some genius had left them on the bus and the bus was blocked in Calcutta's chaotic traffic jam.' Of the presenter he said: 'I did not choose Saeed Jaffrey . . . I did not even know who he was' – one in the eye for the man who needed no introduction. After all of this apologizing and excusing, you had to ask: what *did* Lunetta choose? Did he have anything to do with the ceremony at all? The answer was simple and lofty. 'I have always belonged culturally to the far left,' he declared, suggesting that this was why the famously effete and mollycoddled Bengalis (as it happens, Calcutta is the home of Indian Marxism) had it in for him, 'because I do not believe in the bourgeoisie'. But he added an unusual rider to this riveting confession. 'Sport, and therefore cricket too, has no f***ing connection with political rage or remonstrance. I have never wanted to enter into politics; that is because I have a real job.' It is one thing to dislike the bourgeoisie, we might think, quite another to disbelieve in it. But Lunetta was not in the mood to care about piffling little details like that. He had a real job to do. 'You do not have to be Einstein or Leonardo da Vinci,' he went on, 'to know that circumstances beyond one's control, such as wind, rain, snow, etc., cannot be attributed to anyone but God.' For some reason he did not add 'Calcutta's chaotic traffic' to the list of God's astonishing acts to which we mortals can never be privy. And as it happens the breeze that ruined the laser show was not a surprise: Calcutta's weather does not move in a very mysterious way, kindly blowing in a sea breeze most evenings. When all the official ceremonies were over, Lunetta's team actually reran the laser spectacular, this time helped by an army of small boys who held down the drapes. It worked a treat.

It was not the best foot that Pilcom had been hoping to put forward. The committee was in enough trouble as it was: India was in the middle of a huge corruption scandal, with ministers tumbling like English wickets. And Pilcom was itself the subject of a tax and foreign exchange investigation into the way it had conducted its sponsorship deals, and the way it had handled the payments to the ICC member countries overseas. The real opening ceremony was taking place in the wings, far behind these clod-hopping togetherness gestures. It was a bit like Dad obstinately putting up the Christmas lights after the whole family has stomped off in a huff.

For the last two days, the various leaders of the cricket-playing countries had been meeting, under the auspices of the ICC, to see whether anything could be done about the games that Australia and the West Indies were refusing to play. There had been some dotty talk of calling in the United Nations, as if the desire to skip a couple of games of cricket were tantamount to an infringement of sovereignty, or a violation of Sri Lanka's human rights. But there were serious issues here: quite apart from the politics of it, big-money contracts were involved. Poor Sri Lanka. Their original agreement with Pilcom did not guarantee them a profit share in the tournament as a whole: they had not been able to put up the $6 million stake, so were entitled only to all the proceeds from the four matches they were hosting. And now two of those games, the two big ones, were going down the plughole. It was a test case. Who was in charge round here? Did anyone have the right to punish Australia and the West Indies? Could they be fined? It was up to Sir Clyde Walcott, one of the great pioneers of West Indian cricket, to chair an eleventh-hour attempt to persuade the refuseniks to change their minds.

Australia and the West Indies were requesting that their games be moved to India or Pakistan, and Pilcom, inevitably, was having none of that. Where would it leave the other games in Sri Lanka, and besides, wouldn't it be 'giving in to terrorism', the ultimate diplomatic no-no? As it happened, the Tamil group's spokesman in Paris (guerrilla movements always have their headquarters in Paris) had announced that no action would be taken against the teams; and Zimbabwe and Kenya had declared their intention to go ahead and risk it. Pilcom instead made these suggestions: 1, For India and Kenya to play in Sri Lanka instead of in India, thus proving that the island was safe (a non-starter: India and Kenya hadn't received death threats, so their survival wouldn't prove anything); 2, that the stadium in Colombo would be emptied and the approach roads sealed – a neat idea, as Sri Lanka was worried not just about losing box-office receipts, but also the much more important consideration of the television rights; and, 3, that Australia and the West Indies would stay in Madras (solving the thorny shopping issue) and be airlifted in and out of Colombo by helicopter. This smacked of *Apocalypse Now*: it wasn't hard to imagine the Aussie players up there in the choppers, sitting on their helmets as they flew over the surf off northern Sri Lanka.

At one point the head of Pilcom, I. S. Bindra (one of the 'chappies' at Lord's that day) came out and said: 'We have adjourned for a coffee break. Hopefully we will not need a dinner break.' Some hope: the meeting was twice asked to move to different rooms to make way for wedding parties, stopped for dinner, resumed late into the night, and eventually agreed to meet again in the morning. Even as the talks proceeded, the captain of Australia and the manager of the West Indies gave press conferences to assert that they were not budging.

The next morning they all met again, and went round the houses one more time. But nothing came of it. Pilcom spoke darkly about their determination to extract compensation ($3 million was the sum mentioned) from the renegade countries. Meanwhile, Sri Lanka were awarded the games, and with two victories under their belts, they were dead certs for the quarter finals. Their coach, the half-Australian Davenell Whatmore, said that it gave him 'an empty feeling'.

What with all this going on, it was quite hard to think about the actual cricket. Before a ball was bowled, it had been quite an interesting World Cup already. There had been a geopolitical row, a glimpse-into-the-future media wrangle, rumours of a financial scandal, and big security worries (not least in Karachi, where England were going, and where murder and abduction were daily events). The credibility of the ruling body, in a game that once thought of itself as a byword for fair play, was in ruins. Of the three host countries, two were practically at war (Indian and Pakistani troops were skirmishing up in Kashmir, and posturing with missiles), and the third was tearing itself apart in a bloodthirsty civil battle. Down in Hyderabad, sniffer dogs were prowling the pitch looking for landmines after rumours about the Maoist guerrilla group known as the Naxalites; in Nagpur, where thirteen spectators had been killed by a collapsing parapet the previous November, a local group was threatening to dig up the pitch unless a memorial plaque was put up; in Calcutta, the municipal corporation, partly prompted by pique over the opening ceremony, threatened to insist on thorough 'fitness certificates' from the cricket ground, after complaints that one of the stands had been shaken by the drumming of feet over the weekend. And a labour dispute had halted work on the stadium in Delhi; it seemed there was no way it could be spruced up in time for the match between India and Sri Lanka.

In short, there was plenty to chew on. The English newspapers had a powerful contingent of highly paid writers out in the subcontinent. No other country puts as much effort and money into hassling its players as we do. And as the first game of the 1996 World Cup approached they reported the major news stories of the week. 'England Alarm as Cork Breaks Down' (England's top bowler strains knee) . . . 'Cork KO'd as Illy Hits New World Cup Woe' (same thing) . . . 'Smith Woe as Hussain and Ramps Wait for Call' (Robin Smith strains groin) . . . 'Smith Patched Up With Needlework' (Smith tries acupuncture) . . . 'New Look Gooch Is Knocking 'em for Six' (former England captain has hair transplant) . . . 'Twose Sorry Now, Illy' (the English-born New Zealand batsman Roger Twose accepts a fee from the *News of the World* for saying, 'I'll make you pay for snubbing me,' to the England selectors who never picked him) . . . and 'Fairbrother Joins Walking Wounded' (England's leading tip-and-runner crashed into a fence and needed four stitches in his head). Best of all was: 'Rubbish Skip – the *Sun*'s John Sadler Gives Athers One Month' – 'to show you're not a flop, Athers'. Was it just me, or were we missing the point here?

Actually, I had contributed a drop of poison of my own – an unadmiring profile of Ray Illingworth, which criticized his ungainly tendency to toss breezy abuse at his own players, the cheek with which he accepted credit and handed out blame. In a way, there was something touching about his chronic old-hat belief in keeping the players unsettled and on their toes – he was like some sergeant-major type out of a black-and-white film, or a seaside postcard. And it wasn't just the Devon Malcolm affair – a clear managerial failure, whatever the rights and wrongs of it. 'I've tried to talk to him in the dressing room,' said Illingworth, asked about Mark Ramprakash's repeated failures in South Africa, 'but he just sits there staring.' Anyone watching could see that Ramprakash, who for years had been one of the great young hopes in English cricket, was simply seized up with nerves, much as Graeme Hick had been when he started playing for England. And so what if he was a bit of a surly introvert? Surely it wasn't the manager's place to excuse himself by embarrassing his player so publicly. It wasn't very nice of me to point all this out, of course – I'd never even met the man. But perhaps there was an omen here. Before the 1990 football World Cup, I had written a much ruder article about English football – slow, witless, heavy, crude, etc., etc. – and had predicted disaster. The lads ended up doing brilliant. Perhaps the same thing would happen here. In Bombay, jokes about England were already doing the rounds: Ahmedabad, Faisalabad, England-are-bad. But England weren't all that bad, or so I thought. Jaded, tired, bored, badly led, yes – but not bad as such. Atherton, Smith, Hick, Thorpe, Cork: okay, only three of them were English, but they were truly fine players. It wouldn't take much for them to come up trumps.

After New Zealand, it looked like I was wrong about that.

In Delhi, I discovered that I had left the plug for my computer (an Apple) in the wall of the hotel room. On the television replay of the match, I could see the big hoarding that said: Apple Computer: Hit this Billboard!

I tried ringing the number on the board, but no one answered. So I went down to the hotel bookstore and bought some notebooks instead.

But I had an accreditation pass, at least. The kind reporter from the Associated Press had picked up a fistful of them in Calcutta, and handed them out as soon as we gathered in Ahmedabad. I might not be able to run off the mains, but otherwise I was ready.

— 5 —

PRACTICE DOESN'T MAKE PERFECT

England vs United Arab Emirates, Peshawar

As it happened, New Zealand's victory over England wasn't the first match of the World Cup. By way of a last-minute gift to the luckless Sri Lankans, Pilcom had sent a joint India–Pakistan team down to Colombo, to give the island something to cheer about and to show the world that Sri Lanka was not one big suicide bomber. It was an implausible event. India and Pakistan were barely on speaking terms in the real world, yet here was a cricket team captained by an Indian (a Muslim, no less) and managed by a Pakistani, flying off to play an exhibition match together. Years before, I had been in Tehran for the last spasms of the Shah's rule. On the day that martial law was declared, I rang the man at the British Embassy to find out what the form was regarding curfew and so on. Alas, I was told, he was out umpiring a cricket match. At the time it seemed comically, stuffily, heroically English. But in all the annals of the Raj there could hardly have been a finer example of cricket's stiff-upper-lip ability to shrug off grudges for the sake of a harmonious game than this whimsical joint venture. You didn't have to read much about the horrors of Partition to understand the depth of the animosity: the refugee trains hacked to pieces by raiders, the babies impaled and thrown on to fires. Ten million people were displaced; how many died was anyone's guess.

A single conscience-stricken English bureaucrat was handed the impossible task of hastily drawing neat lines on the map of a country he had never visited, boundaries (a term neatly borrowed from the great game) that would define the new nations. In the east he handed all of Bengal's jute to Pakistan, and all the jute mills to India. In the west, he lopped in half the great fertile heart of the subcontinent, the Punjab. And in the north, he gave Kashmir to India. The Pathans of Pakistan invaded anyway, but were held just short of the capital, Srinigar. The nations have been warring along that jagged line – the so-called line of control – ever since, and cutting whatever historic links remained (India, for starters, is named after Pakistan's river, the Indus). For the World Cup the governments had agreed a visa deal: a thousand Pakistanis would be permitted to go to the semi-finals in India, and a thousand Indians would be allowed to travel to Lahore for the final, and it was a sign of the times that this was a significant concession. In Pakistan Indian cricket reporters had to check in with the police every day, like convicts on parole.

On the other hand, there were touching reunions. At the opening ceremony Pakistan's wicket-keeper, Rashid Latif, met his brother for the first time in twenty-four years. In the week of the final, one family from Bombay came to Pakistan for the first time since 1947. The daughter was taking her aged mother to see the old family house in Rawalpindi; fifty years earlier, they had fled in haste to save their necks. The same books stood on the bookshelves, beside the same curtains. The same cups bore the same cracks.

All these deep wounds and bad memories . . . and suddenly you had two sets of players joking on the plane on their way south to Colombo. Talk about last minute. Wasim Akram didn't have his kit; none of the Pakistan players did. And the Indian batsman Navjot Singh Sidhu had forgotten his passport. There was a flurry of faxes in the night and he ended up making a little bit of history, becoming perhaps the first Indian (not counting smugglers and terrorists) ever to fly to Sri Lanka without the proper documents.

But the island jumped for joy. Rows of schoolchildren lined the road leading to the Premadasa stadium (named, as fate would have it, after an assassinated prime minister); banners carrying loyal messages – 'We salute your magnificent gesture' – fluttered over their heads. Some of the slogans were more caustic: 'Aussie PM is Keating,' read one, 'Australians are cheating.' Another went: 'Murali, you are not guilty – you were convicted by the grandson of an ex-convict.' Not very original, but the feeling was plain enough. 'London bombed,' said a sheet waved by someone who had obviously been reading the papers. 'Where will sissy Warne go shopping?' Probably the neatest banner was the one that said: 'Bombs in London – Ashes contested in Tahiti.'

The players weren't worried about bullets, or at least they said they weren't. 'I just hope we don't nod off,' said Azharuddin. They had hopped on to the plane at midnight, arrived at three in the morning, and here they were, only a catnap later, walking out on to the pitch. And look . . . they were wearing whites – traditional cricket costume. One of the nicer aspects of cricket has always been the pleasant formality by which both teams wear the same clothes, an attempt to dissolve national distinctions instead of inflaming them, an optimistic assumption that any differences can be submerged in the game. Who needed the us-and-them tribal posturings of other sports? One of the alarming things about the present trend in television commentary was its desire to reproduce, on the airwaves, the rivalry out on the field. Already, during the first match, New Zealand's Ian Smith had engaged England's Geoff Boycott in some wearying my-dad's-better-than-your-dad repartee. It was supposed to be impish. In the games coming up, there would be many more instances of ultra-partisan commentating – Sunil Gavaskar on India, Imran Khan on Pakistan, Tony Greig on everyone. It wasn't commentary; it was cheerleading. So, on this doveish day, a drop of the white stuff was just what was needed.

The players were greeted at the stadium by a band, a boisterous crowd, drummers from Kandy and a decorated baby elephant. As the match began a group of fans ran around with flags shouting, 'Sri Lanka, Zindabad . . . India, Zindabad . . . Pakistan, Zindabad . . . Australia, very, very bad,' a variant on the England-are-bad gags doing the rounds further north. The Sri Lankan foreign minister, the man who called Warne a sissy and followed it up by sending sarcastic flowers to Australia's foreign minister, stood beside the High Commissioners from India and Pakistan as they hoisted their countries' flags. This was a genuine opening ceremony, and it made one wish they'd thought of it before. Instead of that waste-of-money laser show, they could have put on a nice little match: Pilcom versus the Rest of the World. Just imagine the teams. For the home side: Tendulkar, Sohail, De Silva, Azharuddin, Inzaman-al-Haq, Jayasuriya, Kaluwitharana, Wasim Akram, Kumble, Muralitharan and Waqar Younis. For the visitors: Waugh, Taylor, Lara, Thorpe, Adams, Waugh, McMillan, Healey, Warne, Ambrose, Donald. Nothing too serious – you wouldn't want anyone to get injured. But a light-hearted slogabout would have whetted appetites for the serious stuff ahead.

Too late for that now. Sri Lanka bumbled their way to 168 off forty overs. When the first wicket fell – Jayasuriya, caught Tendulkar, bowled Akram – the applause, recognizing the historic scorecard entry, was as raucous as if it had been a six. Then Tendulkar, Azharuddin and Jadeja whacked away and won the match with five overs to spare.

The following day, all the schools in Sri Lanka were closed indefinitely on security grounds after the Tamil Tigers issued the following breezy warning: 'Start making smaller coffins.' The police suspected military involvement in the murder of twenty-four civilians. A truck filled with high explosive was discovered a mile from the stadium. And in another diplomatic joint venture, the Indian and Sri Lankan navies teamed up north of Trincomalee and destroyed a flotilla of boats that included a Tamil Tigers arms shipment. Perhaps Australia's fears were not groundless, after all. We would never know. They had declined even to practise in Madras, on the grounds that it was too close to Sri Lanka, and from Calcutta they flew to Bombay. It was ironic, in a way: the facility they had been planning to use in Madras was the Pace Cricket Academy, where the coach was one of Australia's own, Dennis Lillee. They weren't taking any chances, and they were keeping themselves to themselves. Shane Warne was so heavily besieged by the media that the management cut off the phone in his hotel room. The Taj in Colombo, meanwhile, kept fourteen rooms vacant, just in case Australia changed their minds, though the truth was that if they didn't come, the rooms weren't going to be full. No one knew who would pick up the bill if they never arrived.

In a nice postscript to the match, Azharuddin wrote an article for the Indian magazine *Sportstar*, which dwelt at length on the significance of the match and suggested that it become a regular event. 'Why cannot we use cricket to bring about changes in the region?' he wrote. He proposed that a World XI go to Sri Lanka after the final to play the World Cup winners. 'It cannot be that difficult,' he said, 'to find eleven men from eleven teams willing to go to Sri Lanka in order to make a gesture of solidarity.' This sounded like a great idea – so good it was bound not to happen. But it was refreshing to see a cricketer willing to see the game as part of life's wider plot, not as some fragile bloom that needed protection from the rough winds of the real world. And it was proof, too, that the meaning of the game is the game itself.

* * *

I wish I had been there. I have a soft spot for decorated baby elephants. But I was busy heading for Peshawar with the press corps to watch England play the United Arab Emirates. In Ahmedabad several journalists were turned away from the ground because they were 'likely assassins' – and perhaps this wasn't a million miles from the truth. The team had copped it for losing to New Zealand; if they lost to the Emirates the papers would let them have it with both barrels.

The ground was small but spectacular. To the north you could see the snowy tops of the Hindu Kush. Just 200 miles to the west lay Kabul, and in between was the lawless hill country that the Red Army had tried, and failed, to subjugate. Peshawar was a dangerous place, *Kim* country, and in the foyer of the hotel a large sandwich board read: 'Hotel Policy – Arms cannot be brought inside the hotel premises. Personal Guards or Gunmen are required to deposit their weapons with the Hotel Security.' Hmmm . . . it was enough, at least, to make you take off your sunglasses and saunter through with that fake-insouciant look you carry through Customs. But the stadium felt anything but hostile. Officially, the capacity was 18,000, but the man from IMG had personally walked every inch of the seating – working on an eighteen-inch backside – and come up with a figure of 14,000. He needn't have bothered: only a few hundred turned up to watch. One of them was a contortionist: with one heel locked round his neck he hopped along the empty terraces; then he put both feet behind his head and bounded along on his arms. Otherwise, it seemed that Islamic solidarity was not sufficient to rouse the population to come and support their fellow Muslims; nor was the presence of several Pakistanis in the Emirates side sufficient to seduce the fans. This was partly because the tickets had been sold through the banks – and the banks had been closed for the past two days – and partly because this was the fasting month of Ramadan, no food or drink in the daylight hours. But mainly it betrayed a deep lack of feeling for these two teams. 'No interest,' said the *Frontier Post*, the day before the match. 'And no thrill.'

In a way this suited England: it drained the game of tension; made it feel like a friendly. Dominic Cork came running in to deliver the first ball (England had lost the toss and were fielding) and rapped the batsman, Saeed, firmly on the pad. His hearty shout echoed around the empty concrete stands, and the umpire shook his head. The second ball was flicked off the batsman's pads for two with a nice flourish – Saeed had obviously been studying Lara videos: he picked the bat up high with his wrists cocked and brought it down late and fast. After the third ball was struck into the covers (no run), Cork complained about the marks that the bat was leaving on the ball. The umpire called for some tape to wrap the blade, and play continued. For once, in this echoing hollow chamber, you could hear everything out in the middle – the grunts, the sound of hands clapping, the eager shouts, 'Come on, Corky, let's 'ave one . . . Nice, nice, like it, yeah.' England's navy-blue suits, with their advertising logos for Wills and Tetley, the multi-coloured sash of chevrons around the chest, the baseball-style pinstripe, seemed especially ridiculous. All the players wore blue hats except Jack Russell, whose dumpy old white tea-cosy was a talisman. 'I'd rather go home than wear a different hat,' he said. I think he meant it, too.

Philip DeFreitas was opening from the other end – a nice birthday present for him. He had played nearly a hundred one-day internationals and was by far the most experienced member of the team. But he had been a last-minute selection for this trip. He hadn't been chosen in the original party, but had played well *against* England down in South Africa, so here he was, back in the fold. But then he hadn't been picked for the first match: like almost everyone who plays for England, he didn't really know where he stood. 'It's funny,' he said. 'I have hardly ever felt secure in the England team. I don't feel like a senior player even now.' One of the traditional means by which the England set-up motivates its players is to unsettle them, keep them on their toes. Often, they don't know whether they are in the team or not until half an hour before the game starts. So, of course, you have to build up to the game as if you're going to play, and then when you're not, it's a bad let-down. And if it happens often enough you stop expecting to be picked, and don't really prepare yourself mentally with any great belief, and then, bang, you're in, and oh, my goodness, give me a minute to take a breath.

Last Wednesday DeFreitas had woken up hoping he'd be playing against New Zealand, but Atherton told him he wasn't. 'I was very disappointed,' he said. 'Especially as I was given no explanation.' It was like the previous summer, when Graeme Hick (one of the best batsmen in the world, by any measure) didn't know whether he'd be in the line-up to face the West Indies in the fourth Test until the morning of the match. No chance to sit up the night before dreaming of what the morrow might bring, no chance for a long nocturnal stiffening of the nerve and will. He had a bit of a clear-the-air with Illingworth, and then went out and scored a century – so perhaps it wasn't such a stupid tactic, after all. DeFreitas had a vague sense that Atherton didn't much care for him – the two had fallen out a little when they were teammates at Lancashire (when DeFreitas walked off injured during a NatWest Cup tie). But he had been handed another chance now, and was eager to grab it. He bustled in hard, as usual, and made the ball spit a little, as usual. The last ball of the over was lifted straight to Fairbrother at cover. Thank you very much.

Up in the television commentary box, Boycott was having a good whine, in his finest told-you-so voice. 'That was an indifferent shot,' he declared. 'He's hitting it on the up, it was never there for driving, he's hit it straight to extra cover, and really it was just a little lollipop, was that.' Boycott has carved out a nice career being colourfully unimpressed, but being a batting critic is quite easy. You only have to point out, when a batsman is dismissed, that he should have done something different. If he attacked, he should have defended; if he defended, well, he should have left the ball. And if he left it, obviously he should have played it – the prat. Actually, it looked fair enough; in accordance with the new policy of attacking the new ball, the batsman was aiming to lift it over the cover fielders for four. He just mistimed it a little. But Boycott wasn't giving any marks for effort.

Commentators often do this: even the experts judge strokes according to the result. One batsman takes a good swing at the ball and times it sweetly through the covers, and they all praise the way he got his foot to the pitch (even if he plainly didn't) and accuse the bowler of giving him too much width. Another batsman plays the identical shot, is caught at cover point, and is slaughtered for playing loose, for not concentrating, for playing a ball he could have left alone, for not moving his feet, for being irresponsibly reckless . . . There's no end to the things he could have done differently. Boycott is unusual in that he is not down-in-the-dumps, like that unbelievable old slagger-off, Trueman 'n' Bailey: he is enthusiastically grouchy. Actually, he talks much as he batted: working away on a small range of well-rehearsed shots and repeating them, with unflagging concentration, over and over again. It suggests an ultra-regimented approach – an assumption that there is a correct shot for any given ball – that risks missing the whole charm of cricket: the play, the game.

After all, the same delivery can elicit any number of responses: the really great batsmen hit the good ones for four as well as the bad, demoralizing bowlers as they go. When England played Sri Lanka later in the tournament, Boycott was pleading with Darren Gough not to bowl that tight leg stump line to the left-handed Gurusinha. 'He's got to get it outside that off stump, six inches outside. He's got to get the batsman playing away from his body.' Another one skimmed down past the pads and was called a wide. 'That's no good,' repeated Boycott. 'He's got to get the ball here' – he drew a little line on the screen – 'there, that's the line.' Gough had another go, and this time got it just right: six inches outside the off stump, curving in towards the off stump. You can guess what happened: Gurusinha's eyes lit up, he gripped the bat hard and dumped the ball first bounce for four over mid-on.

The silence was, as they say, deafening. You fancied you could hear tittering in the commentary box. Boycott said nothing (never explain, never apologize). But when they showed a replay of the shot, well, he had to say something. 'That's the right line,' he said. 'But see, it's much too full a length . . .'

Of course, in this he is merely aping the self-righteous conversational habits of the average fan. One of the pleasures of watching cricket, or any sport, is to have a good moan about how useless they are out there. It's our way of taking revenge for the disappointments they hand out. This is a key part of the way sport lets us down; it is always, or nearly always, less entrancing than we hoped or dreamed. Golfers imagine that their best shots (flukes, strictly speaking) are actually a true reflection of their game: in their fantasies, all those duffed slices and hooks are mere aberrations. Batsmen too fondly see themselves hitting the ball decisively to the boundary, and bowlers dream of endless unplayable balls. These don't really exist. Some days they work: the batsman is flummoxed and the ball clips the top of the off stump; but on other days the same delivery is nicked straight to first slip, and away it goes through his hands for four. Or you shape yourself, when batting, to hit the perfect straight six, but the ball holds up a fraction on a soft part of the wicket and you end up skying it vertically to mid-on. To whinge that it could all have been different is quite natural, and certainly true; but very dreary.

Boycott's pleading, sorrowful Yorkshire vowels are an influential noise in the English game these days; and this is fitting, since his cautious, judgemental attitude is also one of the besetting vices of English cricket: the idea that cricket is a job. In recent years coach after coach, pundit after pundit has emphasized the importance of the work ethic, but the work ethic has a nasty flip side: it takes the fun out of games. If there is any point to sport at all (and there is, of course) then it is to do with joy, a sense of physical revelry, the pleasures of an arm successfully chanced. A work ethic that stifles the spirit of adventure by demoting the importance of play in the game is a deadly burden. This is not a plea for blitheness or sloth – as it happens, these are encouraged rather than dispelled by the idea of game-as-job. Jobs are things you're supposed to want, and certainly need; but they are also merely what you have to do. They are a duty, a chore, a necessity. Some days you wake up and wish you didn't have to do them. Here, in the silent, evacuated stadium at Peshawar, you could hear the lads encouraging each other. 'Come on,' called Jack Russell. 'Let's go to work.' And you couldn't help thinking: Work? You call this work?

But in England, cricket really is a job – that's the trouble. We have a substantial cricket industry employing some 400 full-time performers. No other country in the world supports such a big workforce. Professionalism ought to help – it raises standards in every other sport – but in cricket it has bred something more like a closed shop: 400 jobsworths, only a small proportion of whom (the ones close to the England team, or the rank newcomers) are truly trying to excel. This has been amply testified in memoir after memoir, quotation after quotation. 'Cricketers do not expect anyone to watch three-day games,' said Peter Roebuck. 'Sometimes,' said Barry Richards, the great South African batsman who played for Hampshire, 'I'm standing in the slips and I start day-dreaming. I think, What the hell am I doing here? What a waste of time.' Mike Gatting didn't beat about the bush: 'Too much cricket will kill cricketers.' And Gary Sobers had this to say about his experience playing for Nottinghamshire: 'You can't consider yourself a county cricketer until you've eaten a ton and a half of lettuce.' Don't get me wrong: you have to be brilliant to get into it in the first place. But county players soon learn how to pick up enough runs or wickets to keep their jobs; and the rest is a breeze. Put crudely, the cricket season is a six-month pub crawl. Some players are pleased when it rains: it means they can put their feet up in the pavilion and watch the racing on telly.

You can't blame them: playing cricket six days a week would be enough to drive anyone to the racetrack. It isn't as if anyone's watching. Attendances at county games are a joke. More people file into any top football match on a single Saturday than visit their local county ground in an entire season. Cricketers are self-reliant, self-made men – their lives depend on their own talent and will-power. So they tend to be Tory-ish in their outlook. Back in the eighties, Ray Illingworth had this to say of the miners' strike: 'It's ridiculous. There's tea ladies at the top of the mine who are earning more than county cricketers. Arthur Scargill ought to come down here and try bowling twenty overs.'

This is a common attitude, and there's nowt wrong with it, except that county cricket is itself a heavily subsidized industry. You only have to tootle along to a midweek championship game to see the truth: it's very charming, a nice throwback to an unhurried age, just old men and children unwrapping sandwiches and snoozing in the sun, or rain. But the box-office takings could hardly pay the match fee for the umpires, let alone the players. Any true Thatcherite would want to cut the grants to county cricket – the cash from television and sponsorship rights to international matches – and see whether the game could stand on its own two feet. One day, this will probably happen. There'll be a bit of a fall-off in Test match attendances, which will trigger panic stations at the TCCB, and bingo: in a matter of seconds some television mogul (a Packer, a Murdoch, a Mascarenhas) will set up an all-star cricket tournament during the English summer, on English grounds, paid for by the lucrative sale of foreign television rights. There's a new advertising technology that will help: virtual hoardings. Soon, television pictures will be doctored by natty software so that different countries will see different adverts, specially tailored for each market, inside the stadium.

This is why Boycott's voice suddenly seemed significant: it was the true note of the English professional, and there was something swan-like about it, a dying, mooning, introverted song that seemed to be growing shriller and fainter all the time. Of all its fatal assumptions, the most damaging seems to be the idea that cricket is suffering. *En route* to the final he flew into Lahore on the same flight as the Sri Lankans. Before the plane took off he ambled back from first class and leaned against a chair to give them a pep talk. He praised them for their performances so far, and thumped his heart. 'If you've got it in here,' he said. 'That's where it counts. You've got to dig deep. If you play to your best, then you'll take a lot of beating.' It was typical Boycott – a beefy platitude served up with enough brio to make it seem like a nugget of wisdom. Not everyone was impressed. When Boycott went back to his seat, Derek Pringle remarked: 'Well, he's got an awful lot to say for someone who couldn't get the ball off the square in the first fifteen overs.' The seats in front shook, and Sri Lankan heads turned and flashed wide grins. It was true, delightfully true: the idea that Boycott, the classic grind-it-out, it's-not-supposed-to-be-fun English cricketer, had anything to teach these vivacious Sri Lankans about the one-day game was just plain silly.

Boycott was a great player, all right – a studious monomaniac, but a great player. And his entertaining willingness to scoff has won him lots of fans. But Mike Atherton isn't one of them. When we arrived in Peshawar the captain wandered up to the hotel bar – the only one in Pakistan – for a beer.

'Oh, Boycott,' he said to John Ethridge, the *Sun*'s cricket reporter, who was also ghost-writing Boycott's weekly column. 'He's got to go. He's got to go.'

Ethridge gamely tried to defend his star columnist. 'Well, you have to admit he does know about batting,' he said. He knew full well, since he'd written it, that Boycott had recently used the space to say that Dermot Reeve should have been captain of this World Cup side. Perhaps this was why Atherton was riled (why shouldn't he be?).

'No,' said Atherton.

'No, I mean about technique. He must be the best actual technician there is. He does know about batting. Who else would you go to?'

'I wouldn't let him near the dressing room,' said Atherton, in that crisp, steady-eyed way of his. 'I did at first. He worked with players in the West Indies. Anyway, I don't know how you can work for that paper. It's a disgrace.'

This wasn't a very controversial view. Among the other notches on its masthead, the *Sun* had printed the number of Keith Fletcher's fax machine during the last tour to Australia, inviting readers to send the manager a piece of their minds. The readers did just that: rude notices tipped into his room. One of the faxes was a crude drawing of a penis, which was nice, because although Fletch wasn't there, his wife was. Ho-ho-ho. The great British sense of humour, eh? (Or an authentic piece of a *Sun* reader's mind?) This time, they were getting excited about a fax sent by Jonathan Agnew's fiancée, which *apparently* was extremely saucy, and which *apparently* had been given in error to Jack Russell, and which *apparently* had been pinned up in the team room to give the lads a good laugh. Poor John Ethridge: he tried to pour cold water on the story, but to no avail. Agnew explained that it was all hokum, and that the sauciest thing in the fax was the description of the weather back home. But who cared? The paper printed it all anyway. Agnew wondered whether to give it a sarcastic mention in his radio commentary that day. But in the end he decided not to.

As it happened, this little spatlet between Atherton and the *Sun* was quite a rare event. The press and the players don't mingle much; they circle each other warily. On a tour such as this, Atherton speaks to the press almost every day, without leaving anyone present in the least doubt that he would much rather be doing the washing up. You can't blame him – nine times bitten, ten times shy – though it is counterproductive. A jauntier supply of quotes would keep the hounds well fed and happy, but Atherton prefers to signal his lack of enthusiasm by playing with a dead bat. It is not as if the questions are ever demanding: 'Happy with the performance, Mike? Pleased with the way Hicky batted? Any thoughts about the decision to bat first?' Indeed, an English press conference is a strange ritual: non-questions and non-answers which somehow wind up as shocking confessions with exclamation marks all over the place.

When Illingworth spoke to the press after the defeat against New Zealand he said – what else could he say? – that we'd fielded poorly, dropped our catches and not batted with quite enough conviction. 'We've put extra pressure on ourselves,' he said, 'and I'm hoping the players will respond in the right way.' Well, of course he was: so were we all. But in the *News of the World* this reasonable assessment of the situation became 'Illy's Blast – Ray Illingworth warned England last night: No more cock-ups or I'll give you a kick up the Khyber.' The players have long since learned to take what the papers say with a handful of salt. But there's no doubting the corrosive, exhausting effect all this hysterical stirring has on the atmosphere of the team. It is one of the reasons why England teams often seem so fearful and worried.

An extra twist is given to this sapping cycle of bad news by the way in which the players enter into the spirit of the thing by taking money from the very papers that routinely hound them. Out here in the subcontinent, Darren Gough was earning £50,000 – reports varied: it might have been £100,000, or £500,000, it hardly seemed to matter – for contributing 'Darren's Diary' to the *News of the World*. All he had to do was chat to the paper's reporter for ten minutes once a week ('More practice. Another long haul in prospect. Leave hotel 6.45 p.m., reach Delhi for overnight stop about four hour later'). It's nice work for Gough, that's for sure. But it is a fairly absurd state of affairs when you have a well-paid journalist and a well-paid cricketer, both of them perfectly articulate, collaborating on a bit of flim-flam in order to maintain the illusion that sportsmen are blockheads. In a way, taking money from the papers is the players' only way to avenge the slights they are liable to suffer, so you can't blame them. What's in it for the papers is much less clear.

But DeFreitas wasn't worrying about all this just now: he had started well, with a wicket maiden. And in his second over he curved one back into the left-hander's pads and trapped him lbw. Maybe England were going to do what they were supposed to, for once. South Africa had absolutely trounced the Emirates, calling into question their right to be in this tournament at all. If they were to give their spirits a lift, England would have to do the same. But Nazhar Hussein, who had once played for Pakistan, started finding the boundary with surprising ease, especially off Cork. Cork didn't seem too impressed – you could see him wagging a finger at the batsman – but it didn't seem to make any difference. Hussein hit five smart fours and the score advanced smoothly until . . . Oh, Gawd, here we go again. Craig White came on to bowl, and in the middle of his second over he tried to bowl a quicker one, and wrenched the muscle in his side. He gave a loud yelp and fell to his knees. It was obvious, even as he was led off, his head tilted to one side in distress, that for him, the World Cup was over. What was it about us? Why were we such crocks? Did we train too little, and drink too much? Or perhaps there was too *much* training. 'If you don't have any muscles,' John Embury said once, 'then there's nothing to pull.'

Neil Smith came on to complete the over and, ten minutes later, he had taken three wickets. The Emirates were fifty for five and the game, it seemed, was as good as over. It was nice for Smith. Like DeFreitas, he hadn't been picked for the New Zealand game, and he'd also been given a few fierce looks when he had started banging on at team meetings about the way they did things at Warwickshire.

If there was one thing the England set-up was fed up with, it was bloody Warwickshire. Bob bloody Woolmer and Dermot bloody Reeve – just because they had won everything in the domestic game for the past two seasons, did that give them the right to go on and on about how they did things? Everyone knew that it was only because they had had Lara to get all the runs one year, and Donald to get all the wickets the year after that. Give us a break, would you? The idea that they might be on to something, that the Woolmer approach that had succeeded so brilliantly both at Edgbaston and in South Africa might have some merit – oh, spare us.

It wasn't going to help Smith much, doing well in this game – it was only the Emirates, after all. But the significance of these wickets was clear. On these low-bouncing tracks, spinners were going to be of more use than fast bowlers. Against New Zealand, England's best bowlers were Hick and Illingworth, and Illingworth bowled well again here – one for twenty-five off his ten overs – to make sure that nothing bad happened in the second half of the innings. The Sri Lankan fast bowler Samerasekara batted nicely for twenty-nine, but when he was run out – a run-out! England! – that was it. The Emirates were all out for 136: sixteen runs fewer than they had managed against South Africa.

Not bad, from England's point of view. It could have been better: a couple of catches went down. But, hell, it could have been a lot worse.

During lunch, Ray Illingworth wandered up to the press box to break the news about Craig White: he was out of the Cup, and would be flying home soon. He then revealed that he had no idea what the rules were about substitutes. Did the replacement have to come from the four men officially on standby? 'We can't seem to get a straight answer out of Pilcom on that,' he said. It made everyone gasp. Quite apart from the fact that it ought not to have been beyond the wit of England's cricket authorities to find out what the rules were, what on earth was the point of naming four players as substitutes and then picking someone else? Why name people you'd rather not pick when the time came? Still, Illingworth helpfully said that they'd know by this evening, so he'd be very happy to tell the press lads who it was going to be. This was a thoughtful gesture – too thoughtful, perhaps.

'Actually,' said one quick-thinking reporter. 'You could tell us tomorrow morning – that would be fine.' The press corps nodded as one.

'Oh, right,' said Illingworth. 'Well, suit yourself.'

The reason the papers didn't want the news was obvious enough. It meant that today's story could be 'A White Old Mess: Craig KO'd in New Blow', which would leave tomorrow (a slack day, otherwise) free for the replacement story: 'Reeve Flies Out on Illy Rescue Bid'.

There had already been a couple of silly public-relations gaffes today. Before the match, the captains went out to toss up and were escorted to the middle by two children dressed in traditional costume, holding bunches of flowers. The deal was that after the toss the captains would accept the flowers and pose for a photo. Sultan Zarawani took his bouquet and beamed. Mike Atherton simply plodded off towards the pavilion, shoulders hunched.

'I told him,' said the children's escort, spreading his arms. 'I told him.'

The little girl walked uncertainly off the pitch, still holding her carnations.

And then the teams lined up for the national anthems – a horrible Pakistani idea; cricket had so far managed to do without these jingoistic fripperies (though this might be just an Englishman talking: our national pride is so guilt-edged and defensive that we can barely hear the national anthem without wincing, or giggling). The first one dragged on, and then came 'God Save the Queen'.

'Oh, no,' whispered the man beside me, one of the event-managers. 'I know what's going to happen. I bet they don't realize that the first one was Pakistan's.'

Sure enough, when the anthem ended the England team peeled away. When the Emirates' anthem struck up, the lads had to fall back into an apologetic line like something out of *Dad's Army*.

It didn't really matter, as it happened, because there was hardly anyone watching. The previous day, in Baroda, 20,000 people had turned up to watch New Zealand score 307 against Holland, a daunting total (Nathan Astle, the centurion against England, was run out for nought – a great leveller, cricket). Down in Hyderabad, nearly 30,000 had watched the West Indies take on Zimbabwe. India, it seemed, was taking to the World Cup. But up here in Pakistan it was a different story: fewer than 3000 had bought tickets for South Africa against the Emirates in Rawalpindi. And the South Africa–New Zealand game had all the makings of a record-breaker: advance sales were 382. There was plenty of passion for cricket in Pakistan: the cities were festooned with banners and flags, and you could see boys playing cricket in quiet roads. In Peshawar, little plywood cut-outs of players teetered on the verges of the roads, and fierce exhortations waved overhead: 'Green is our colour, and green are our thoughts.' Local businesses took out adverts in the papers to wish the Pakistan team luck. Even the government pitched in: '120 million people and their prayers go with you.' In Karachi, a camel was sacrificed in the national cause. But no one was coming to the matches. It was an ominous sign that the love of the nation was keener than the love of cricket.

And these empty surroundings made you wonder: what were we doing here, exactly? Beating the Emirates was, to be honest, a bit like beating Scotland or Ireland, though as it happens there are many more cricket pitches in these countries than there are in the Gulf, which boasts just one grass wicket. The Emirates playing cricket? It was about as plausible as a Swedish bullfighter. They'd already been absolutely whacked by South Africa, and now they were struggling again. Actually, South Africa had taught them a sharpish lesson in cricket etiquette while they were about it. At the airport in Calcutta for the opening ceremony, the Emirates players made mock-brave hooking motions at Allan Donald, and you had to hope they enjoyed it at the time, because it rebounded on them in Rawalpindi. When Sultan Zarawani, their suave, Lamborghini-driving captain, came out without a helmet, Donald gave him a welcome-to-the-big-time bouncer, which crashed into the side of his head. Zarawani was carried off.

When he turned up in Peshawar, he grinned and said he'd probably wear a helmet from now on. 'You don't have anyone like Donald, do you?' he asked. (No, we didn't.)

It seemed to sum up the Emirates. They were a whimsy, really, a folly: the creation of a single cricket-mad potentate who had successfully made Sharjah one of the key stops on the international circuit. In England, of course, Sharjah made only a small dent in the public imagination: our team didn't take part in the glitzy one-day tournaments staged in the Gulf state. But it was big news in Asia. Sharjah was where, for the past decade, the great rivalry between India and Pakistan had been played out. In 1986, in a famous match, Javed Miandad needed five to win off the last ball, and hit a six, and that put Sharjah on the map in a big way. Film stars from Bollywood (Bombay's film industry makes more movies per year than California's, though slightly fewer than Madras's) and high rollers from

Karachi flocked there to watch the colourful one-day tournaments.

It was a glamorous, high-stakes cricket party. But this Emirates team . . . only two of them were Arabs. The rest were Pakistani and Sri Lankan expats. Nazhar Hussein, whose neat batting had threatened to give England a small fright, was from Lahore: he had played for Pakistan before moving to the Gulf. Samerasekera, the Sri Lankan fast bowler, had a brother who had played for his home country; he might have played for Sri Lanka himself had he not, as it were, emirated. In his case, safety was an issue: his father was a policeman engaged in anti-terrorist work, so he would have made a tempting target for the Tigers. The ICC had just ruled that from now on seven members of each team had to be citizens of the country they were playing for – a fair enough idea. But for the Emirates it was going to be a killer: importing players was their only way to raise consciousness at home. The new rule looked specifically formulated to keep them out of future competitions. So they needed to make the most of this chance – and so far they hadn't.

It wasn't even as if this performance by England, however efficient, could raise anything like a cheer – merely relief that they hadn't cocked it up (so far). On the other hand, because of the way the tournament had been planned, there were only two important matches for England, and this was one of them. The other was the one against Holland, coming up at the end of the week. These were the only games England absolutely had to win to make sure of qualifying for the quarter-finals, the only ones that really mattered. And they were both, strictly speaking, non-contests. It requires some fairly impressive bureaucratic interventions to make the big games – the ones against Pakistan and South Africa – next to meaningless, and the walkovers charged with significance; but that was what Pilcom had managed.

And however much one applauded the idea of spreading the gospel according to cricket to new lands, these so-called lesser nations weren't half spoiling the competition. Why couldn't four of them have come and played a little round-robin among themselves, with the winner going through to the World Cup proper? They'd have been hard-fought, close matches. Whereas this . . . the place was echoing. Even on television it looked like a practice game.

It seemed, frankly, a long way to come for a match like this. Peshawar had taken quite a bit of getting to. We had flown via Delhi and Karachi, which was a little like going from London to Edinburgh via Berlin and Manchester – three two-hour flights which took over twenty-four hours in all. The journey hardly deserved the pasting it took in the papers back home. The *Sunday Times* called it a '27-hour marathon', claiming indignantly that the players had paused in Delhi for 'a few hours' sleep' – an interesting way to describe a schedule which got the team to its hotel in time for dinner, and didn't leave till late the next morning. But there we are. Every trip in the subcontinent can be described as a hell trip, if that's the way you want it.

Anyway, in their ostentatious red-white-and-blue shell suits and sponsored T-shirts ('England Thirst and Foremost') the players filed into the departure lounge in Ahmedabad, a featureless concrete bunker that had been inventively decorated to resemble a cargo hold, and settled down with their ghetto blasters. You can always tell, in the hotels, which rooms the players are in because of the loud music pumping through the walls, and here in the airport they had the volume up high. The other passengers shuffled in their seats. 'If it was anyone else,' said the Indian business traveller next to me, 'you'd be asking them to turn that bloody stuff down. But I suppose they want to make sure everyone notices them.' I didn't think it was that at all, quite the opposite – a way of keeping the rest of the world at arm's length.

Eventually the plane was ready and we climbed aboard. 'Anyone know what happened to Man City?' asked DeFreitas.

Otherwise, the main topic of conversation was the rain in Rawalpindi. It was absolutely gushing down, and the match between South Africa and the United Arab Emirates had been postponed until tomorrow. The technology for mopping up the moisture was a nice mixture of the primitive and the advanced: a swarm of labourers squatted down with sponges, and an army helicopter swatted up a breeze from above: a huge air-dryer. But suddenly an ugly ghost reared its head: if tomorrow was washed out too, and the forecast was not good, then England could find themselves in very deep water indeed. Just suppose that England's own match against the UAE was rained off (and it was pouring in Peshawar as well, apparently), well, then the UAE would have two points from two games, and England only one. So if the UAE went on and beat Holland, they'd have four points, which might well be enough to see them through to the quarter finals at England's expense. That defeat against New Zealand might turn out to be costly, after all.

The other topic of conversation concerned Cork's knee, which was clearly not in good shape. During the match against New Zealand you could watch him walking back to his mark, stiff-legged, head back, teeth grimacing with pain. 'It's the plague of English cricket,' said the team doctor, Phil Bell. 'He doesn't need surgery or anything. He just needs a rest. But if you are England's best bowler it seems inevitable that you are bowled into the ground.' The plan was to play Cork, but to let him put his feet up between games. He didn't bowl in the nets on the day after the match in Ahmedabad, and was under instructions to take it easy. Was it worth resting him entirely for the next two games, against the Emirates and Holland, which England ought to be able to win without him, and get him fit for the harder contests to come? Of course it was. But such was the nervousness in the England camp that they dared not risk it. As the Muslim newspaper put it: 'If England continue to play like they did against New Zealand, Cork may be able to put his feet up sooner than expected.' This game against the Emirates was beginning to form itself, like a cloud slowly sculpting itself into a new and ghoulish shape, into a looming nightmare. If Hick's hamstring ruled him out, then the half-fit Robin Smith would come back in, and he'd be a bit rusty and tentative so he might eke out a slow thirty or so, and then if one of their batsmen got lucky and middled a few, then anything could happen. It hardly bore thinking about.

Some people, of course, were saying that defeat would be the best thing that could happen to English cricket – a real, thorough, unmistakable, inexcusable humiliation that could not be explained away with a lot of waffling about tiredness, travel, food or wives. A defeat against the Emirates, ran this gloomy argument, would finally shock the ruling bodies in English cricket into action: the clamour for change would be irresistible, and the long-awaited transformation would finally come about.

Still, it was a pity about the rain. England knew nothing at all about the Emirates – they'd been issued with some 'pen-pictures', so they were well up on their star signs and favourite pop songs, but not much else – and had been hoping to catch them on the telly playing South Africa. As it was, they had to leave for the airport shortly after the match began. South Africa were batting and Gary Kirsten, that famous stick-in-the-mud, had scored fifty in no time. That change of tempo seemed to be working.

The West Indies were on television too, playing Zimbabwe down in Hyderabad (there were games going on all the time now). And if

England fans thought they had worries . . . well, the West Indies were in another league, and not only because their clothes were too small. It was the opening-ceremony sarees all over again. Obviously it hadn't been easy for an Indian tailor to imagine that anyone could seriously be as large as Ambrose, Walsh and Bishop, and the results were embarrassing. But that was trivial. For twenty years the West Indies had been an unbeatable force in cricket, their fast bowlers simply too fast, and their batsmen too flamboyant, for everyone. It had seemed like something more than mere sporting brilliance. Cricket seemed to crystallize the swirl of life in the Caribbean – a defining expression of the island culture. The West Indies had its Nobel Prize winners, and reggae music, but its raw, displaced and enslaved history was still legible in the dead sugar plantations that littered its damp, dark hills. No wonder there was a course at the University of Barbados in the sociology of cricket. In Sobers, Richards and Lara, not to mention Hall, Roberts, Holding, Marshall and Ambrose, the West Indies had produced batsmen and bowlers of outsized, never-seen-before gifts. In tiny nations increasingly studded with yachting marinas and resort complexes for wealthy American and European tourists, cricket was one place where West Indians could be lordly.

But it had all gone badly wrong in the last year or so. Mostly it is totalitarian states that seek to pin their national reputations on sporting prowess – a risky endeavour, since sport has a habit of humbling the high-and-mighty. And the West Indies was anything but a totalitarian state: it wasn't even a country. There was a Caribbean trade federation, for squabbling with America about tariffs. But it was cricket that transformed the tiny tourist paradises of Barbados, Jamaica, Antigua, the Leeward Islands, Trinidad, Guyana and the rest into a coherent force. In the opening ceremony's laser show, each of the teams had their flag displayed on the gusting screens – except the West Indies, who had to make do with a badge. When Trinidad play Jamaica or Barbados in the 'domestic' competition, it is still international cricket, with intense sovereign rivalries. When the West Indies went into a Test match in Barbados without the Bajan player Anderson Cummins, the crowd angrily boycotted the game. Likewise, when the Guyanese Shivnarine Chanderpaul was preferred to the local man Phil Simmons at Port of Spain in 1994, 70 per cent of callers in a radio poll urged a similar boycott. In Trinidad there has long been a feeling that their players have been ignored by the West Indian selectors, and there is something in this. Under Lloyd and Richards, the West Indies became synonymous with a kind of clenched-fist, African-nation pride; but this is not the whole story of these islands. In Trinidad and Guyana, the Asian and Latin populations make a mockery of the Afro-Caribbean myth.

This uneasy cocktail was stable enough so long as the side was victorious, but the recent string of disappointments was exposing the cracks. Letters appeared in the Jamaican *Daily Gleaner* suggesting that Jamaica secede from the union and go it alone in world cricket. The West Indies arrived at the World Cup having been beaten at home by Australia, only managing to draw in England, and losing all round in a World Series one-day tournament Down Under. They still had some hot bowlers, and in Brian Lara they had the best batsman in the world (you could make a case for Tendulkar, though it was Lara who had the records to his name). But Lara was patently unhappy with the present West Indian regime and it was, in a way, a miracle that he was here at all. Still, he looked in good shape.

Zimbabwe hadn't scored anything like enough runs. Ambrose, Walsh and Bishop were too quick and straight for them. And the West Indies set about their small total – 151 – with panache, though they stalled briefly when Paul Strang took four quick wickets in three overs. But those same three overs went for forty runs. Lara evidently had little faith in his colleagues, and decided to get it over with fast. He began by pulling the fast bowler Heath Streak for a flat four over square leg, and went on to hit five fours and another six in a thirty-one-ball score of forty-three. With just three runs needed (off twenty overs) he skipped down the wicket, fired Strang for an unnecessary six over long-on, and walked off. His bat was already tucked under his arm by the time the ball landed. On the way out he paused to shake hands with Zimbabwe's hapless captain, Andy Flower.

Or maybe he was worried that the floodlights would fail. With an almost-scandalous sense of priorities, the cricket authorities in Hyderabad had staged a day-night match despite the acute power shortage in the state of Andhra Pradesh. The twin cities – Hyderabad and Secunderabad – were suffering a five-hour power cut every day. Electricity was a burning issue elsewhere: in Karnataka, a petition had been filed in the High Court demanding a guaranteed power supply during World Cup matches for the sake of the television audience. It didn't please everyone that the VIP areas had been targeted for special effort in Delhi. 'Let us concentrate on the VIPs,' said one official, at the weekly meeting of the power rangers, 'and fortify the sub-stations in other areas, especially in East Delhi, to prevent enraged citizens from going on the rampage.' On the rampage? Because the cricket transmission failed? The crowd in Hyderabad sounded especially vivacious, and this was partly because cricket, even more intensely than usual, offered an escape from the day-to-day. They came, you could say, to see the light: watching the floodlamps burning was a pleasure in itself, rather like gazing at a waterfall on a parched day, even though the power they gobbled up would have lit the city for a week. The previous day, Zimbabwe had been at the ground practising under the lights when they failed; in the gloom, the Africans threw a rugby ball about by way of training. But today the power didn't falter. When Lara was batting, the lights seemed, if anything, to glow brighter.

It was no more than anyone had expected. But if the cricket world had been waiting with bated breath for the chance to see a small, whippy left-hander flaying the bowling to all parts, they might have been looking in the wrong place. Up in Rawalpindi, Gary Kirsten was busy thumping 188 against the Emirates, a record score for the World Cup and just one shy of the all-time record in one-day internationals. There was something about these South Africans . . . More and more, it was looking as if Nelson Mandela would have to fly into Lahore for the final, wearing Hansie Cronje's shirt and smiling benignly on his rainbow-nation warriors.

England still had a bit of batting to do before they could risk a smile of their own. It looked as if they would be able to knock off these runs without too much bother, but what was really needed was something haughty and dismissive, to make them feel like hot stuff again. Atherton, in particular, could do with some runs. He had scored eighty-five in the second of the one-dayers down in South Africa, but since then he had gone: nought, seventeen, six, three and one. Here was a chance to find some form. So it was a bit of a surprise when he didn't open the batting: Alec Stewart came out with Neil Smith. In theory, this didn't seem too bad an idea: Atherton was a top batsman, but he didn't exactly frighten the horses. Perhaps it would suit England to start with someone bolder, and then have a steady run-accumulator like him coming in later on, when the field was pushed back to save boundaries. But was this the time to try it, when they were chasing only 130? Even if it worked, what would it prove? The whole point of sending an all-rounder like Smith in first is to encourage him to hit over the top and get the innings off to a flying start. But England didn't need a flying start.

It was another dismaying sign that they did not have a clear idea what their best strategy was. Out in South Africa they had experimented, but the experiments quickly became more and more experimental. They juggled round with the batting order, tried opening with Russell, White and DeFreitas. But they never tried anything twice, they never gave an idea time to work. This wasn't experimenting. It was casting around for straws. If Smith succeeded, would he get the job, and go in first against South Africa next week? Illingworth kept saying that he knew his onions, but now it seemed he changed his mind as easily as all his predecessors. Naturally, after the match, he lobbed the buck to his captain. 'That was Mike's decision,' he said. 'I'd rather he went in first and got some runs. He needs a big score.' This might well have been true, though it would have been nice if he'd kept it to himself.

Stewart and Smith put on fifty pretty slowly – nothing special, but solid enough. Smith, for his part, was plainly ill. At one point he beckoned for water, and you could see him asking if he could come off. His teammates were not sympathetic: they told him to carry on, then lined up on the balcony with their cameras. They knew what was coming and, sure enough, Smith was soon doubled up and spewing vomit on to the edge of the square. 'Apparently he had a pizza last night,' said Ray Illingworth. 'And now it's out there.' Smith became the second victim of Italian food in the competition so far: half the Dutch team were in bed after eating spaghetti. Several home truths came to rest at once. When in Rome, do as the Romans do, which translates loosely as: when not in Rome, don't eat pizza.

England ambled towards victory. Thorpe was in no trouble, and Atherton paddled the ball around easily enough. In one sense it was just the sort of sensible, undynamic, professional performance England had been looking for. But it hardly made the pulse race.

No one watching had really expected it to. On the eve of the match, England had turned out for nets at the ground in Peshawar, and you couldn't watch without feeling alarmed. It was the usual ramshackle story. The players yawned through their physical jerks – talk about been there, done that. Then they had a bat. And it was a truly mortifying sight. Illingworth stood silently at the end of the nets, or fifty yards further back, watching. And the players fell back on schoolboy ribbing. 'Yay! See you later!' said Richard Illingworth, when he bowled Jack Russell. 'Bye-bye!' called Craig White, when he beat the bat. 'Christ,' muttered Russell. 'I'm batting like a donkey's arse!' He slapped his thigh angrily, perhaps to demonstrate to the manager that he wasn't pleased with himself. There is always with England a strong sense that nets are the worst thing they could be: an audition. If you play well in the nets, the feeling goes, then you might get picked. Well, that's pretty motivating. But it hardly encourages anyone actually to practise anything. It hardly encourages anyone to think.

Robin Smith was a case in point: he had a bit to prove here, form as well as fitness. DeFreitas, Illingworth and White were bowling, and Smith wasn't finding the middle of the bat at all. 'Fucking arsehole!' he swore, as another one sprang into the net behind his groping bat. Outside, Graeme Hick was practising his sweep shot: the team doctor lobbed the ball up to him and he swept it into the side of Robin Smith's net. This looked sensible, rehearsing a shot you think you might need. Graham Gooch had done just that the day before his match-winning century against India in the semi-final of the 1987 World Cup. He took one look at the pitch, predicted low bounce, grooved his sweep shot for half an hour, then went out and swept the spinners to death. But otherwise England didn't seem to be practising anything; they were just batting. If anything, it seemed thoroughly counterproductive. It was knocking the batsmen's rhythm out of kilter, and wearing out the bowlers without adding anything to their armoury.

It was tempting, watching, to play fantasy management. Atherton had wafted all round a leg stump yorker in the first match. Why not get a bowler – Darren Gough, say – to bowl a bunch of leg stump yorkers at him? Hick was the only batsman who had succeeded, and he'd done that by playing the bowlers up and down the ground with a straight bat, not trying to dab them away behind square. Why not get everyone playing that way for a while? Atherton, seemingly off his own bat, ran singles when he hit the ball – why not get everyone doing this? Come to that, why not take the sides of the net down and spread a few fielders around to see if they could run him out? Why not . . . oh, never mind.

Fairbrother came in for a bat, but who was he facing? Thorpe, the physio Wayne Morton, and the tour manager, John Barclay, an Old Etonian former Sussex off-spinner. 'Bye-bye! Bye-bye! You nicked that,' called Morton. No one wondered why he had nicked it, or suggested a way not to nick it – there wasn't a coach in sight. After a bit more of this, his time nearly up, Fairbrother was set a target: ten off the last six balls.

'That's two,' he shouted, slogging the ball on the off side.

'Never,' said the bowler. 'Had a man there.'

'Nah, he'd be wider. That was two.'

'Okay, eight off five.'

'Four!' cried Fairbrother, slashing another one away.

And on it went, a constant jolly bickering about how much each shot was worth. I was only an outsider, someone who hadn't seen England practise much, but you had to think: jeepers creepers. Too quote that Indian reporter, on the subject of England's fielding: was it always like this? Did anyone think that this was doing more good than harm? The English idea of nets seemed to be that you could acquire, by catching a few in the middle of the bat, a feelgood factor you could take into a proper match. But all these chaps liked golf. Hadn't they noticed the way golfers practised, drilling themselves in certain shots, aligning themselves to the conditions? Working on a draw, for instance, if the course was predominantly right-to-left, or rehearsing the low chip-and-run if it was hard, long and bumpy. Golfers know that they are the last people to understand what's going on in their swings, and batsmen should be no different. But nothing like that was happening out here. The idea seemed to be that if you were good enough to be picked you ought to be good enough to sort yourself out. This was another way of saying that no one was going to help you; they'd just drop you if you did badly and get someone else. Sportsmen are constantly playing for their places – that goes with the territory. But English players, more than others, seem always to be on trial.

In the centre of the field, people crowded around the wicket: it looked like the kind of ground you set land-speed records on, or one of those shots of empty reservoirs during droughts – parched, broken into flat hexagonal cracks. Aged men squatted on the outfield, grooming the grass by hand. One perfectly bearded old man was badgered by photographers into posing by the nets for an atmospheric old-and-new picture, which duly appeared in the papers back home: 'England practise under the watchful eye . . .'

It seemed truly amazing that England didn't have a coach, though this was nothing new. The English professional game has always taken a surprisingly dim view of the idea that improvement is possible, or necessary. 'In twenty years of cricket,' Mickey Stewart said once, 'I only received half an hour of one-to-one tuition.' Richard Hadlee, the all-time leading wicket-taker, played in England for ages, and did anyone pick his brains? 'In the ten years I was at Notts,' he said, 'only a couple of young players ever approached me for advice. Maybe some guy learned a bit from watching me, but as far as talking to me about technique and attitude, forget it. Nobody ever wanted to know.'

Certainly, here in Peshawar, no one was taking players to one side, working on any one particular shot, or recommending that you think about tilting your shoulders – like *this*, for instance. Darren Gough was having a bat now, but look who was bowling: the physio, the doctor, and the gallant captain, who never bowls these days because of his seized-up back. Now Gough had looked quite spiffy as a batsman when he first came on the scene. But since then he seemed to have lost the knack entirely. His normal exuberance had a tense, uncertain edge; and his shots seemed loose and incoherent. If ever there was a case for some special remedial work, here it was. It was important that Gough be in a sprightly mood with the bat. More than likely, he'd come in with twenty or thirty needed off the last few overs – that's what had happened against New Zealand. But England seemed to be leaving him to his own devices. It was almost inevitable that in the coming matches he'd be facing fast, end-of-the-innings bowling; yet here he was flailing away against lobs.

Selection . . . strategy . . . training . . . fitness . . . public relations: England seemed to be off the pace in every area, comically so. They knew it, too. Even the players admitted that they were 'behind' Australia and South Africa. But no one seemed to want to do anything about it. It was obvious that they would have been better off swimming, or playing golf, or hiking up in the mountains, or going to some local school and playing with the kids, or going on a tour of the fort – just about anything. A game of footy wouldn't have been bad. They just needed to have some fun.

Things were going well enough out in the middle, however. England were sailing smoothly towards a nine-wicket win, and what more could anyone . . . Aiieee! Atherton leaned back to chop the ball away behind square and was bowled. His shoulders sagged: getting runs was no great shakes, but being out was a bit of a downer. Still, it didn't make much difference: Fairbrother came in, and a few overs later, England had won.

A few barmy soldiers had trekked up from Ahmedabad to watch, and if the English team thought that *their* journey was a drag, they should have tried their supporters'. There weren't many of them; they could have shared a cab. As it was they took a three-day bus ride through Amritsar and up through Pakistan. One hung a banner on the fence: 'Uwe Rosler: the Cream of Manchester'. Maybe this inspired DeFreitas, the City fan. But Peter Martin, the Peshawar rep of the Man Utd supporters club, soon put a stop to it. He disappeared into the dressing room, came out with a sheet of paper, and stuck 'Eric Cantona' over Rosler's name. The long arm of the Premier League reaches even the North-west Frontier.

They hadn't done very well, the Emirates. But they were having fun. That night there was a dinner for them at a rambling old hotel in the middle of Peshawar. The streets were lit up and alive: every evening is a festival during Ramadan, and as soon as the sun dips beneath the trees the people have what I suppose we must call breakfast. Up on the roof of the Pearl hotel, the armed police assigned to protect the teams headed up in relays, leaned their AK47s against the parapet, knelt in prayer and helped themselves to some buffet chicken biryani. Each floor had a couple of these men stationed outside the lift. Sometimes they dozed off, guns between their knees. On the way to dinner one or two of the Pakistani members of the team experimented with Arab costume. Nazhar Hussein looked pretty good in flowing Lawrence of Arabia white robes. He had been to Lahore University; now he worked for a bank in Dubai. He'd looked pretty good this morning too, hitting the ball crisply for his thirty-three. It must have been fun. 'Oh, it was great,' he said. 'Cork goes, "Fuck off, there's no way you're playing me off the front foot." And there was constant jeering. But it was good. Hey, don't drink the water.' I didn't.

The day after the match, England headed for the golf course to play a Ryder Cup-style North versus South competition (the North won, though the two left-handers, Thorpe and Fairbrother, had only three clubs between them). There were two more days here, and then the team would take a bus for a three-hour hell-trip to Rawalpindi, to play Holland. It was going to be the same thing all over again

– a lurching sense of how appalling it would be if England lost, followed by a routine England win. I decided to skip it. Down in Gwalior, a hundred miles south of Delhi, cricket was beginning to stir.

— 6 —

DAWN TRAIN TO GWALIOR

India vs West Indies

The first real match of the tournament was a while coming. New Zealand had beaten England in that uneventful curtain-raiser, and then put Holland in their place; the West Indies had beaten Zimbabwe, India had seen off Kenya, and both South Africa and England had overpowered the Emirates. So what else was new? Even the jockeying for position hadn't really begun yet (since the leader of one group would play a quarter-final against the fourth team from the other group, there was a notional advantage in doing well). But when Manoj Prabhakar came running in to deliver the first ball for India against the West Indies the crowd was screaming as if there was one to win. The huge roar fizzled into a huge sigh when Sherwin Campbell left it. And he left the next one, too. Then – third time lucky – he pushed the ball into the covers and dashed a quick single. Richie Richardson, the captain who had promoted himself to open because of Carl Hooper's late withdrawal from the World Cup, took guard, thumped his bat into the dry, grassless crease and flicked the ball past mid-on for four. Then he dropped it on the leg side and trotted up the pitch for one.

Over they went. Javagal Srinath, India's best fast bowler, marked out his run and came in with that still, crouching, snaky run-up of his. He's a yoga fan, and there is in his run-up an echo of the lotus position: his pointy legs seem only just uncrossed. The first ball bounced nicely enough, and Richardson watched it go by. The next one was even shorter, and went cracking through the covers before anyone moved. Then a no-ball. No problems so far.

Campbell looked neat as well. We had seen plenty of him in England the previous summer: if nothing else, he gave the lie to the race-tinged idea that Caribbean cricketers were born, not made. He looked like a drawing in a coaching manual; when the left elbow yanked the bat through plumb-straight like a robot's arm, you could almost see the little arrows and dotted lines explaining the arc of the shot. Prabhakar overpitched, and Campbell unhooked a lever, firing the ball for another four. Eight balls, ten runs.

It was a crisp start, not at all what the local crowd wanted. The West Indies seemed to be showing already why they were going to win this match. They looked purposeful, compact, assured – everything they hadn't looked for the last year or so. Perhaps the stories about the new-found harmony in the Caribbean camp were true. Perhaps that smiley-smiley television commercial, showing the players beaming as they fizzed the tops off their sponsors' lager, wasn't a put-up job. Richardson was wearing his trademark floppy hat – no helmets, please, we're West Indian. It all felt just so.

It looked even better when the next ball reared up off the wicket, beat the bat by a mile, and zinged into the keeper's gloves at head height. Ambrose, Walsh and Co. might not mind bowling here. Suddenly it seemed that if India were a bit off the pace, they could wind up getting slaughtered. Heaven knows how the crowd would have taken it: their heroes had been turned into little godlets by celebrity. It seemed unimaginable that they could fail. They hadn't played much before the World Cup, so there'd been nothing but build-up, build-up, build-up. And in their first match they had been momentarily caught on the hop by Kenya, who batted smartly for a while before falling away. And then Tendulkar swatted a century to see them safely home. But the West Indians had also seen off Zimbabwe without much trouble, and, more tellingly, had been making threatening noises. For them there was a lot at stake: they had enjoyed a rotten year, and seemed to be in the mood to come out all guns blazing. Having forfeited the game against Sri Lanka, they didn't have much room for manoeuvre, and given that no one fancied their chances against Australia, this was a game they were keen to win. India were going to need to be on their mettle.

There was something else, too. Travelling from Peshawar had involved another overnight stay in Delhi, and I seized the chance to gatecrash dinner at the apartment of a friend from the paper, the correspondent here. Miraculously, he came up with a spare lead for the computer, so I was wired again. When I got back to the hotel it was about two in the morning, and the man at reception, guessing that I was following the cricket, proudly said that the Indian team was here too – downstairs in the nightclub right now. I went for a look. Sure enough, there they were, most of them anyway, glinting under the flickering lights. It wasn't exactly England footballers ripping their shirts off in Hong Kong, but neither did it look like what you would call ideal preparation: they had a match the day after tomorrow. On the other hand, they had flown in late from Cuttack, scene of their game against Kenya: why shouldn't they unwind? It was all right for them, I thought: they could afford to dance till dawn. They were probably booked on to some swanky private jet to Gwalior. I sat for a few moments in the zonking global-village music – 'Don't hurt me . . . Don't hurt me' – watching the beautiful young girls with their gushing dark hair and gushing dark eyes (symbolizing India); it was enough to make anyone feel old and jealous and tired. It was hardly worth going to bed, since I had to be up at five to catch the dawn train, but a couple of hours would be better than nothing. I found my room and fell asleep with my clothes on.

At six the next morning the station was packed. On the concourse people crammed and clamoured. And suddenly, from nowhere, the Indian team stepped on to the platform. The only thing I could be sure of was that they'd had even less sleep than me. So much for the private jet. A ripple of recognition shivered along the crowded platform. People nudged each other, pointed with their heads, and began to drift in that direction as if tugged by a magnet. There was Azhar, clutching his portable phone-fax machine. There was Sachin, everybody's favourite son, chunky in jeans and with a goatee beard struggling to decorate his young chin. They were all here: Kambli, the rebel, with his ear-ring; Sidhu, who had had a close shave with the law when he was involved in a road-rage killing; the wicket-keeper Mongia, who appeals every time he catches the ball. They stood for a moment and then, when the crowd started fluttering around them like a flock of pigeons landing on crumbs, leapt aboard.

I couldn't follow suit: I didn't have a ticket yet. Apparently the train was full, and it took a long haggle to find a seat. In the end the steward accepted my money, crossed someone's name off the list on the side of the train, and wrote mine on instead. I climbed on and hunched down, throwing guilty glances at the platform, expecting to see an irate displaced passenger waving a ticket and demanding to be let on. But no such passenger arrived. When the train pulled out I was in a sea of empty seats.

I wandered along the swaying corridor as we gathered speed south of Delhi. The train was full of French, German and Japanese tour groups *en route* to Agra. The Indian players lay back with their heads tilted and their eyes shut – business travellers accustomed to cat-napping on demand. When the train stopped, people hopped out and wiped the windows with bottles of mineral water. 'It'll be light soon,' they said, 'and we might get a view of the Taj Mahal.'

It did get light, but we didn't get a view.

There was a big crowd waiting for the team when the train pulled into Gwalior. Up along the crest of the hill you could see the fort where the Rani of Jhansi, India's Joan of Arc and the martyr-heroine of the Mutiny, was killed by the final, successful British assault. The town was full of rose gardens – no wonder the river was empty. It was tempting to see these perfumed borders as an echo of England but, of course, the reverse was true: roses offer, in England, a whiff of Asia. Anyway, the effect was characteristically Indian – half familiar, half very strange and remote. This is a place, after all, where the temples feature wild erotic carvings, not a sight you often see in the naves and transepts of Salisbury, Exeter or Lincoln.

The hotel I had been booked into for the last couple of months was full, so we were shunted elsewhere. As a newspaper contributor, I was starting to develop the routine reflexes of foreign correspondency: I walked into the room, pulled back the bedside table and winced when I saw the mass of wires and dead insects. The key to happiness, for a travelling reporter, is a phone into which you can plug your computer. In Peshawar, the Reuters man found himself idly turning the pages of a brochure advertising the World's Greatest Hotels, and realized with a shock that his first thought was not for the Louis Quinze bureaux or the glittering chandeliers – he just squinted at the phones. Oh, well. I dumped my stuff and headed for the ground.

Before leaving I turned on the television for a quick look at South Africa against New Zealand. If nothing else, the game would provide a form guide to England's loss against the Kiwis. And surprise, surprise: New Zealand were 100 for five. Nathan Astle had been out for nought again (as he should have been against England, come to think of it). I was still adjusting the brightness when Adam Parore set off for an easy single, Jonty Rhodes plunged on the ball and from a kneeling position hit the one stump he could see. Parore wasn't even hurrying until the last minute and, sure enough, he was out. A few overs later Gary Kirsten sprinted in from the boundary, picked up on the run and threw down the stumps for another run-out. That made it 116 for seven. There was something possessed about the way these South Africans fielded, Rhodes especially. He was famous for it: on the sponsored lager cans in South Africa he is listed as a specialist fielder – the only one in world cricket. He was one of those infuriating fidgety types, the sort who can't wait for a lift without jabbing the button every five seconds. But he had certainly cracked fielding, and his approach seemed to be infectious. None of these South Africans ever seemed to miss: that was the third run-out. New Zealand had been lulled into a false sense of security by playing England.

Down at Gwalior's neat ground all the talk was that the upcoming game was a duel, a shoot-out between the two best cricketers of the day: Lara and Tendulkar. People in responsible positions pooh-poohed this idea. 'Anyone who thinks that the game is just about Lara and Tendulkar,' said the West Indies' manager, Wes Hall, 'doesn't know anything about cricket.' Of course he had to say this, for the sake of his other players, if nothing else. But he was wrong. Lara versus Tendulkar wasn't the match – everyone knew that – but it was certainly the little piquant match-within-a-match that was going to make this game special. And special in a way intrinsic to one-day cricket. Purists, especially English purists, look down their noses at one-day cricket, regarding it as a debased version of the real thing, as a sad misshapen orphan. 'I call them cricket and crack-it,' said Raman Subba Row, the match referee in Gwalior. He wasn't being rude. 'There's no doubt that the one-day game has changed public attitudes, and we've got to catch up with that. All that old-fashioned administration of the game has got to go out of the window, really. The trouble is, as fast as we've made changes,' he drew an imaginary curve in the rose-scented, mosquito-humming Indian air, 'so life has changed like that – an even steeper curve.'

Subba Row was in on the ground floor of the World Cup, chairman of the TCCB marketing committee that staged the first tournament in 1975. Back then, Prudential sponsored the event for £100,000. This time the title had been sold to Wills for more than a hundred times that amount. Many of modern cricket's accoutrements – adverts on sight-screens, logos on the outfield, racing-driver costumes, umpiring by TV replay, match referees to control the players' behaviour – were not even dreamed of back then. One-day cricket seemed a mere frolic. But these gaudy pageants had turned out to be a life-saver. The old idea of cricket as an established fact of life in England's streets and parks had been going up in flames for years, and not only because the parks and streets have become crime zones, places to be feared. As this World Cup was making clear, cricket was now a zillion-dollar sport, competing for the public's attention and wallets like any other.

And there isn't much point, any more, in being snooty about the one-day game. Most cricket reporters hate it, finding it repetitive, formulaic and unmemorable. But these men are in the unusual situation of having sat through several hundred of the things, many of which finish inconveniently close to deadline. Of course, it is true that one-day eventing is a less roomy, less subtle, less testing and chancier game than a Test match. And by abolishing the draw, it fosters a win-lose mentality that has certainly crept into the Test arena – there are many fewer draws than there used to be. In seventy Test matches before the end of 1995, England drew just nineteen times. In the seventy games before that, there were forty-seven draws. It is as if the players have given up on the idea: if they can't win, they might as well lose and get it over with. Whether this is entirely a bad thing is an open question. A draw is a beautiful idea, that sense of the game being bigger than the result, that sense of two teams giving it their best shot and agreeing that honours are even. The mere possibility of the third outcome makes the idea of straightforward winning and losing seem simplistic: no game without grey areas can truly stand as a metaphor for life. But draws can be murder, too: deadly, pointless and dispiriting.

Tactically, to be sure, one-day cricket is limited. The fielding captain has only one aim, to save runs, so the whole delicate balance between wicket-taking and protecting the boundary is ruined. And the strict time control puts a lid on the glorious, open-ended freedom that runs through Test cricket: the possibility (however remote) of a batsman scoring 200, 300, even 400 (why not?). The action on the field might be more striking in a limited-overs match, but there is far less to think about, much less that *could* happen.

But as for the effect of one-day cricket on technique, which so many ageing pundits hold responsible for the frailty of modern batsmen, I'm sceptical. Sure, heavier bats have coincided with strict rules about short-pitched bowling, with the result that hooking and pulling are dying arts. But the main difference is psychological. Bad batting gets you out in one-day cricket every bit as easily as it does in Tests. Everyone talks about the ill-effects: the playing across the line, the shortened attention span. But what about the benefits? In the coming fortnight we were going to see some extraordinary strokeplay from Tendulkar, Waugh, Jayasuriya, Lara, De Silva and others – batting to make the purest purist purr. Could it be that the extra pressure in one-day games had forced batsmen not to be sloppy but innovative? These days they routinely eased straight balls through the leg side for four, or gave themselves room to find the gap on the cover boundary. These days we had reverse sweeps, and deliberate uppercuts over the slips. Good length balls, which Test cricketers block on pain of death, are often lifted back over the bowler's head or helped to deep midwicket. Is this bad? Sometimes, these days, you see batsmen in Tests playing a parody of patient cricket: leaving alone balls they could have hit for four. One-day cricket truly was Frankenstein's monster: it could make Test match batting seem distinctly low-throttle.

And it made you think. I mean, if these sides could score 300 in fifty overs, with the field set back and the bowlers exclusively trying to save runs, then how come they could so often spend ninety overs – a day of Test cricket – scoring only 200, with the field forward and gaps all over the place? The experts say, 'Hah! Well, in Test cricket you have a slip cordon waiting to snatch up an edged shot, so one of the most lucrative strokes in the one-day game – the behind-square dab – becomes too fraught with risk to attempt.' But if this is true, if slip cordons really do make strokeplay too hazardous, then why don't they have slip cordons in one-day games, to keep the runs down? It's ironic: one of the aims of batting is to force the field back, to make room; but in one-day cricket the fielding captains do this for you. Why don't bowlers pack the slips, guard the off-side boundary, and bowl a foot outside off stump?

Because they'd get hammered, that's why.

The truth is that one-day cricket has spawned an entirely different mentality from the one that prevails in the traditional game. The conventional wisdom is to survive first, and score later; stay in, and the runs will come. There is lots to be said for this: Pakistan played this way in the 1992 World Cup and won the final. But it is not clear any more that positive batting is really riskier than timid batting. Boycott is fond of wondering how many runs Gower would have got if he had applied himself harder. But perhaps he'd have scored fewer. No perhaps about it, actually: it would have been disastrous. Fiery batting has great side-effects: it alarms the bowlers, spreads the field, and introduces a healthy margin of error into the equation. The greatest run-getters are nearly always free-scoring. Perhaps the best hope of survival, let alone run-scoring, is to get rid of the slips by rasping a few through the empty covers for four.

This is only thinking out loud. But as one-day scores get higher and higher, so Test match scores seem to get lower and lower. And the more resolutely the fielding side tries to defend, the more runs they seem to give away. The know-alls keep saying that modern batsmanship has gone to pot, yet records keep being broken. Ah, they say, that's because modern bowling has gone to pot as well – anyone can hit the rubbish they serve up these days. But is it obvious that Trevor Bailey would have made mincemeat of Ambrose, Donald, Waqar Younis and Warne? Is it clear that Fred Trueman would have blown away Lara, Tendulkar, Waugh and Hick with those pitched-up, fastish away swingers? It feels like fantasy cricket to me, though if it makes you feel better . . .

Anyway, even leaving all the technical point-scoring aside, there remains something wrong with seeing one-day games as a coarsened, diminished version of the great game. When one-day cricket was 'invented', back in the 1960s (in England, of course), it was an immediate success. It was introduced as a response to a crashing fall in attendances at county cricket, and it worked: crowds loved it. The reasons given for this are usually to do with its plebeian appeal: it encourages slogging, it is all hasty and risky and not really cricket, which is why ignoramuses like it. But this isn't the whole truth. One reason why people like one-day games – the Lara versus Tendulkar reason – is because they guarantee you a glimpse of your heroes: both teams will bat, both teams will bowl. You can see Lara and Ambrose in action on the same afternoon. Test cricket is a marvellous game, but a dodgy spectacle: you catch the train up to the ground to watch a great player and spend five unproductive hours seeing a bunch of tailenders saving the follow-on instead. Most of all, one-day cricket offers completion: a beginning, a middle and an end.

But the main reason why it is so popular is that it is, in the best sense, demotic. One-day cricket *is* cricket, the game as it dwells in villages, schools, clubs, parks and playgrounds. Perhaps we should start looking at things the other way round, and think of five-day cricket not as the staple but as the treat. It is, after all, a high and rarefied form of the game that very few people have ever played. In the one-day game, we can see the best players in the world playing *our* game, the one we give up Sundays to play; the one where a long innings is two hours, where five an over is the least you expect, where it often comes down to the last few balls and could go either way. Nothing is grander than a Test match that after five days of see-sawing remains in the balance until the last few overs, but how often does this happen? Once every couple of years, if we're lucky. The rest of the time teams are winning or losing by huge margins in three or four days; or batting the possibility of a result into oblivion and spending the last five or six hours of the match just going through the motions.

You could even say that Test cricket offers a refined, delightful and ample extra dimension – but that it isn't cricket.

Maybe I was getting carried away. To be honest, I had come to Gwalior a paid-up killjoy on the subject of one-day cricket as compared to the senior form, but now I wasn't so sure. This felt . . . perfect. A raucous crowd, waving their '6 plus 4 = 10dulkar' banners and shrieking every time an Indian player looked in their direction. A gorgeous outfield, mown in broad criss-cross stripes to imitate Lord's. A nice, compact, tree-surrounded stadium – up in those oaks a few fans were tearing off branches to improve the view. The two best batsmen in the world; two of the best bowlers as well. What more could anyone want?

Here came Srinath in for another go at Campbell. One of the awkward things about playing the West Indies is that with Brian Lara at number three, you can't be sure if you want to take a wicket or not. An early breakthrough here might expose him to the new ball, but it would also give him more time to strut his stuff. There was something unreal in the atmosphere: the crowd was too partisan for words. What was all that about the knowledgeable Indian cricket-watcher? When Venkatesh Prasad picked up the ball at mid-off and lobbed it back to the bowler, the stands shook as if he'd taken a flying catch. When the ball caught Campbell high on the bat and squirted off the inside edge, there was a vast, stunned *oooooohh* as if he'd got away with murder. Which didn't mean there wasn't plenty left in the barrel when Campbell pushed a rising ball back into his own stumps and was bowled. Arms waved, horns blew, bottles flew in the air. And it was all very well saying that the West Indies looked determined; fact was, this was like walking into a gale. Even for the best batsman in the world, it had to be unnerving.

It'd be nice to say there was a big hand for Lara, but there wasn't. The noise of celebration tailed off and he came dinking out to the middle in something like silence. His first task would be to defuse the atmosphere. If this crowd got restless, the Indians were not going to enjoy fielding out there. The impatience was tangible. Actually, Lara looked too relaxed by half. After just a couple of balls he strayed out of his crease, didn't exactly hurry back as the throw cannoned into the stumps, and . . . oh, no? The umpire called for a judgement by replay, and the crowd shouted and held up cards saying, 'Out!', as if wishful thinking could sway the slow motion in their favour. Here it came – there was the bat, and . . . *blimey*, that was close.

That really would have been something: Lara out for nothing. Talk about an anticlimax. Actually, it was a miracle he was here at all. The previous summer, in England, both he and the West Indies had all but fallen apart. After they were beaten by Sussex – thrashed, in fact – they had a three-hour team meeting at which Curtly Ambrose gave the team a piece of his mind. He laid into Richardson, Hooper and Lara, the team's top batsmen: he shouted and raved about their lack of effort. It was, said Wes Hall, a 'virtuoso performance'. But it didn't work. After the second Test match, Hooper had just about had it: complaining of physical and mental exhaustion, he said he needed help and a break. In the end, after a consultation with Mike Brearley, he stayed with the team but later announced his unavailability for the World Cup. Richardson, meanwhile, was shrinking further and further into some sad, silent place far behind his dark glasses. Lara was disenchanted. He walked out in a huff after the fourth Test and went to stay with his friend Dwight Yorke, Aston Villa's Trinidadian striker.

He had been protesting for a while about the behaviour of the touring party, and Hall finally called a meting to sort it all out. It took place in the Holiday Inn, Manchester. 'I spoke,' he said, 'of the issue of players taking drinks in their hands from the dressing room on to the coach, wearing sponsor's caps with peaks behind in public and in the hotels, the general loud talk in the dressing room, which seemed to upset players, and Ambrose's refusal to sign autographs for the sponsors, Cornhill.' The mood of the team had been sour for a long time. The big fast bowlers, Ambrose especially, had become well known on the circuit for a brand of bullying rudeness, which no one much liked. Kenny Benjamin had once been suspended for six months for slagging off (the official report said, 'wilfully refusing to obey') the parking officials in Antigua; and Ambrose had been censured strongly after the sullen contemptuous way he once snatched a winner's medal from Sir Clyde Walcott, then President of the West Indies Board of Control. Here in England, they were at it again, ignoring the dress code and every other code. Ambrose threw a wobbly on the team bus when the caterers at Paul Getty's ground failed to come up with hot food, and Benjamin pissed everyone off so royally that he was sent home in disgrace.

So there was plenty to talk about at this particular team meeting. Ian Bishop accused Ambrose and Benjamin of plaguing the team with their noisy and disruptive ways, and said that Benjamin should have been sent home a lot sooner. And then Lara said that the real problem was not the bowlers, who had worked hard, but the captain, who had let these things drift. 'I felt some of the players were undermining the spirit of the side,' he said later. 'I told Richie Richardson he should do something about it. He said he would take no notice of someone who "had his own captaincy agenda". I said, "If you think I have hidden motives then I retire."' Hall let him go, and the meeting continued. Ambrose, rather crestfallen, said he 'thought he was popular'. Nothing really happened. Afterwards, Hall caught up with Lara and tried to persuade him to change his mind about retiring, but Lara refused. 'Cricket,' he announced, 'is ruining my life.' It was one of the quotes of the year. It was like Kafka saying that literature had ruined *his* life (probably true, as it happens). Lara had been offered £3 million by a batmaker on condition that he continued playing Test cricket, but sod that. For once, this was about cricket, not money.

Three days later the President of the Board of Control, Peter Short, went to Somerset to see Lara. He succeeded in persuading him to rejoin the tour. Lara turned up at Trent Bridge and the Oval, and his ravishing centuries saved the West Indies from being beaten by England, which really would have been embarrassing. But Wes Hall's end-of-term report inspired the Board of Control to reprimand and fine Lara 10 per cent of his tour earnings for indiscipline – kind of ironic, since it was indiscipline he was complaining about. Benjamin turned up for the hearing wearing a T-shirt showing an unrepentant clenched fist, which earned him more black marks.

And Lara was furious: in a shocking (to the high-ups) bit of player-power, he refused to go on tour to Australia, and suddenly it was by no means certain that he would play in the World Cup either. Did the board dare punish him further? Would the public wear a shrill attempt to blackball their only genius by a board of control hardly anyone respected, for the cricketing equivalent of wearing a wonky tie? Obviously not, especially since without him the West Indies did dreadfully on their winter tour. They were beaten by an Australian Academy team (the cue for a national outcry when it happened to England a year earlier) and pipped in the one-day series by Sri Lanka (though this, as we would soon see, was nothing to be ashamed of). Without Lara, they never looked like getting enough runs. Back in the Caribbean, opinion was divided as to whether Lara was an unjustly maligned superstar, or a spoiled brat. Someone leaked Hall's report to a Trinidad newspaper. The Caribbean board's response was to drop the last word from its name. It had, it was obvious, lost Control.

Out here in India Lara had been making some ominously confident noises. The team arrived a day late – engine trouble forced the plane to turn back to Barbados – but as soon as it landed Lara started asking about what the records were. If he was in the mood on these good batting pitches, who knew what was possible?

Against Zimbabwe he didn't have too much time to impose himself, but even in that brief stay at the wicket he looked the business. He always did. For the last three years he had batted with dizzy, intoxicating ease. English players are reared to defend first, and to attack only if the coast looks clear. Lara did the opposite. He played with a classical straight arc of the bat, wonderfully balanced on his mesmeric tap-dancer's feet, but as a grace note added a unique high flourish to his backlift. It gave a drumroll even to his defensive strokes. I had been a dyed-in-the-viscose fan for several years, ever since I saw him on his home patch, in Trinidad. At that time he was only a local hero: his 277 against Australia had brought him to the attention of the world, but he was adored mainly for his single-handed triumph against Jamaica, when he scored 180 out of 230 to win the match for his team. One Trinidadian trainer named a horse after him: Lash Dem Lara. And it was remarkable to see the effect he had on his supporters. Desmond Haynes and Phil Simmons (another Trinidadian) opened the batting that day, and after only a few overs the chanting began: LA-RA, LA-RA, LA-RA. The Port of Spain fans couldn't wait for the wicket that would bring their hero to the crease. When Simmons lifted Caddick for two consecutive sixes there was polite applause, but still the cry was LA-RA, LA-RA. People in Lara caps and Lara T-shirts drummed their feet in anticipation, and when a wicket finally did fall, they simply roared. There was a brief pause, and then out he came, all tippety-tappety, a dainty little matador with a bat like a wand.

He didn't last long that day. But a few weeks later, in Antigua, he scored 375, the highest Test score ever. I was back in England by then, but it was a remarkable event, even in London. Cricket is slow enough to allow news to travel fast; and as his score mounted – he went past 100, then past 200 – phones began to hum around the world. Are you watching? It's amazing. It felt like fate: centuries are hardly rare, and do not usually encourage people to start talking about world records. But, in Lara's case, you couldn't help it. He wasn't just batting, he was helping himself. As Angus Fraser said, after bowling at him in Test after Test: 'Sometimes it's as if he's taking the piss.' Lara had talked about a big score himself, promising that he'd be looking for 'a double or perhaps a triple'. And his talent was so outrageous, so obvious, that there didn't seem to be any clear reason, apart from bad luck or a rush of blood, why he couldn't get triple centuries every time. Most batsmen begin watchfully, but Lara always seemed to start as if he was on eighty not out. He went to bed that night on 320, like a mountaineer bivouacking on the south col, ready for the final push tomorrow. The world tuned in and waited.

It didn't have to wait long. Lara rose early and played golf – a smart move. If he could crack that tiny white pellet, a cricket ball would seem a piece of cake. He started nervily, even missing a couple, but as the bowler (Fraser again) said: 'You can hardly tell someone they're a lucky bastard when they're on 347 not out.' The moment slowly approached. Eventually Chris Lewis pounded one in short, Lara swivelled ('I knew he'd bowl a short one') and pulled it with a rifle crack to the leg side boundary. As he swivelled he brushed against the off stump, but the bail didn't come off. It was fated, after all. The police assigned to prevent a pitch invasion raced out to the middle and took photographs.

Lara's life changed after that. He had signed to come and play for Warwickshire, and I, calling on a deep reservoir of shrewdness and expertise, predicted failure. In an article written the day after his great score, I suggested that cricket in Birmingham in April might be a wholly different matter. We could hardly blame him, I said, if he stood there shivering in three sweaters as fat grey clouds sank towards Wolverhampton, while some slow-medium seamer got one to stop in the mud and lolly up into the air . . .

I could hardly have been more wrong. His scores went like this: 147, 106, 120, 136, 26, 140, 501. Six centuries in seven innings, capped by that historic 501. He walked out in the morning on 111, and scored 390 in a single day's cricket – an unbelievable feat. In the space of six weeks he had exposed two truths about English cricket: first, that the standard allows a true star to shine with ease; and second, that the six-days-a-week grind is enough to curb anyone's enthusiasm. After a couple of months, you could see Lara twigging that the only way to get a day off was to be out. He would find it hard to rise to anything but a special occasion. A week or so later he went down to play Northamptonshire, where he would come up against his Test teammate Curtly Ambrose. Many English fans have wondered for years how these West Indian batsmen would fare against their own fast bowling, and Lara provided some sort of an answer: he scored 197.

One more truth about the county scene. Lara was hired for £40,000 to play the season for Warwickshire. Between the time of his 375 in Antigua and the beginning of the season in England, the club gained 1000 new members, each paying £60 apiece. Lara paid for himself even before the first ball was bowled.

The day after that amazing 501 I went to watch him again. He was playing in a one-day match at the Oval against Surrey. You had to feel sorry for him: no sooner had the match ended the previous night than he'd had to drive down to London, dozing in the car, grabbing forty winks in some motel, getting to the ground to find, oh, shit, we're fielding. Surrey got a few runs and the stage was set. I arrived at teatime and was charged £20 to get in, even though I'd missed two-thirds of the game – it must be TCCB policy to discourage people from going to cricket matches. Actually, the Northern line down from the City was crowded with suits sneaking the afternoon off to go and see Lara; but the steep entrance fee was enough to make sure there weren't many West Indians in the ground. Still, the atmosphere was keen enough, even though Warwickshire were doing depressingly well. For a while it looked as if they'd win by ten wickets, and Lara wouldn't get to the crease. And even when wickets started falling, and the crowd hunched forward, necks craned to see the exact moment when the star would come clicking down the concrete steps in front of the pavilion, he didn't appear.

Warwickshire were trying to win this one without him: Lara had his legs up in the dressing room. But eventually he had to take part. He walked to the crease at number six, like someone with a hangover, someone who didn't want any sudden movements. And in an hour or so he had scored seventy-odd without breaking sweat, just clipping boundaries away off the front and back foot. It was rather like a teacher who'd been hoping the kids would be able to figure it out for themselves, but – oh, all right then, look, this is how to do it. It was like his dêbut match for Warwickshire, when he scored 147 just like that. Afterwards, someone asked if he was tired. 'Not really,' he said. 'I didn't have to do much running.' Over a hundred of his runs had come in boundaries.

It went wrong after this. In the second half of the season Lara spent an awful lot of time not fielding, and had a fair few run-ins with his captain, Dermot Reeve. And when he rejoined the West Indies he was fined and suspended for cursing the square leg umpire during a Test in India. When Richie Richardson took a sabbatical, citing stress, Lara was ostentatiously (and stupidly, if you want my opinion) not made captain.

He sent a tremor through English county cricket by tearing up his contract to play for Warwickshire the following season. The cat was out of the bag – county cricket was too hard a slog, not worth playing, if you could possibly avoid it. Allan Donald was busy bowling Warwickshire to a second successive championship in 1995, but when he returned to South Africa he practically broke down. 'For a few weeks I couldn't get out of bed, I couldn't do anything,' he said. 'I was completely drained. In the end I went to see a psychologist.'

I asked him if he would consider playing in England again.

'I reckon I'd have to hang my boots up if I did,' he said.

County cricket had long been an attractive option for overseas players: summer in England is winter for the rest of the cricket-playing world, so county cricket is a nice, if hard, off-season earner. England was going through one of its periodic whinges about this: Illingworth, and Atherton too, felt that the presence of the overseas stars (who might or might not be trying their best) was hindering the development of young English players. It sounds logical, though it is really the older English players, the ones who are evidently not going to make the step up to international cricket, and can't even be role models, who are hindering the development of youth. Anyway, the idea that the best players might stay away is even more worrying. During the World Cup, Surrey signed the powerful South African all-rounder Brian McMillan, only for him to be dissuaded by his own cricket board, who feared it would burn him out. Warwickshire had once made a similar overture to Shane Warne, only to be told that the Australian Cricket Board would not consider allowing him to play an English summer. Whether we wanted the world's best players or not was irrelevant: they didn't want us.

But right here, right now, Lara was back. Normal service could be resumed. Srinath crept in, and Lara whipped his bat into line almost apologetically, but with a certain snappy relish. Then he turned one off his hips for two as if he was giving someone their ball back. He lifts his shoulders when he plays this shot, to keep the ball down: it looks like he's shrugging.

And then, well, wouldn't you know it? Srinath bowled an absolute beauty, which pitched straight and leapt away towards the slips. It shaved the outside edge of Lara's bat and flew to the keeper, Mongia. Would pandemonium be too strong a word for what followed? Not really. But underneath the thunderclap of delight that shuddered into the warm air of Gwalior there was a faint bass rumble of something like shock; perhaps even dismay. Talk about an anticlimax. It might still be a good game, but it wasn't, now, going to be one of those special days. That's the trouble with cricket: there's no script. Romeo goes to the ball, gazes into Juliet's eyes, but then says, oh, sod it – and gets drunk with his mates instead. Lara didn't move for a moment; his shoulders sagged and he looked pleadingly up the pitch. This was teetering on the edge of dissent. Headlines began to form, like clouds, in newsrooms. 'He didn't quite go over the top, but he bloody nearly did,' said the match referee afterwards. It wasn't like Goa a year ago, where he had had a real go at the square leg umpire and was court-martialled. But a prickle of alarm scurried through the stands. Don't say it was a dodgy one. There were a few television sets scattered up in the press box. Reporters ran down for a closer look. This was Srinath bowling, that was the ball sliding away from the bat, here came the outside edge, and *whoooooooaaah* – that looked like pad. You could clearly see the ball clipping the top of Lara's back pad as it went through.

Would you believe it? Lara fingered for just two runs.

Let's have another look, in even slower motion. Ball . . . pad . . . and was that a bit of bat in there as well? In truth, it was impossible to say for sure. But then someone turned up the volume, and Richie Benaud, sitting about five yards away, said: 'Now just take a look at the bowler here. Keep your eye on Javagal Srinath [Richie loves to pronounce people's names with studied care, like someone calling out the winners in a school prizegiving, or a radio announcer lingering over the name of some rare composer]. Now: does he go up for this?' It was true: the bowler wasn't even appealing until the slips started going crazy. It was a bad sign, possibly a clincher. It looked like a poor decision, all right.

Opinion in the press box divided on fairly predictable lines: the Indian reporters thought that Lara had visibly nicked it; the rest were sure he had missed it. Luckily, there was no question of this being a home decision: the umpire, Khizer Hyat, was from Pakistan. He was, as they say, no stranger to controversy: indeed he had been one of the umpires involved in Australia when Sri Lanka were accused of ball-tampering. When the protests came in from the Australian players (who asserted that they had heard the umpires saying: 'They're playing with it') the match referee wanted to confiscate the ball as evidence. Umpire Khizer Hyat declined: the protest was registered, but since the Sri Lankans carried on using the same ball the case against them collapsed. By allowing the ball to remain in use, the umpires effectively ruled that there was no case to answer.

As it happened, Australia were in the process of scoring 500 runs in that innings: they kept whacking the ball into the concrete stands for six. Now there's ball-tampering for you.

Naturally there were a few dark mutterings, Down Under, about the role played in this incident by the Pakistani umpire. Wasn't Pakistan the home of ball-tampering? Wasn't Pakistan also the home of all the gambling and match-rigging allegations? Wasn't it obvious that Hyat, simply by virtue of being a Pakistani, must in some vague, conspiratorial way be in cahoots with Sri Lanka's attempt to bend the rules (and the ball)? This was careless talk – racist talk: a casual attribution of villainy based on nothing more than his nationality. But in Lara's case he was in the clear: why would he do India such a blatant favour?

I ran into Khizer Hyat at Delhi airport, a couple of days after the match. We were both queuing for the flight to Lahore. He, like me, was having trouble securing a seat. Correction: I was having trouble securing a seat; he was waiting for his upgrade to first class.

'Perhaps they don't know who you are,' I said. 'You must be the most popular Pakistani in India at the moment.'

It might not have been the most tactful thing to say.

'What did you think?' he asked. 'Did you think it was out?'

'Who, me?' I said bravely. 'Well, I mean it's hard to tell from the television, isn't it?'

'Yes, but what did you think?'

'Well, I must say it looked like pad,' I said. 'But you can never tell.'

'I thought it hit bat first,' he said – a little sadly, as if he knew no one believed him.

He didn't sound too sure, unlike the third umpire, Stephen Tovey, whom I had bumped into in Gwalior. He was the Dutch umpire on the list, and he did look typically Dutch, fair and open-faced. So I chose my words carefully, not sure how good his English would be (though, of course, all Dutchmen speak English like natives).

'Ex-cuse me,' I said. 'Can I just say hello? I was won-der-ing if I could just . . .'

''Ang on a sec. Be wiv yer in a minnit.'

It turned out that Tovey was from Reading. He went over to Holland fifteen years ago for a lark, met someone, got married and stayed. And he had no doubts at all about the dismissal.

'Nah, it was out,' he said. 'Nicked it, didn't he? These your fags?'

He was having a whale of a time. In Calcutta he'd been along to see Mother Teresa with his co-umpire, Darryl Hair. 'Darryl went twice,' he said. 'He was well rapt.'

He was on £50 a day; the more senior umpires were on £100. Not bad, as a holiday job, but not great as a professional wage, given that your number of employable days is so limited. There have been strong moves towards professional umpiring in recent years – the umpires panel has a sponsor, National Grid. But most of them still have other jobs, and it's a tough balancing act. 'Someone like Darryl,' said Tovey, a housing officer in The Hague, 'he's a teacher. It's hard to know if he can afford to keep taking so much time off.'

You couldn't blame him if he decided to quit: the umpire's life has been invaded by television. In a game that has lost faith in the idea that bad decisions are just an agonizing, inevitable part of life, a game that wants to iron out its grey areas, umpiring is controversial.

And there's nothing anyone can do about it. How can the umpire's word be trusted when he is so frequently, visibly wrong? The finality of the umpire's word has for an age, of course, been cricket's equivalent of papal infallibility. Television was exposing this as a sham. Heaven knows how many bad run-outs there must have been in the past; now we are forever imagining that a batsman was easily in, only to find that he was inches out. Players don't help, either: they appeal like fury every time the batsman sniffs, while reserving the right to glare if the umpire has the nerve to give them out when they missed it.

Could the West Indies survive the loss of Lara? For a while it seemed as though they might. Azharuddin, perhaps forgetting that this was a one-day match, immediately brought on his leg-spinner, Anil Kumble, and stationed himself at silly point – a good attacking move: it was obvious that Richardson and Chanderpaul, for a few overs at least, would have to batten down the hatches, stop the rot, stick a finger in the dam, er, put up the shutters, dig in, retrench and what-have-you. So it was a good chance to put a bit of pressure on. But perhaps the whiff of crisis would shake free in Richardson the memory of the swaggering player he once had been; perhaps with a young pup like Chanderpaul at the other end, he could bat with something like his old authority.

The two of them did quite well. They saw off Kumble, then began to pick holes in the field. If anyone overpitched, Chanderpaul tapped them quietly through the covers. If the ball was short, Richardson lashed it with that wristy cut-slash of his. After twenty overs the scoreboard – a huge scaffold full of busy bodies hooking and unhooking names and numbers; there were even a couple of chaps with calculators working out, and posting, the ongoing run-rate at the end of each over – had moved to seventy-eight, only a twitch below four an over. There were signs of an acceleration. Chanderpaul lifted Prabhakar to the midwicket boundary (in total silence: the ball was showered with paper darts as it ran up against the crowd-control fence); when the off-spinner Kapoor came on, he was swept politely for another four. The score rolled towards 100 without any fuss; if these two batted sensibly there was no reason why they shouldn't lay down the basis of a defendable target.

The previous day, asked what he thought would be a good total on this wicket, Richardson had squinted through his sunglasses and said, 'The boundaries are small – 350 would be good.' He was joking, but perhaps the joke undid him. The boundaries *were* quite small, which is probably why when Prabhakar bowled an absolute clonker, short, sitting-up and begging to be hit, he went for an extra-big one. It looked like six as it left the bat, but it just seemed to steeple up and die, and in the end it fell about a foot short. And Vinod Kambli, running round the deep square boundary, grabbed it and leapt into the air with delight. He wasn't the only one. It was a big breakthrough, and the whole stadium knew it. Out came the banners, the balloons, the flags, the bits of paper. Someone held up a picture showing a pair of juicy lips, with the word 'Vinod' scrawled underneath. Off went Richardson, dragging his bat. Another ounce behind the shot and he'd have been fifty-three not out, the West Indies would have been 100 for two, and the stadium would have been quiet.

As it was, his dismissal ushered in ten overs that decided the match. Amidst rapturous noise, Roland Holder came out, leaned back in an attempt to give himself room, attempted to chop Kumble down to third man, and was bowled. We wouldn't see many stupider shots than this in the entire tournament. Holder had never faced Kumble before, but anyone could have told him that the one thing not to do – the only thing, really – was what he had just done. Kumble is a leg-spinner in theory, but most of the time he bowls hurrying-through inswingers. The previous season he played for Northamptonshire and took 100 wickets, not one of which was a stumping: he's simply not that sort of spinner. This was his trademark: kidding the batsman he was dropping one short, trapping them on the back foot, and hustling it into or through their pads. Last time England were here he took twenty-three wickets in five Tests, nearly all of them bowled and lbw. Holder's shot was doomed from the moment he lifted his bat. His sponsored leg stump sagged back in dismay.

And then Chanderpaul went to pull Kapoor, caught the ball high on the bat and Azharuddin, the only man within range on the leg side, plunged to take the catch.

Suddenly the West Indies had run out of batsmen. Bizarrely, they had selected Courtney Browne as wicket-keeper instead of Jimmy Adams, who frequently took the gloves in one-day cricket and was the number-three-ranked batsman in the world. He came out to join Roger Harper, the off-spinner, but what could they do? Neither was a front-line batsman, but they still represented the West Indies' last hope of a serious partnership, so they couldn't afford to take any risks. They blocked. In the twenty-fifth over, before Richardson was out, they were ninety-four for two; ten overs later they were 114 for five. Twenty runs for three wickets was not at all the sort of acceleration they had been hoping for.

After that, well, there were a couple of big blows from Harper, and a thumping six from Otis Gibson. But wickets kept falling. Azharuddin must have thought he'd gone to heaven: every time he changed the bowling, someone was out. Prabhakar came back, and bowled Browne: Kumble came back, and yorked Harper. The West Indies straggled to 173.

It was all a bit of a let-down. At practice the day before the West Indians had seemed cheekily confident, even Richardson.

'How do you feel about Kumble?' asked an Indian reporter. 'You had some problems with leg-spin against Zimbabwe.'

Richardson shook his head. 'We didn't have any problems,' he said. 'Who won the match?'

So, who would open the batting? 'Wait and see. Maybe Ambrose or Walsh.'

What plans did he have for Tendulkar?

'Our plan is to get him out first ball.'

What if it doesn't work?

'We'll try and get him second ball.'

These were better than brave sounds: they were authentically lighthearted. At one point Richardson saw the reporters writing down his words and said, just in case, 'Don't worry. I'm joking.'

There was a long history of cricket jokes in Gwalior, home of one of the last surviving maharajahs of any prominence. Way back, they used occasionally to play cricket with the heads of their enemies – a lovely instance of a polite ritual being swallowed up by the ornate cruelty of the Indian aristocracy. The maharajahs became Britain's imperial stooges, indulged and pampered in their excesses. One of them was advised that silver could be pounded into an aphrodisiac, and all but bankrupted his exchequer attempting to prove it. Here in Gwalior, along with other mementoes of extreme opulence – the cut-glass Belgian rocking chair, the erotic marble statues and a ludicrous number of flea-bitten tigers – the palace contained a famous curio: a train set that delivered decanters of brandy and cigars to the dining table. The present maharajah was in a bit of a fix: he had recently resigned from the government because of some piffling hoo-hah to do with currency transactions and airline contracts; but he was also the energetic leading light of India's cricket board, which was why there was a plum match here. He strolled across the pitch on pre-match day, congratulating the groundsman, checking that the sign above the special enclosure for pupils at the Scindia School was in order, glad-handing the foreign press and urging them to go to the *son et lumière* up at the fort.

Outside, electricians tested the lorry-generator that would run the new floodlights: the World Cup was paying for a major upgrade in India's cricket facilities. Up in the press area, workmen drilled holes in walls and tried to install telephone lines. Neon lights were screwed into the ceiling of the concourses – they'd never had a night game here before, and at the last minute it had occurred to someone that these concrete corridors would be pitch dark. One of the lights crashed to the floor as soon as it was turned on. Everywhere there was the sound of hammering: bits of railing were welded into place, clocks were hung on the pavilion wall, televisions were lugged up the stairs. The impression was of a stadium dressing up for a party. Everything was hand-made, even the lettering of the Gwalior Division Cricket Association. And everything was temporary: it would all be dismantled the day after the game.

A game that was in India's hands now. The West Indies' hopes were pinned on Ambrose having one of his special hot days.

I went down and stood behind the sightscreen. This accreditation pass I had was great – below my passport photo, it clearly stated that I was not welcome at this match, but it seemed I could go anywhere. I had wandered out to the middle during the toss-up, where Azharuddin entertained the match referee, Raman Subba Row, by jokingly proffering a double-headed (or double-tailed) coin. I had strolled into the VIP enclosure, where rich red carpets protected the shoes of the affluent, and where one of the match sponsors, the manufacturer of a betel-nut breath freshener, kept giving me mouthfuls of his product: a disgusting, sour-cinnamon pink crunch. And now I was down by the sightscreen, next to the groundsman, a handful of policemen with snub-nosed guns, and the boys whose job it was to lift the black drape over the advertising hoarding – er, I mean the sightscreen – when the bowling was from this end. It felt a bit sneaky, and I sympathized with the Indian cricket writer who noted: 'If an Englishman were to introduce himself as Jack Horner from the IRA who wishes to meet Mike Atherton, he would be escorted right to the dressing-room door.' But it was a great vantage point. The pitch had a slight crown in it, so Ambrose's huge feet were about the height of my shins – he seemed supernaturally tall. There is, in his action, a moment of deadly stillness: his long snakelike arm coils above his shoulder like a cobra about to spit. Sometimes the hand with the ball in it gives a little shiver of impatience as he prepares to let it go, like a warning hiss before the strike. And he runs in arrow-straight with light, bouncy, greedy strides.

Tendulkar turned one off his thigh and the place went berserk. 'The decibels on that roar,' said Benaud, 'you'd normally associate with a four or a six. But India are off the mark.'

Ambrose promptly took two wickets with identical balls, inslanting white flashes that streaked through the batsmen's defences and bowled them. Was anyone going to be able to stand up to this? Ambrose made something of a speciality of these blazing patches. A couple of years ago, an Australian (rumour had it) made the mistake of thinking that victory was inevitable, and that it was safe to start calling Ambrose rude names. The next thing he knew, Ambrose had taken eight wickets and Australia had lost. Against England, in Trinidad, he turned on its head a match England looked to have a good chance of winning, ripping seven men out for forty-one runs. Perhaps the same thing would happen now: there was a charming banner over there saying TAILLESS MONKEY AMBROSE; maybe that would sting him into action.

But Sachin Tendulkar didn't look fazed. He stood dead still as the bowler charged, his broad bat grounded, eyes bright under the fierce floodlamps, like someone who hadn't even unsheathed his sword yet. Forgive me: it was hard not to think of David and Goliath. It felt like a bullying giant bearing down on a boy – Ambrose is a good foot taller than Tendulkar. And body language counts for a lot in cricket, especially when fast bowlers are involved. Their main weapon is fear – standing there, I could barely imagine what it might feel like to face a man that fast. The fastest bowler I ever faced (I think) was by these standards a gentle medium-pacer: he was opening the bowling for Berkshire, and the first ball hit me just above the pad before I had figured out where it was. And it *hurt* – Christ. I didn't know whether to rub it, shriek, smile, or what. I wasn't worried about machismo: it's just that if you show the bowler you're not keen he'll bowl faster, straighter and with even fewer inhibitions. I think, in the end, I settled for a couple of squatting exercises, as if I was getting warmed up. And I am sure I looked pretty nervous.

But Tendulkar – his whole demeanour seemed to suggest the opposite. Think you're fast, eh? We'll see about that. Bowlers are predators, so they can also be cowardly. They like picking on weaklings. If their prey seems unafraid, it takes away half the fun.

Ambrose came striding in, long and sharp, and Tendulkar took a tiny pace forward, leaned towards the bowler, and rifled the ball to deep midwicket for four. The whole world knows that you couldn't afford to bowl at this man's legs; he has a way of punching it through the leg side that is unique. There are others who can glide and work it that way, and a few who can short-arm it round the corner with some vigour. Lara helped it away with a classic trademark shrug. But Tendulkar is able to catch the ball on the rise and smack it on the rise, like someone slamming a door, to the boundary. Actually, Ambrose hadn't even bowled at his legs. He had bowled pretty much the exact ball that had just done for Jadeja and Sidhu. But it was like firing at a revolving door: Tendulkar simply gathered up the slant and catapulted the ball out again with added speed. And then he cocked his wrists up through the ball like a sharpshooter lifting his gun. Ambrose put his fingers to his chin in that thoughtful-menacing gesture of his. Tendulkar jiggled his helmet, waggled his box, shuffled his thigh pad and settled down.

A few balls later, Ambrose found that length again, the ball arrowing in towards the off stump. This time Tendulkar took half a step forward, half a step back and struck the ball hard, off the top of the bounce and with a bat as straight as a plumb-line, past Ambrose's flailing boots. It ran into the gutter full of television cables and paper cups only yards from where I was standing. 'You won't see a better shot than that,' said Benaud. He says this so often that it can't be true. But in this case it felt fair enough.

Another one went flashing through the on-side. This was remarkable. After five overs India were twenty-four for two, and Tendulkar had twenty of them. Not for the first time, he seemed to be playing in a different game from everyone else. A couple of days earlier he had run riot against Kenya, whose total of 199 didn't look too bad until Tendulkar set off in a flurry of fours, scoring 127 and winning the game with nine overs to spare. By English standards it was very odd indeed to see him opening the innings at all, let alone attacking with such abandon. English teams take the view that you need a solid start, and don't want to risk your best players until later on. Sometimes they believe that you can send in some down-the-order slogger to have a whack early on – but no one whose wicket you can't afford to lose. Asking your best player to bat so freely seemed an exorbitant risk. But Tendulkar had been opening in one-day matches for a while now, with great success: the licence to hit out suited him. He seemed to begin with a wounding flurry of boundaries and only started playing straight once he got his eye in.

So it was disappointing when, on twenty-two, he gave his wicket away attempting to lash Ian Bishop over the infield. The ball caught the top edge of his bat and skied up in a gentle arc, glowing in the floodlights like a mortar, towards Sherwin Campbell at short square leg. Campbell ran in to take it, and a shudder ran round the stadium: the chanting ceased. Without Tendulkar, nothing was certain. Courtney Browne, the wicket-keeper, called for the catch, trotted underneath it, stopped, reached out . . . and dropped it.

Unbelievable. The easiest catch in the world had gone to ground. Poor Courtney Browne. He was sharing a room at the hotel, once the palace for the maharajah's unmarried children, with Brian Lara. That was going to be one unhappy hutch tonight. Head bowed, he returned to his post as the crowd cackled and jeered. That wasn't the worst of it. Taking a catch is great: you are immediately accepted into the bosom of the team. Grateful happy colleagues run a hundred yards to shake your hand – or, if you're West Indian, slap your upturned palm. But drop one, especially a sitter like that, and you are left alone to brood. These are the moments when you decide that you hate cricket, that you have just played your last game.

For India it was an amazing let-off. There's no way of knowing what would have happened had the catch stuck. But the loss of their charismatic, talismanic star might have dented their self-belief as thoroughly as the loss of Lara had sabotaged the West Indies'. Could, might, may have, if only . . .

Two balls later, Azharuddin (the batsmen ran a single while the catch was being dropped) flashed the ball viciously behind square for four. It was almost unfair.

What followed was a brilliant Tendulkar innings: the dropped catch was, perhaps, just the warning Tendulkar needed. He was not a godlet, after all. It was possible, in theory, for him to be out. He settled down into the model of correctness he had always been, ever since he was coached in Bombay's dry meadows by the celebrated old master of the maidans, Achrekar Sir. His daily routine, in his early teens, required him to reach the ground by seven-thirty in the morning, practise till ten, and return in the afternoon for more. He had a crazy bottom-handed grip as a result of borrowing his brother's too-large bats, but Achrekar let him keep it.

He stroked and pushed his way to an emphatic seventy, and looked to be heading for his second century of the tournament when he set off for a quick single, was sent back by Kambli (the two used to open the batting for their school team, and once put on 600 for the first wicket) and was run out. Azharuddin had just been out for thirty-two, lazily hoisting a catch to deep mid-on, and suddenly it wasn't all over. Two new batsmen, fifty to win, four top men out – funny old game, cricket. When Azharuddin took his stooped, mournful physique off to the pavilion, you couldn't help feeling for him. The weight of the crowd's expectation was frightening. And he was just going through the closing stages of a truly shocking (by Indian standards) divorce: his wife and children had moved in with his own parents, whom he had outraged by his adulterous liaison with an actress. 'He's no great man,' said his father. 'Just an ordinary cricketer.' Actually, the freakish thing about it was that it wasn't bigger news. Imagine if Botham had run off with Naomi Campbell . . . it didn't bear thinking about.

Richardson responded well to this brief upturn in his fortunes. For two decades West Indian captains hadn't been required to think of anything more subtle than taking off one very fast bowler and bringing on another. But now, with Roger Harper bowling low-arm off-spin, he brought seven fielders inside the circle to save the single (only four were required by the rules), posted a silly point right under the batsman's nose, and a leg gully. Another wicket now and the West Indies would be in with a serious shout. The crowd fell silent – they didn't want an exciting finish; they wanted triumph. They wanted capes and swords and tassles and Kambli's autograph.

It looked like real cricket now. Prabhakar didn't like the feel of those close fielders, and drove the ball straight back at Roger Harper, who popped it up in the air and caught it on the rebound. Walsh bowled a maiden (his second in a row) at the new batsman, Mongia. Seven overs went by, and only eight runs were scored. Walsh had bowled nine overs for just eighteen runs – exactly the kind of dogged, unspectacular performance that could turn a match like this. His reward was to be pelted by fruit when he went to field on the boundary. But the West Indies were putting a good squeeze on here. One more wicket and we'd be talking.

Eventually, Mongia sprang the locks by heaving Gibson over the top for four. It was like opening a window: a gale of fresh air raced across the pitch. The crowd relaxed. Another one went slipping away fine to the boundary.

There was time for just one more confrontation. Ambrose came back to have a final crack. Kambli was not renowned for his nerve against the fastest bowling; perhaps he would wilt.

He did precisely the opposite. Ambrose dropped short, aiming to give him a good scare, and Kambli thumped him high into the crowd for six. That, surely, was that. The next one was an Ambrose special, a totally accidental don't-you-dare-hit-me-for-six beamer which Kambli luckily managed to avoid, and the crowd began to dance. Matches flared and burning scorecards lit up the night sky. Within moments the whole stadium was ablaze with flickering orange torches. The final runs felt like a ceremonial parade: smoke drifted across the pitch and the chanting took on organized shapes. India won by five wickets: cricket was coming home.

So much for Lara versus Tendulkar. The one had been fingered for two; the other had been given the biggest let-off of his life. Anyone vexed or disappointed by this could only reflect that it was close to the essence of cricket: no one can bend the game entirely to his will. There are too many chance occurrences, too many slips between cup and lip. You can go mad wishing it were fairer, or more logical, or more controllable. You can do everything right and get nothing in return; you can do everything wrong and get away with it. There is no such thing as plain sailing in cricket, though sometimes, in retrospect, it can look as though there is. There are always reefs in the water. If a golfer hits a perfect shot it'll go close to the pin – a golfer's idea of bad luck is when his caddie gives him the wrong club. But a cricketer can do everything by the book and still end up with egg on his face. This might be why cricket is productive of suicides (there's a whole book on this subject). The knowledge that there is an area of the game that is quite beyond you claws away at your resolve and self-esteem, leaving you stranded on some vertiginous precipice of wishful thinking. There is only one ferocious rule: only cricket can cure you of a loss of cricketing faith. Failure at cricket can only be mended by success at cricket. Back in England Lara had enjoyed one of those honeyed periods when it seemed that nothing could go wrong. Perhaps it was this that scrambled his seemingly even temper: the illusion that the game was masterable. No one since

Bradman had known such a feeling of supremacy. It must have been a hard, high mountain to come off.

Anyway, India had won two games, and the path ahead was bright. The West Indies had lost two (one of them forfeited), and the outlook was grim. When they flew north to Delhi they looked anything but happy: Richardson sat alone and motionless, a guitar between his feet, staring into space. Lara and a few others played cards. Arthurton clamped headphones to his ears (he had plenty to think about – more than he knew: in this tournament, he would bat four times and score two runs). When they climbed on to the plane, a slow stopper from Bombay, with no reserved seats, there was a small comedy of who-sits-where. Ambrose struggled to fold his giant legs into what seemed like a baby seat. Arthurton sat alone in an empty row, ignored by the others. And here came Lara. He looked at the seat next to Arthurton, thought better of it, and carried on.

Several Indian passengers beckoned him. 'Mr Lara, sit here. Please, Mr Lara. Here!'

Lara climbed over someone's legs, smiled and wedged himself between two fans. Then he took out his pocket Gameboy and played computer games for the entire flight.

Can the rest of us imagine what it must be like to be recognized and badgered wherever you go? These players were not safe even in their hotel rooms: an endless procession of cleaners, shoeshiners, flower arrangers, stewards ('Is everything all right, sir?'), minibar monitors, chocolate-on-the-pillow distributors, fruit dispensers and waiters streamed through in search of autographs, tickets, predictions and tips.

Of course, there's a good side too; but sometimes even this goes wrong. Arriving in Delhi, Ian Bishop stooped to get under the door of the terminal and was met with garlands by two extremely gorgeous women in flowing dresses.

'Hello?' he said.

'Hello,' they said. 'Are you Brian Lara?'

Nothing was going the West Indies' way. The only thing in their favour was that they were not, like England, permanently answering to a large press following. Only a single West Indian reporter (the former Test-player Bryan Davies) was chasing them round the sub-continent, and his presence here was salutary. He was travelling off his own bat, drumming up sponsorship from Angostura bitters – a Trinidadian world-beater – among others, and developing a network of pledges from papers all over the Caribbean. The lengths to which he had gone were in stark contrast to the extravagant ease with which the English papers sent people flying around the world. Many of them went so far as to foot bills for correspondents to sit in hotel rooms reporting games off the TV, which they could have done without leaving England.

Being there, of course, allowed you to bump into people like the marketing man for Yes mineral water, who claimed that 48,000 bottles of his product had been hijacked outside the ground. 'It was chaos,' he said. 'They just emptied the lorries. And lunches too. When the lunchboxes were delivered people just helped themselves. 8000 lunchboxes never made it.' In the posher seats, lunch had been included in the price of the tickets. It never arrived. Scandalous? An attractive touch of the Robin Hoods? No one in the shady seats, after all, would die if they skipped a meal.

Before leaving Gwalior I saw England playing Holland on television. It was exactly as predicted, only worse. Atherton dropped himself down the order again (and was out again) but Graham Thorpe struck a bravura eighty-nine, which allowed Graeme Hick to assemble a calm century. England posted a large, if not dazzling, total. Naturally, Hick was the man of the match – an award that goes as a formality to the highest-scoring batsman on the winning team, not to the decisive performance, which was Thorpe's. But it was still an impressive performance by Hick. In two innings he had, like Tendulkar, scored eighty and 100. There the comparison ends: we persist with our misgivings about Hick, while India dances attendance on Tendulkar as if he were a king. Some of what we see is, indeed, in the eye of the beholder.

England duly went ahead and won, but Holland succeeded in embarrassing our bowlers. Bas Zuiderent, a seventeen-year-old who had been obliged to obtain permission from school to play in the World Cup, struck out boldly and scored fifty-four in partnership with Klaas van Noortwijk, who scored sixty-four. They were both students, but this was some kind of lesson they were handing out. At one point Van Noortwijk hit an enormous six. 'That's more like a twelve,' said Robin Jackman, commentating. Holland fell only forty-nine runs short: they scored the same number of runs as England had against New Zealand, an emphatic margin of victory, but hardly expressive of the gulf in class that was supposed to separate these two teams. 'The thick line between minnows and professionals,' said the *Pioneer*, 'is smudged.'

In the tabloids the next day the main story was that Darren Gough had nearly been hit by a 'sharpened stick'. 'Spike Could Have Killed Gough', sang the *Mirror*, describing the 'gauntlet of hate' run by England's fielders. It can't have been nice. But at least it diverted attention from his hapless performance with the ball. His three overs, against two young amateurs, cost twenty-three runs. There was an alarming lack of variety about England's bowling, and still no zizz in their fielding. But the win at least secured their place in the quarter-finals. And suddenly a hidden benefit of the seemingly perverse structure of this World Cup revealed itself. Relieved of the need to obtain points, England's two games coming up – against Pakistan and South Africa – were now nothing more than that. They truly were only games. Which is what this was supposed to be all about.

I flew to Rawalpindi via Delhi (of course) and Lahore. That was nothing. The commentary team (Greig, Benaud *et al.*) spent nearly two days trying to get to Australia versus Kenya at Vishakhapatnam on the east coast. They flew to Delhi, then headed for Calcutta, but had to turn back because of rain. By the time they got to Calcutta there were no planes to Vishakhapatnam, so they flew to Bhubaneshwar and took a train down the coast. They left Gwalior on Wednesday night. By the time they arrived, at Friday lunchtime, the game had already started. Michael Slater, Australia's stylish opening batsman, was holding the fort in the commentary box.

By these standards, my own little three-flight leapfrog was a breeze, even if I did need the help of a woman heading for Islamabad to queue-barge the mob at the Lahore check-in desk. And the first thing I saw on arriving was a headline claiming that England had attempted to bribe the groundsman before the match against Holland. 'England At It Again,' it said.

Oh, Christ, I thought. Welcome back to the frying pan.

— 7 —

HERE WE GO AGAIN

England vs South Africa, Rawalpindi

As luck would have it, the sky was cool, grey and damp when England took the field against South Africa in Rawalpindi, and there was talk of drizzle later. Typical English conditions, in other words. A lot of fingers were crossed against the fear that this might inspire a typical England performance. The recent drubbings in the Cape were still a painful memory.

The early signs were not good. The wicket-keeper, Palframan, opened the batting with Gary Kirsten, and the pair of them came out of the blocks fast. Luck seemed to be on their side. Kirsten scuffed one just over Gough's head; Palframan top-edged to within feet of Peter Martin. And then Palframan skied one to Cork, and goodness gracious me, he dropped it.

The press box slumped. It has been exhausting work following England in recent years. How many ways are there to say the same thing? This time last winter, down in Australia, they had run out of words. If sublatives are the opposite of superlatives, then – well it doesn't matter, actually, because they were all used up. England hit rock bottom . . . England set new depths of ineptitude . . . England rotten to the core . . . Where do England go from here? And these were the broadsheet papers – the tabloids were much saltier. The what's-wrong-with-England article is one these chaps have written many, many times; at the same time it is a subject they shun. They know that grandiose generalizations can quickly be shot down by a single flash-in-the-pan next week. And you can't fire all your bullets at once; you need to save a few, as it were, for a sunny day.

The thing was, everyone knew that South Africa would have caught that catch. When they are in the field and the ball goes in the air the collective shout of 'Yesss!!!' is almost tangible. With England, the opposite happens, something to do with dread. Oh, cripes, you can feel them thinking. Looks like it's coming to me.

This is hardly fair on Cork, as warm a zealot as England has produced for years. But it felt true, on this wet Rawalpindi morning. He never looked like catching it.

After ten overs South Africa were fifty for nought. For England nothing was going right at all. The fielding was indescribable. Atherton, crocked back and all, made about four terrific plunging saves in the gully, but otherwise it was business as usual. Cork, trying furiously to redeem himself, went for a direct hit and gave away four overthrows; Martin trotted to his right to pick up a flash to third man, only to see the ball cannon into the boundary just where he'd come from. Thorpe tried to whip the bails off at the bowler's end, missed, and fell over, the ball stuck in his hand. Fairbrother went for one of those glamorous pick-up-and-flick jobbies, overran the ball and ended up headbutting the stumps as he dived. Jack Russell thought it was so funny he couldn't see the next couple of balls for the tears in his eyes. It was a comic masterpiece.

The crowd, if you could call it that, guffawed. Most of them had South African flags, which some clever marketing clogs was handing out at the gate. 'British Are the Pits', said one banner. 'England Tamper With Their Balls', read another. You couldn't help feeling sorry for the players. They knew that everyone was against them, but weren't sure why. 'It's amazing how much they hate us,' said Thorpe.

Not that amazing, perhaps. In *The Autobiography of an Unknown Indian*, Nirad Chaudhuri said that 'servility and malice were ingrained in every fibre of our being'. It was a combination that led, he suggested, to 'grotesque antics of alternating genuflection and defiance'. This continues to ring true, in Trinidad and Antigua as well as in the subcontinent. Cricket, the emblem of colonial intrusion, and a bulwark against social change, has also been an energetic emancipating force. Beating England is a significant historical event: one up for the sugarcane slaves, the coolies, niggers and wallahs, the rejects and refugees. In Australia they used to have a cheeky song, which went:

Sing you a song, won't take long
All Pommies are bastards
Second verse, same as the first
All Pommies are bastards.

This was basically the cheap-seats version of the famous cultural cringe. 'No Australian had written *Paradise Lost*,' said Thomas Keneally, the Booker-winning author of *Schindler's List*. 'But Bradman had made a century before lunch at Lord's.' In the former colonies cricket is simply a more urgent matter than it is in England, where it remains, sadly for those who like it, a dwindling game with dying facilities (all those school sports grounds sold off) and an ageing following. Cricket comes low in the latest surveys of what schoolchildren like. And it wasn't only a political question: there's an aesthetic dimension as well. In England, cricket grounds suggest a rural idyll, all twittering birds and long, somnolent shadows on summer evenings. In the subcontinent, cricket grounds make a more forceful impact: in the middle of parched, arid wastes, or squeezed into rickety, crowded, dusty cities, these magical green circles seem vivid and rich. Even the spaciousness, the smell of grass and water seem unbelievably luxurious.

It isn't surprising that English cricket has a drab flavour. But the players pay a price for this when they travel overseas. In Ahmedabad there was vociferous support for New Zealand; and even the tribesmen of Peshawar were happy to be Dutchmen for the day. But South Africa . . . excuse me, but wasn't that the home of apartheid? England has plenty of reasons to reflect on its past; but in this match we were in good company. We had Amritsar (not far from here) but they had Soweto – it was a close call. I don't mean to be offensive, only to point out that there's no pipping England when it comes to infamy. Not counting Australia, of course, which to subcontinental eyes looked increasingly like England's cocky grown-up son – the same, only tougher. Actually, it was hard not to like South Africa: they were committed, modern and very conscious of their importance as representatives of a new, happier country. They knew they were lucky, too: most of the team had grown up imagining that international cricket would not be on the menu unless they emigrated to England. And, anyway, cricket wasn't to blame for apartheid; indeed, it had been anxious to break down the race walls, if only so it could regain Test-match status. South African cricket felt aggrieved and maligned during the boycott, and it had a point: in the year of the Gleneagles agreement, the year the world confirmed its high and admirable reluctance to permit sporting links with South Africa, the IMF lent Pretoria a billion dollars. Cricket felt picked on. But there seemed to be no hard feelings now, just a powerful urge to show the rest of the world what was what.

And then there was the Jonty Rhodes effect. South Africa's springiest little bok had star quality. His fans up in the commentary box (Jack Bannister, mainly) liked calling him a 'real live wire'. Even the official 'Share the Magic' World Cup poster showed Rhodes diving. If you looked closely it was clear he'd missed the ball and was clutching the air, but never mind that. It was a strong image of out-and-out effort. His prominence was enough to make cricket purists want to scream – he represented the triumph of vulgar acrobatics over patient endeavour. But no question, he was the one they were supporting up here in Rawalpindi. 'Jhonty I am your proud Pakistani fan,' said a banner, pretty sure there was an 'h' in there somewhere. When a gaggle of fans started waving 'Kashmir Must Be Free' flags, and sang and waved, the police moved in to make sure there was no trouble. They needn't have bothered. When you got closer you could hear what they were singing, and it wasn't anything to do with liberation theology. 'Jon-ty!' they went, drumming their feet. 'Jon-ty! Jon-ty!'

Poor old England. On that horrendous tour of Australia last winter they had been a terrible laughing-stock. 'If the Poms Are Batting,' said one banner in Sydney, 'Tell the Taxi to Wait.' When they finally had a good day, one newspaper headline couldn't resist it: 'Dull Day at the Cricket: England Fail to Collapse.' It must have been awful. This was the tour when it became clear that the management of our team was . . . well, what management? Remember that time Illingworth announced that Neil Fairbrother was flying out to replace Craig White (poor old Craig White, the intercostal muscle got him again)? Keith Fletcher promptly insisted that no such thing was the case, that neither he nor his chairman had called for anyone.

Who to believe?

Fairbrother arrived two days later.

Illingworth hadn't been in Australia long himself; he flew out half-way through, after delivering plenty of long-range criticism from his television lounge. When he landed he was asked: 'Does it worry you that there's a generation of children who think that England Test collapse is one word?' It was not a happy tour.

And here we were again, being knocked around by a second-string wicket-keeper. It felt especially awful because it didn't matter; we were probably going to have to endure all this again against Pakistan down in Karachi.

Eventually, with the score on fifty-six, Palframan was out, edging a Courtney Browne-style catch to Jack Russell. But Cronje looked in good form, and we knew about Kirsten now. South Africa had got off to just the start they wanted – and you'd have put your house on them driving home the advantage.

And then something truly amazing happened. Kirsten took a quick single to Alec Stewart at mid-on and was run out by a direct hit. Take that! A run-out! It was a taste of their own medicine all right. And it lit the fuse so far as England were concerned. Gough (six overs for twenty) and Martin (six for eighteen) started bowling really well. Cronje was caught behind, and the worm had turned. South Africa were eighty-eight for three. The first fifty had taken ten overs; the second took twice that. Cullinan grew impatient, aimed a big one at DeFreitas and was bowled, South Africa were 139 for four, with only seventeen overs left. England were back in it.

Or were they just 'at it again'? That groundsman-bribe scandal had turned out to be nothing at all. Unhappy with the nets in Peshawar, England asked the groundsman if he could mow them a wicket on the edge of the square, and said they'd be happy to meet any costs that might be incurred. Sounds reasonable enough – though, of course, 'meeting costs' is another way of saying 'name your price'. Here in Rawalpindi, England had tried to train on the wet outfield, ignoring the people attempting to sponge moisture out of the grass. That didn't go down well, either. 'Brash Brits Bother Groundstaff,' said the *News*.

If they wanted a quick lesson in public relations, they were playing the right people. South Africa had wasted no time in declaring they would have been happy to play in Sri Lanka – an easy trick to pull since they weren't going there whatever happened. Plus they owed Sri Lanka one. Back in the dark years of isolation the islanders, desperate for top-class opposition at a time no one else much wanted to play them, sent a touring side to South Africa. Payback time.

Jonty Rhodes hadn't got many runs against England in the recent series, but he played a nice hand here, dashing and darting a quick thirty. But when he was out South Africa were in danger of failing to set a decent target. At 202 for eight England had them cornered, and there was one sunny moment – Thorpe taking an excellent diving catch to get rid of Symcox – when they were all over each other, running, clapping, slapping and laughing like a real team. Because in the end, whatever you say about the management, the system, the media, the conditions and so on, the truly corrosive thing is defeat. England were defeat junkies: they had been swaying from match to match in pursuit of the losing habit, and it had made them bleary.

South Africa wouldn't lie down. The fast bowlers, Matthews and De Villiers, struck out bravely, and the innings ended on 230 – gettable, but not easy. England needed a solid start.

They didn't get it. The fourth ball of the innings was a rising ball outside off stump (from Pollock) at which Atherton took a hasty little stab, edging it to the keeper. Poor Atherton. It was too soon to start talking about 'a weakness', for he had been England's steadiest batsman for years. But he was shuffling across his crease, peering up the wicket, like a man who'd mislaid his glasses.

Having said that, it was a cracking good ball.

Hick, the man in form, was far from his commanding best. He scratched around until he flicked one off his pads straight to short square leg. This was a bigger victory than it looked at the time. Hick had been out-thought. 'He was the one we feared,' said Woolmer later. 'So we were aiming simply to frustrate him. We know he likes to score fast, so we concentrated on cramping him for room. It worked because everyone knew what we were trying to do – the bowlers, the fielders, everyone. And the plan was to limit his scoring. Not try to get him out, just bowl good length to a field, frustrate him. And that's what happened. He took a risk and swatted a catch.' You could sense a bit of this in the way South Africa congratulated themselves out on the pitch. It bolstered their already keen faith in each other, in the coach, in the game. They were on a roll.

Thorpe, as usual, batted neatly while wickets fell at the other end. Perhaps the answer at the moment was for *him* to open; maybe the others would do better if they came to the crease with a score already on the board. Neil Smith had kicked off with Atherton, which at least showed consistency. But with the score on twenty-two for two he might have realized that his job was no longer to slog (sorry, I refuse to use the meaningless 'pinch-hit') but to bat steadily. Instead he lashed out at De Villiers and was bowled. Alec Stewart did one of the most foolish things you can do in a cricket match – he hit the ball straight to a South African fielder, tried to pinch a single, and was run-out by a direct hit. Did these people never learn? The *coup de grâce* came when Russell hit a crisp uppish cut and Rhodes bounced up like someone on a pogo stick and came back to earth with the ball in his hands. England eventually managed 152 – the same as the United Arab Emirates had scored against the same opposition. It was lucky Allan Donald was in bed with a bad stomach.

You would have expected England to dig really deep here, after the drubbings they had received in South Africa a few weeks earlier. But this . . . well, it was Cape Town all over again. Now, as then, our players looked tired and dispirited. It had, in truth, been a long winter. For many of these players, it had been a long year. They had returned from the humiliations of Australia to spend the summer facing the West Indies, and then gone out to South Africa for three and a half months. There was only time for a quick week at home before jetting off to Lahore again. Atherton, for one, could count on three hands the number of non-cricket days he'd had in the last twelve months. And you can fake effort, but you can't fake enthusiasm.

It is easy to laugh at the players for being poor tourists. But overseas tours are claustrophobic occasions, mainly because the press are always blocking the light. I don't know quite why they put up with it – though it isn't easy legitimately to ban newspapermen from the hotels at which the team is staying (usually the second nicest in town). But what it means for the cricketers is that at breakfast, at the bar, in the lift and in the cab rank outside there are always pressmen eyeing them up, or studiously not catching their eye, which is almost as bad. You could order room service, which is okay if you're pampering yourself, but not much fun if you are simply avoiding the world. But *en route* to your cup of coffee, you can't help passing the *Times*, the *Guardian* and the *Sun* all having a good moan about what happened yesterday. Over there the *Mirror* and the *Standard* and some bloke you've never seen before, who might be the new man from the *Express*, are reading the papers and laughing. Their conversation seems to die as you walk past with a polite nod – does that mean they were talking about you, agreeing that it was time you were put out to grass?

Or maybe you don't nod politely; maybe you just ignore them. You know you'll get a fearful ribbing from the other blokes if you're caught fraternizing with the press boys – it looks like you're sucking up. Over there's the *Independent*, carefully staring down at his muesli – what do you suppose *that* bastard wrote this morning? But it isn't easy to ignore people you have met, and see every day. It gives you a funny feeling. So you go over to the buffet knowing that if you help yourself to that delicious-smelling scrambled eggs and bacon and hash browns, which is exactly what you feel like before a long day of butterflies in the stomach, the *News of the World* guy will immediately start proposing a feature on England Fatsos – With Egg on Their Faces. And it isn't just the press. As they patrol the hotel lobby the players can't help being aware that over in the coffee lounge people are nudging each other and whispering, 'Look, there goes Athers, he looks cheerful, considering . . .' If you are the captain, especially, you know that an awful lot of ghastly nationalist urges are riding on your shoulders, and the air in the hotel is thick with them. It isn't natural. Celebrities in other fields do not have to endure such persistent close inspection. Inevitably, cricketers grow thick skins: they start by affecting not to care and end up not caring, slouching around in crappy shell suits with ghetto blasters turned up to frighten away intruders.

The players were on their own for the World Cup; all lads together, as usual. But wives, girlfriends, children and nannies had flown down to Cape Town for Christmas during the South Africa tour. It was hinted that the sudden arrival of the players' families contributed to the team's decline – a seedy-sounding and unattractive thing to say: old-fashioned, jealous and false, as if normal life was hostile to cricketing excellence, or as if 'wives' were by definition a bore. I mean, given that England usually did okay at home, and dreadfully abroad, maybe it was because they were *away* from their families that they struggled. Perhaps they would do better if they toured like adults, instead of squaddies or schoolboys, two-to-a-room. It sounded pathetic, actually, especially when it was immediately distilled into a crazed 'Too-much-bonking' cry by the tabloids. The *Sun* swiftly produced a galley of understandably dejected wives ('No Sex Please: Wives in Fury Over England Love Ban'), who wondered, as one, who the heck Illy thought he was to say that the players shouldn't see their own families – at Christmas, of all times! 'The last time England beat Australia,' said Kathy Botham, 'wives and girlfriends were there nearly the whole time.' The idea that any real-world emotions would somehow seduce away the concentration and energy of the boys is well entrenched: but it was rare to hear it articulated so blatantly.

On the other hand, anyone could see what a difference it made. And, of course, it wasn't bonking that was the distraction – that, as everyone knows, is extremely helpful; eight out of ten coaches say their players would be lost without it. It was simply real life; and its sudden appearance into the odd, collegiate regime of international cricket was bewildering.

You only had to watch the players having their breakfast. There was Graeme Hick with his wife and little Hicklets; there were the baby Watkinsons, and goodness, was that an infant Cork? Up on their own, sniggering slightly at the sight of their teammates (who only last week were making ribald jokes about the air stewardesses) clutching baby milk, were the younger lads. And hang on a minute, who was that over there, trying to persuade a bit of muffin into a toddler's mouth, trying not to glance at his watch? Alec bloody Stewart, that's who!

Now this was serious. In most senses it was a great thing for Stewart to have the family out there. He had, after all, been away for nearly three months. But on this particular morning, well, for goodness sake: it was the middle of a Test match, England were on the rack, and he was one of the not-out batsmen. This was the morning after South Africa's last pair had snicked Malcolm all over Newlands. They had a first-innings lead of a hundred, and Atherton had already been out. If ever the team needed a big innings from Stewart, today was the day. He owed it: except for eighty in the previous match, where he'd batted tenaciously all day, he hadn't scored a run this winter. The hour had cometh, and it was about time the man cameth as well. Victory was still possible if they could bat decently and go past 300. Surely Stewart needed to be doing whatever batsmen do to pump themselves up (pace around smoking, yogic meditation, rehearsing shots in the wardrobe mirror, whatever). His ideal breakfast – surely – was a quiet contemplative coffee on his own; or a High-Energy FibrePlus Vitabrew or whatever sportsmen need, these days, with Fraser, the nightwatchman, or Hick, the next man in, discussing how they were going to set about the task, what to watch for with Allan Donald, which shots to emphasize against Shaun Pollock. Instead of which he was sitting here holding the baby. And I'm sorry, but it was hard not to imagine that his wife was thinking, Alec, no offence, but if you could just hold him for a minute, and the unspoken implication was *because, you know, I've got him all day* – and the unspoken implication behind *that* was that, yes, of *course* it's lovely that we could come out here, it's just a pity you're playing cricket all the time.

This is all entirely natural. And it would be absurd to suggest that Alec Stewart's day was so important that he should be insulated from his own family. In most jobs, it wouldn't be regarded as an impossible distraction for a man to have breakfast with his wife and child – quite the opposite. But cricket isn't like other jobs. If Stewart did well today, there'd be 20,000 people watching, talking about (laughing about) and analysing his every move; his face would be on television screens all over England and South Africa for hour after hour. Of course he was used to it. But this wasn't a run-of-the-mill day, even by the never-ending slog standards of modern cricket. This was a big occasion. And it probably did call for a mind uncluttered by everyday worries. It wouldn't have been so bad if the family had been out here for the whole tour; then this would be a special morning in its own right. And this had turned out to be anything but an ideal time for conjugal visits: England were playing two Test matches over Christmas and New Year, with only a one-day gap in between. But there hadn't been any choice about that: this was the specified time when wives were permitted.

It vaguely beggars belief that the powers-that-be had decided the ideal time for families to join the tour was when the players had absolutely no free time. Why didn't they create a free week in the schedule, and have the families out then? But *c'est la vie*: the methodology of English cricket is based on the idea that cricket is a hard grind, and that if you had a week off you might lose touch. It is staring-you-in-the-face obvious to everyone who watches England that what they need more than anything – more than *anything* – is a week away from cricket now and then, a bit of time to think and dream. As it was, the family had come all this way to see their chaps and here they were, fretting about their late bloody cuts as usual. Stewart is a thorough man, and had booked an extra room in the hotel, so it wasn't as if he'd been up all night with the baby or anything. But unless he is inhuman, it is barely possible that he didn't feel a teensy-weensy bit guilty or vexed about all this. I mean, here he was: he hadn't seen this gorgeous little baby Andrew for months, and now he had been durdling and dandling for about five minutes and . . . HELP!

What could he say? So, darling, what about *you*, what are you thinking of doing today? Um, 'cause Mrs Hick said something about going to the Seaquarium. Or the botanical gardens are really nice, apparently. Or I know: the Watkinsons are going somewhere for a barbecue, maybe you could . . . Yes, I know, it's a real shame the hotel hasn't got a pool. I know, I just sort of assumed it would, I'm sorry. I think one of the other hotels – hey, Corky, is there a pool at the Holiday Inn? Or the beach is nice, though the sea's a bit cold, they say. I know! There's a penguin colony somewhere, I'm sure the people behind the desk would know how to get there. God, I wish I could come too, but the bus goes in about . . . oh, no rush, we've still got five minutes.

Luckily for him, his child was too small to talk. Otherwise it would have been: Daddy, don't go. Stay with me. But I have to go. Are you playing cricket? Yes, that's right. But you played cricket yesterday morning. I know, I know. Can I play cricket with you? Yes, of course – but not today. But I want to. I know you do, so do I. Don't go. I have to. Why? Well, 'cause I have to. But I want to come with you. No, you're going to have fun, you're going to the Seaquarium to see dolphins – won't that be great? But I don't want to see the dolphins, I want to come with you. I *know*, but . . . AAAAGH!

It is hard for fans to imagine that cricketers live normal lives, partly because they don't. And this is why a sudden sighting of a typical family breakfast seems so shocking. We armchair spectators don't expect our screen heroes to have ordinary habits – it seems selfish of them to be preoccupied by anything but the game. Soap stars complain that their fans doggedly think of them as the characters they play. Cricketers have the opposite problem: they are real, but we see them as fictional figures, as 'cricketers'. The previous evening, outside the England dressing room, you would have expected long looks and furrowed brows – the team had done badly, so surely the players would be chastising themselves somehow. Not a bit: they did what anyone else would do after a bad day at the office, they made plans for dinner. Well, I said I'd be at the Vines at nine, and Beefy's picking up Lamby at ten and going straight to Hemingway's, so we'll see them there. Want to come? Nah, better get back. Beth said she was going to book somewhere.

International cricket is tough on wives with children – impossibly tough, maybe. They know, if they glance at those anthologies of cricket quotations in the loo at home, that they are the enemy. Back in the 1960s, when the spinner Tony Lock said he wouldn't tour Australia unless his wife came with him, Wilfrid Wooller, one of the old greats, said: 'It is a sign of the times that the star player is making so much money . . . that unless Aunt Clara and the two poodles are allowed to tour with him he is not disposed to represent England overseas.' That's what the wife amounts to – Aunt Clara and the two poodles, a ludicrous, embarrassing burden. Tying this into the idea that modern players were making too much money is a curious bit of counter-intuitive thinking: it implies that wives – er, I mean Aunt Clara and the poodles – are simply an acquisition, part of the soft-living habits of today's youth. Probably it is just embarrassment that provokes these defensive twitches in cricket circles: the presence of women on tour is a daily reminder of how exclusive and time-consuming the game is. Obliging them to be mere spectators, day after day, week after week, month after month, is a glum fate to impose on anyone, let alone a so-called loved one.

Alec Stewart had been away since October. He'd been away most of the summer as well, tooling around the motorways of England (25,000 miles in the average season). The previous winter he'd been three months in the West Indies. The one before that: Australia. On one level, well, that's just the way it is. But does it have to be? One of the whole troubles with cricket is its antique sociology, and the whole concept of these three-month tours, which no other sport imitates, is a product of the steam age, when it took five weeks to sail to Australia so you might as well stay for five months while you were about it. But that was an age when women were supposed to stay at home and keep the kitchen snug. Life wasn't like that any more, was it? These days, what with new-fangled gadgets like the aeroplane, players could fly off to Cape Town or Karachi, play a few one-dayers and a Test match, and be home inside a fortnight. So why don't they?

That was the last thing on Stewart's mind. He grabbed his kit, climbed on to the coach, rumbled down to the ground, changed (oh, shit, where's my bloody sunblock – hey, Thorpy, got any zinc I can borrow?), took a few deep breaths and came blinking down the steps into the bright sunshine (Holy Christ! Look at all these people) to face the music. And the music was loud. He was out with the taste of toast and Marmite still fresh in his mouth.

I felt for him. I, too, had a pair of tiny children back in London. I was faxing little drawings of animals from the hotel business centre. I was especially good at camels – you could trace them straight off cigarette packets. To be honest, this really would have been a hell-trip with two children to ferry around, what with all these pre-dawn flights and late nights at the cricket. But for me, at least, this was a one-off. The thought of living like this all the time made me dizzy.

After the match in Rawalpindi, South Africa came in, said generously that England had bowled magnificently but that they always thought 230 was a good score on that wicket, and gave way to Atherton and John Barclay, the tour manager. Illingworth, they said, was 'unavailable'. Atherton started right in: 'I thought we bowled really well, and I thought we'd get close to 230. But . . .'

'Could he speak up?' someone asked.

'No.'

It's such a pity. Atherton's media tactics – surly, work-to-rule non-cooperation – might sit well with his persona: uncompromising tough guy, out to do for England what Allan Border did for Australia. But it has a shrill edge: it's as if he's determined that no one's going to call him a southern pansy just because he went to Cambridge. I for one wouldn't blame him in the least if he non-cooperated properly by not giving these conferences at all. Let the quote-mad tabloids go hang; let them write about the game for a change (as it is, in Tabloidland the game is merely the surface trace of the real story – the personality clash). Or if he could lift his eyes and imagine not that he's talking to the people in the room but to some imaginary codger in an armchair in Accrington, even that might help. As some old sage used to say: Journalists are in the publicity business, and there are only two products – good publicity and bad publicity. And if you want the former then you have to sing for it. Perhaps in press conferences, as in cricket, attack is the best form of defence.

There was a whiff of danger in the room. You had to feel for Athers. He'd had a rotten bloody day, and having to face the music like this, like a schoolboy reporting for a slap across the wrist from these guys . . . but that's the job.

A Pakistani journalist asked something no one understood.

'Sorry,' said Atherton. 'Don't think I caught that.'

The reporter had another go.

'You've lost me,' said Atherton.

Third time: still no one could make it out.

Atherton decided he needed to bring this to a halt. 'We're playing Pakistan next week. We'll prepare hard and practise hard. I hope that answers your question.'

It was good: polite but firm, ironic but tolerant.

'Thank you,' said the man, writing it all down.

'Pleasure.' Atherton looked up, and as he did so muttered, under his breath, 'Will someone get rid of this buffoon?'

Don't say it! Don't! But it was too late. It was sort of meant to be a joke; a clumsy shot at matey humour, a way of acknowledging what everyone in the room felt. But it backfired. It simply wasn't funny enough. The room froze. If it hadn't been so damn hot in there you could have felt frost forming on the windowpanes. And it's tough, because we're allowed to call him Captain Grumpy or Captain Calamity or Captain Miseryguts to our heart's content. But one mild rebuke from him and we're outraged.

'We're not batting with any flair or confidence,' Atherton continued. But no one needed to hear anything else. Today's story was in the bag. I wrote about it myself, I'm ashamed to say. It was a hard subject to avoid.

'I thought he called me a baboon,' said the reporter in question, adding a forlorn touch.

The Rawalpindi Journalists' Association demanded a formal apology. England tried to insist that the matter was 'closed', which it plainly wasn't. Eventually they issued a statement. Ever wondered how statements get 'issued'? In this case, it meant John Barclay nipping down to the pool to find the Reuters man and whoever else was around, and reading out a brief text: 'At yesterday's press conference after the match against South Africa I am sorry if I caused offence to a local journalist or journalists.' It was charmingly delivered but, as apologies go, it was a C minus: mealy-mouthed and grudging. Everyone ran off to get a reaction from Illingworth: eventually they caught up with him, playing bridge.

Obliging as always, he agreed to chat, and the papers filed into his room. The telly was on: Pakistan were playing Holland. They had already trounced the Emirates, and their opening batsmen – Sohail and Anwar – looked truly alarming, flashing the ball all over the shop from the word go.

'The captain's not playing,' said Illingworth. 'Lubbers, is that his name? Got runs against us, didn't he?'

Er, no.

Someone congratulated the chairman on his suite.

'Well, after forty-five years I need a bit of comfort.' He chuckled.

He began by explaining that he had not, repeat not, been unavailable. 'I wasn't unavailable, I want to make that clear. I was sat at one end of the dressing room. Normally someone comes to get us, but that didn't happen for some reason.'

This was a startling piece of news. Even the connoisseurs were speechless. There's almost always a press conference immediately after play. There's almost always a little runaround while people establish where it's going to be held. It was very bad luck indeed to have missed it. But there was hardly time to brood on what this meant, hardly time to enjoy the thought of Illy sat in the dressing room with a towel over his head not knowing what was going on out there – because he was proceeding to hand out at least six extremely dishy 'stories':

1. Illy Blasts Hosts: 'We've come here to play cricket, and to be fair we've tried to get good wickets to practise on. But the ball was turning square in the nets. And we were promised dot bowlers. These things were agreed in writing. But it hasn't happened.'
2. Illy Slams Skip: 'I spoke to Mike about dropping himself down the order against Holland. He said he felt all right. But it's not a matter of feeling, it's a matter of getting runs. He needs the runs now. He'll definitely have to open now.'
3. On Tha' Bike, Stewie!: 'I was amazed when I saw the run-out on the playback. A normal running position would have got him safe.'
4. Illy Raps Smith: 'To be fair, Smithy's not been fit. He was batting with one bloody pad in the throwdowns and got hit. Now you tell me why they bat with one pad on, it's just as easy to put two on. I don't know.'
5. Illy Gets the Ump: 'We got the rough end of the weather. And I just think it's unacceptable to go on playing for forty minutes in rain. To me, that's what the second day's for.'
6. Illy's World Cup Woe: 'It's not ideal, but we've got to put up with what we've got. To play every three days is a far better way. It's spaced out a bit too long, really.'

This last one was a whopper. England spent half their time complaining that there wasn't time to practise; now they were saying there was too much time. But the details of what Illingworth was saying were submerged by the overall impression, which was an astonishing self-portrait of poor old Illy, surrounded by fools and incompetents and pettifogging bureaucrats. You had to admire the man's invincible self-belief.

Meanwhile, bad news was swirling across the wires. Dennis Silk, chairman of the TCCB, had been out here for a look, not to mention some major carpet-buying, and his conclusion was grim. Before the game in Rawalpindi the South African High Commissioner turned to him and said: 'May the best team win.' Silk's reply was terse but pregnant with meaning. 'I hope not,' he said. We were a low-ranking cricket nation, he was saying, perhaps seventh in the international league table – alarming when you considered we had the only professional structure in the world. He went on to suggest that county cricket be divided into two divisions to add a competitive zest to the games, and that the top players be employees of the national board instead of the counties.

When the chairman of the TCCB talks like this you know that reformation is in the air. But actually, everyone knows what's wrong with English cricket: it is run by the counties for the counties, at a time when no one really gives a hoot about county cricket. It's a fairly absurd situation. The lucrative international scene is milked to finance a domestic industry that has almost no customers. It's as if the revenues of the Crown were spent subsidizing public executions, on the grounds that it would be a shame to put all those nice executioners out of work. It would be worth it if county cricket were enchanting in itself, or if it produced clever teams for England. But it doesn't seem to do either of these things.

Other countries do not imitate our domestic structure. None of them would think of supporting eighteen fully professional teams with the money they earn from international cricket. Instead, players begin at club level and enter the shop window for national selection by being picked for their state – or island, in the West Indies – teams. In Pakistan the leading clubs are banks and airlines. Players get paid, but there aren't many who can call themselves pros, in the English sense. Cricket remains a game, not a career.

And, of course, the English way is self-perpetuating because the chief officers of our cricket, not to mention many of the writers and commentators, are former county pros. They have filled their boots with benefit money, having been underpaid during their actual career, so it would be truly ungracious to turn on the hand that fed them now they are safely free. But the players you meet are almost unanimous in agreeing, glumly, that county cricket is a painful, draining slog that knocks the glimmer out of its brightest stars.

So, yes, it's the system. But it isn't only that. England had a shocking record of taking very good players – *very* good players: Hick, Smith, Thorpe, Ramprakash – and squeezing below-par performances out of them. Everyone who came into contact with the team during the World Cup could feel that there was something unwell in the atmosphere, something besieged, worried, bored and cynical, something that was smothering the players' *joie de vivre*. Some of it was temporary: the team seemed not to have recovered from the four-letter tongue-lashing Illingworth handed out after the Test defeat in Cape Town, when he lost his temper good and proper and went, by all accounts, so red in the face that someone had to give him water to stop him choking. But some of it seemed permanent, an inevitable by-product of the professional approach. England, in recent years, have looked like a hard team to play for.

I mean, we all know that if Graeme Hick had qualified for Australia instead of England the positive-thinking wizards would have fine-tuned him into a run-machine. And take Tendulkar. When he was fourteen he was selected to play for India Under Fifteens – a great moment in his life. He was, admittedly, an absolute exception: he kept scoring triple centuries for his school. On his way to the match, he asked his brother what would happen if he did well. His brother said that maybe he'd be picked for the Under Seventeens, and if he did well then perhaps he'd get a go with the Under Nineteens, and if he did well there, well, we were talking Ranji Trophy – first-class cricket!

It was a nice joke. But it came true. That is exactly what happened.

What if he'd been English? It's hard to imagine, but here goes.

He doesn't get many triple centuries at school, because there isn't time – there aren't many two-day games for fourteen-year-olds. But he plays some county colts games and does very well, so gets picked for a couple of Young England tours abroad. He plays the odd game for his county second XI in the school holidays (there's no question of his playing for the firsts, because there's a pecking order of established pros). The senior guys are encouraging, but distant. They talk about cricket as if it were trench warfare, not an extremely technical game. And they want the good young players, but not just yet, if it's all the same to you. It's their benefit coming up.

They recommend him to one of the best league clubs to get some experience. And that's what he gets, all right. It goes brilliantly at first – three centuries in a row. But word soon gets out, and if there's one thing these league boys know, it's how to bring a fellow down to earth. They jeer when he comes out to bat, tell him to fuck off home to Mum where he belongs. At tea, some prankster puts a bottle of baby milk in front of him. Half an hour later, their Antiguan fast bowler digs it into the green, patchy wicket and cracks him on the shoulder a few times. He's out fencing at a wide one. Word gets back to the county that he's got a bit to learn. He works the bar on Saturday nights, which everyone thinks is hilarious since he's not even allowed to drink. To prove he's not a wimp he downs the odd pint just to show them, and is sick in the car-park. God, how they laugh.

Eventually his runs talk. He is taken on by the county and given a try-out in the second XI. Four seasons have passed since his glittering fourteenth year, his *annus mirabilis*. The feeling around the county is that he hasn't quite fulfilled his potential yet. But because of injuries he gets a chance in a big game – a cup final – and scores an imposing, fluent fifty to win the match. Immediately he's talked about as a possible England player. First, though, he has to get a stack of runs for his county. Which isn't easy. He comes up against some bloody good bowlers, most of them from overseas. Ambrose, Donald, Walsh, Waqar – it sure wasn't like this in the seconds. The coaches advise him to cut out the more extravagant shots and concentrate on survival. He opens up his stance and starts playing from his crease, looking to nudge and glance. He's still a brilliant player with a good eye, so it works: the runs start to flow. But it's all incredibly tiring. Some days you finish a game and drive half the night, stopping for steak and chips in a motorway service station, to another match the next day. It's so frustrating, too. It's impossible to bat properly when you can hardly keep your eyes open, and there's no one watching you anyway. You know there's a selector at the game so you're keen to impress, but you get a rotten lbw decision before you're off the mark. You throw your bat across the dressing room in disgust and have a row with the captain, who says it was a stupid, selfish shot you played. You end up being fined and dropped.

And the press go, Well, he's young, he'll grow up eventually.

You go on a couple of England A tours and do quite well. And then one day, eight years after your great year, you get picked for the England team itself. You have a haircut and make sure your kit is extra clean, and spend a few nerve-racking hours at the nets the day before the match. You go to bed early in the team hotel, order breakfast in your room, and then the phone rings. You haven't been picked. Your county wants you in Chelmsford today – if you leave now you should just make it.

You drive down the M1, churning. So near yet so far. You go in at number three and are bowled not playing a shot by Wasim Akram.

For the next Test match you are not even in the final thirteen. No one tells you why.

But your turn comes eventually and you don't do too badly – no big scores, but plenty of decent contributions. So it's crushing when you're not picked to tour Australia.

By now you're just about ready to give up cricket altogether. County cricket . . . Well, take last week: you drove five hours all night to Cornwall to play a NatWest game, and didn't even get a bat, then straight back in the evening; didn't get home till half two. The next day there was a four-day match, with the Sunday League in the middle. On the Monday night after the game you tore up to Headingley for the Test, and spent Tuesday and Wednesday practising with the team. You were twelfth man – brought on the drinks, helmets and so on. And then the match finished in three days, and the county wanted you for the Sunday. So down you drove first thing in the morning with a hangover from the party the night before. Tried to wash it away with a bumper brekker at Watford Gap. Your back was killing you – all this driving, probably.

You're Sachin Tendulkar. Everyone knows you had it in you to become a great player. But somehow it didn't quite work out. Nice boy, the committee men agree. Never quite had it up here, where it counts. The England manager is on the radio saying that we're just not producing the batsmen any more. He thinks covered wickets are to blame.

That, roughly, is the career so far of Mark Ramprakash. The previous summer he had scored more than 2000 runs for Middlesex. But he wasn't out here in Pakistan.

England had a week off now, but the rest of the tournament was taking shape fast. Sri Lanka had nailed their colours to the mast. In a hysterical atmosphere in Colombo, they played host to Zimbabwe and everything that people had been saying about their batting turned out to be true. Zimbabwe scored 228, and when both Sri Lanka's openers committed suicide there was a lot of work to be done. But De Silva and Gurusinha simply destroyed the bowling. Blocking, they seemed to have decided, was for sissies. In twenty-seven overs they put on 172; Gurusinha hit six sixes, De Silva two. Sri Lanka had gone out of their way to thank Zimbabwe for turning up in the first place; now we knew why.

Australia, too, were making a mockery of the idea that they'd be uptight when the action finally started. Kenya gave them a small fright by dismissing Taylor and Ponting for not many, but then Australia declared Waugh. Mark and Steve put on 207 – a World Cup record. As coincidence would have it, that was exactly how many Kenya scored: they lost by nearly a hundred runs. Their opening batsman Kennedy Otiemno had a fine day, though. He scored 85 and might have got a century if he hadn't wrenched his leg and retired hurt.

Australia certainly sounded chipper enough in the post-match presentation (a feature of which was that you could hear them on television, but not at the grounds – such were the priorities around here). Mark Taylor spoke into Tony Greig's microphone.

'Looked like a pretty good wicket out there,' said Greig.

'Oh, I don't know,' said Taylor. 'I thought it was a nightmare, personally. No, Mark and Steve played tremendously well. I should have got out sooner.'

'And now for the big one down in Melbourne.'

'Bombay, I think,' said Taylor. 'Yeah, we're looking forward to it.'

The Kenyan captain, Maurice Odumbe, climbed up for a word.

'Well done, mate,' said Greig, scanning his notes. 'How's the leg?'

'Er, that was another player.'

Greig didn't seem to mind. He just blazed on. His finest moment was yet to come. Before the semi-final he spoke over a few scenic shots of Chandigarh. 'A beautiful city,' he said. 'Designed, of course, by the French architect Le Causy-Buzet.'

I know. It's mean to laugh. And I like Greig. That unflagging multi-exclamation-mark enthusiasm is deliberate – a calculated attempt to rev up what can sometimes be a dull day.

Anyway, it seemed as if the real action was happening elsewhere. I headed down to Bombay to see India play Australia . . .

. . . And only got half-way. I left Rawalpindi at midnight, flew to Karachi, and that's where I discovered I didn't have an onward ticket.

I was met by an extremely nice travel agent who rummaged around in the airline computer and found no evidence that they were expecting me. They did, as it happened, have a seat. But I didn't take it, because they sure as hell didn't have a seat back. My schedule was tight: the way things stood, I'd arrive in Bombay a few hours before the match, go straight to the ground, watch the game, dash to the airport and catch the midnight flight back to Karachi. The idea of being stuck in Bombay didn't appeal: I had visions of a few more night-stopovers in Delhi. And it was about four in the morning by now. I headed for the hotel, swapping photographs of children with the travel agent on the way.

The next day I watched India and Australia on television with some chagrin – it was one heck of a good match. Waugh and Taylor began streakily, both edging just short of slip. But then they took command. Taylor, usually a sticker, was throwing the bat, a bold and self-sacrificing attempt to give his partner, who had all the aces up his sleeve, time to settle in. There was a tradition of close matches between these two: Australia had twice won by a single run. The rooftops around the stadium were crammed, partly because only 7000 of the 40,000 tickets had been released to the public. Oh, and the floodlights looked like they'd been there for years.

After twenty overs Australia were just two runs short of a hundred – a great start. They had been cocky coming into the match. Their media manager (yes, other teams have those) was telling the press about the post-match conference. 'It will be attended,' he said, 'by the Australian captain Mark Taylor, and by Man of the Match Shane Warne.' Nice.

And he was only three letters out. Mark Waugh unwrapped his second successive century (126, to follow his 140 against Kenya), and if anyone had stayed with him the match could have been over by dusk. Waugh isn't like Tendulkar: he doesn't club you to death. You wouldn't be quite so nervous if you were bowling at him. But at some point you'd look at the scoreboard and find he had eighty-three not out. He guided the ball freely and easily all round the wicket, with no great fuss. It was astonishing to watch: you kept thinking you must have missed something. He was timing the ball so well that when he dabbed away the winning single against Zimbabwe, the ball went fizzing past mid-off for four. And here again he kept streaking the ball past helpless fielders. Something had happened to him in the last year or so. He had always been exceptional, but there was something in his yawning, gum-chewing, no-worries demeanour that suggested a careless approach. His twin brother Steve had always been made of sterner stuff, so much so that Mark spent a few years being called the forgotten Waugh. Maybe it was that bribery business; maybe it was seeing his brother rise to number one in the world batting table, maybe it was the switch from Allan Border's get-the-bastards style of captaincy to Mark Taylor's sunnier approach, but all that had changed. Where once he looked merely unflappable, now he was implacable.

Australia blew it rather in the slog overs, losing five wickets for fourteen. But 258 was still steep.

Tendulkar didn't seem to think so. He picked up where he left off against the West Indies. Glenn McGrath's first three overs were maidens; the next two went for twenty-seven. When the fifty came up, Tendulkar had scored forty-one of them. He dominated the commercial breaks too, stabbing a stump into the ground to show how fizzy and liberating and unofficial Pepsi was, or holding up a credit card: 'I've got Visa power – now you go get it!'

Here came another contest everyone had been waiting for: Tendulkar versus Warne. There were rumours that the bowler needed surgery on an arthritic finger, rumours that turned out to be true (after the tournament he went to New York for the operation). But he was still a fearsome opponent. Crafty, too: he spent so long exercising and flipping the ball to mid-on that the umpire had to walk over and tell him to get on with it.

The crowd booed and roared, and Tendulkar didn't disappoint them. The first ball was bludgeoned back into the sightscreen behind Warne's head. Tendulkar tried to wallop the next one too, but succeeded only in almost being caught at extra cover. The third ball was greeted with another great whirl of the bat – this time it sliced away for four to third man. It was a great over, and it went for ten runs. Round one to 6 plus 4 = Tendulkar.

Round two went to Warne, though. His next nine overs cost only eighteen: even Tendulkar had to come to his senses and watch his step. The ball was turning furiously. It still looked as though he would go on and win the match single-handed, however, until Mark Waugh saw him advancing down the wicket and shrewdly bowled a wide. Tendulkar was stumped (for ninety) and so were India. They battled on, and fell sixteen runs short.

You couldn't help noticing that all the fun cricket was in the other group. Up here in the empty stadiums of Pakistan there had been nothing like that. Perhaps it would change now that Pakistan had entered the fray: they had been waiting for the end of Ramadan. They had certainly looked the part in their two outings so far, against the Emirates and Holland. Saeed Anwar, in particular, had prevented anyone else getting any batting practice. So far he had scored 123 not out (forty and eighty-three), and Pakistan had only lost three wickets.

One way or another, the World Cup was coming alive.

— 8 —

THE GAUNTLET OF HATE

England vs Pakistan, Karachi

South Africa arrived in Karachi the morning after me, so I went along to their press conference. Bob Woolmer tapped the microphone like a pop star.

'Testing, one, two,' he said. 'Hello, Karachi.'

A few reporters settled in their chairs.

'I feel a little like the woman,' said Woolmer, 'who knew what to do, but didn't know how to make it interesting.'

The press lads relaxed. An innocuous crude joke! Their kind of guy! Then Hansie Cronje sat down, unfolded a piece of paper, and read out a prepared statement.

'The South African team wants to thank the Karachi people for coming to meet us at the airport,' he said. 'We're sorry we couldn't stay as long as we'd have liked, sorry if we missed some of the children. But we really appreciated the trouble people took. Thank you.'

There. That wasn't very difficult, was it? Those words would be reprinted in all the local papers the next day, and everyone would agree how much they liked these nice polite South Africans. It is called public relations, and it isn't very complicated, really.

Apparently, it had been quite a shindig out at the airport: bands, camels and thousands of people. Naturally the English reaction, when they arrived a few hours later, was more subdued. 'Bloody chaos,' said one player. 'Took us three hours to get to the hotel.'

Apart from myself, there was one other English journalist at this press conference. 'How are you finding the practice facilities?' he asked. This isn't a question other nationalities would bother asking, because it's obvious what the answer has to be. But with England, under Illingworth, you never knew. It was worth a try. But Woolmer wasn't falling for it.

'We have nothing but praise for the wickets we've practised on,' he said. 'They've been absolutely magnificent – the best surfaces you could wish for. It's enabled our batsmen to find their form really well and quickly. Actually the whole tournament has been run really well. We've been looked after really well. One of the reasons we want to beat Pakistan next week is so we can stay in Pakistan for the quarter-final round. We're very happy here.'

Wasn't he doing really well? The local journalists swooned. One of them asked Cronje why he thought things were going so really well.

'I'm going to praise Bob a little here,' he said. 'He's done a lot for us as a team. We communicate better about game plans, the batsmen have a lot more options. And fielding practice – none of the practice sessions I've been to in the last year have been boring.'

Well, that was a nice mutual-congratulation society, wasn't it? But you couldn't help feeling they meant it. They were happy with each other.

I was curious about these brilliant practice facilities, so asked if I could come along and watch. Sure thing. Off we went. The defence ground was out on the edge of town, in the middle of a new housing development. The ground looked okay, but the net area out back was truly awful. Soft sand on the run-ups: it would be like sprinting through dunes. The wickets in the nets themselves looked reasonable – flat and shiny. But it was not very good.

Cronje called his men round and told them that, well, the facilities might be rubbish, but there was no use worrying about that now, since here they were; and they all knew what they had to work on today, so let's go to it.

And that's what they did. Every now and then Woolmer would take a batsman off to a net on his own, and throw balls from five yards. Occasionally he'd take the bat to show them what he meant. There he was with Rhodes, demonstrating that there, just at the top, see? Like taking a tennis ball early, on the rise. Rhodes was working on the top-of-the-bounce whip: Tendulkar's shot. Well, you might as well imitate the best.

'Yes,' said Woolmer. 'Jonty's such a talented sportsman. But he's a hockey player really – a great eye, great hands. We're trying to make him a real batsman, and he's doing well. I just hope he has time, because this fellow Kallis is really something.'

Darryl Cullinan strolled out of his net to ask Woolmer something about his feet.

'See, I find if I go back, then forward, it feels okay.'

'That's fine, that's like Lara, look.' Woolmer took his bat. 'Da-dah ... Dah-dah ... Da-dah. Back and forward, back and forward. That's fine, gets your feet moving nicely. If you're comfortable, stay with it.'

Woolmer gets a lot of praise for his coaching methods. People talk about him as if he were some sort of guru. The truth is that he does what you would expect a coach to. He was working on a book about it all with a sports scientist in South Africa. 'It's an experiment in how to prepare a team,' said Woolmer. 'It's important that we document what we're doing.' He was desperate to do well (really well) in this World Cup, to vindicate his methods. This contrasted nicely with the present England views on such subjects. Illingworth's were famous: 'It's fifty per cent head, fifty per cent heart, and bugger technique,' he once said. So there.

England were working hard – as hard as South Africa. But not as intelligently. When they arrived in Karachi a day later, for their game against Pakistan, they set up at the smart Gymkhana club and went through their usual routines. One new fielding drill (Atherton's invention) was to set up the stumps and get two batsmen to hit the ball into a ring of fielders, then go for the run. It was a good idea – at least people didn't know who the ball was going to, unlike the customary take-it-in-turns routine – but it was only semi-baked. For starters, the batsmen might have worn two pads instead of one, and helmets (it would have been hot, but real). Worse, the field was set back to save two, and guess what – they always succeeded. The batsmen ran the first fast (as per the textbook), turned to look for two like true Australians, and then decided against it. Why? Why on earth didn't they run the second? That way they would have found out how often they could make it, and would have pressurized the fielders too.

The National Stadium in Karachi was full to the brim when their heroes came out to bat, but they were chanting only one man's name: Ja-ved, Ja-ved, Ja-ved. Javed Miandad had been persuaded back into the fold by the Prime Minister. He was the oldest man in the World Cup and some doubted his ability to cut it these days. But as a talisman he was priceless. The previous night he had dedicated a giant bat to cheering crowds at one of the city's main roundabouts. Ja-ved, Ja-ved, the crowd roared. They didn't know he wasn't actually playing. The word was, he had refused to bat at number five or six, and this had led to a row with the captain, Wasim Akram. With Pakistan you never knew: it was possible.

They had wiped the floor with both the Emirates and Holland, bowling the former out for 109, and knocking off the runs in eighteen overs. And Waqar Younis had been much too fast for the Dutch, taking four for twenty-six off his ten overs in a total of 145, a target the batsmen treated with disdain.

They were looking good again here. Sohail and Anwar looked identical: two left-handers of similar build. And they hit the ball like the proverbial shell, slotting it into the breech with unhurried panache and blasting it across the trim grass. After eleven overs Pakistan were fifty-two for nought and going well. Hansie Cronje's response was to bring himself on to bowl and stick a short extra cover in for these slightly lofted drives. Immediately he had Anwar caught by McMillan – the Hick dismissal all over again. And then he got one to straighten on Ijaz Ahmed, and everything changed. Pakistan had a problem now: they'd won their first two matches so easily that most of them hadn't had a decent bat. Inzaman-ul-Haq was run out (of course) and Sohail and Malik found themselves sinking. They took no unnecessary risks – fewer, perhaps, than were called for. Sohail got his century in the end, but the total (242) looked no better than okay.

You would have expected the crowd to cheer when the captain, Wasim Akram, came out to bat. But there were loud boos when people realized it wasn't Javed. When Rashid Latif went out to the middle, you wished someone had given him Javed's shirt, just to get the crowd going. They still didn't realize he wasn't playing. But they were having fun: swaying and roaring. You couldn't call it a Mexican wave, but it was trying. It was a Pakistani wave; it had crashed into the rocks and was sloshing about all over the place. There had been serious worries that the match could not take place, Karachi being the murder-and-kidnapping capital of Asia. Then there had been worries that people would not dare go: there hadn't been a big social gathering like this for months. But the atmosphere was stupendous: it would take a while, once the game was over, for the roar in our ears to subside.

South Africa set about the total with their by-now-typical composure. Wasim Akram, on the other hand, looked a shadow of his usual self. So it wasn't a surprise when he took himself off and handed the ball to Mushtaq Ahmed. Ah-hah – more leg spin. Be interesting to see how South Africa coped with this.

Brilliantly, was the answer. Hudson plopped forward and swept the first ball for four. The second ball he swept for four as well. For variety's sake, he took another sweep at the third ball, and scuffed it. It was pretty clear, at least, what the plan was; and they were wasting no time in executing it. Fourth ball: sweep for two runs. Fifth ball: sweep, miss, four byes. Mushtaq Ahmed scratched his head. Perhaps he ought to bowl somewhere else. He tossed the ball up outside off stump, and Hudson, expecting no less, leaned back and cut it for four. It was early days, but it felt like a matchwinning over. He'd scored eighteen runs off six balls: the fifty had come up after only seven overs. Who was it who said that there was no room for flair in the South African mentality (Mike Atherton)? They had the game cold, now.

They didn't change the plan, though. Gary Kirsten was out sweeping, and in some dressing rooms this would have triggered a flood of stern warnings against trying that shot again. So what happened? Jacques Kallis walked in, took guard, and swept the first ball he faced. They weren't going to let the fall of a wicket change a plan that had brought them 105 runs in fifteen overs. The score rattled on. Wasim Akram seemed to have something against leg-side fielders, which was odd, since that's where the ball was going all the time. His three on-side men were all on the boundary: South Africa swept, swept and swept again. Jesus swept! They were winning this at a canter. Eventually he twigged and moved a man across. Kallis promptly unhooked the reverse sweep instead. They were almost teasing. The 200 came up in the thirty-fifth over: plenty of time to fiddle the rest. Waqar Younis came back – too late, one felt, but the crowd got behind him as always: he tears in with something like a hot wind raging behind him, made of yelling and rhythmic stamping. He had been suffering badly from a squiffy back, and the consensus was that he had lost the toe-crushing pace that had made him such a scary force a couple of years ago, but he was doing a very good impression of fast bowling here. His third ball cut in and drove back the stumps of Darryl Cullinan. But then Salim Malik came on and bowled a few full tosses, almost as if they wanted to get this over and done with. When Pollock hit the winning run there was absolutely no applause at all.

'There are always butterflies,' said Cronje afterwards. 'But luckily for us they seem to be flying in formation.' Even the quips seemed well prepared.

Wasim Akram seemed relaxed too. No, he said, the team wasn't worried about the prospect of going to India to play a quarter-final.

Not everyone believed him. And there have been so many conspiratorial gambling stories written about Pakistani cricket that even optimists couldn't quite dismiss the grim thought that Pakistan had seemed to be playing at half cock. Betting was all the rage. During matches there was a constant barter: how many fours this over, how many dot balls, what were the odds on a six? Several local cricket fans insisted that gambling was essential – it was putting money where your mouth was. Everyone should do it, they said, especially journalists. They don't remind you, though they could, that cricket began, back in the eighteenth century, as an excuse to gamble. In that sense they are merely being traditional.

But the more sombre stories persist. The big bookmakers are held to have enormous clout, and everyone you meet believes that it is possible, if not likely, that the players are in bed with bookmakers and that half the games we see are fixed. It seems a bizarre, overheated allegation, but so did the one made by Mark Waugh, Shane Warne and Tim May – that they'd been offered those huge sums to play badly. None of it made sense. Why bribe bowlers, who would be swiftly taken off if they bowled rubbish? On the other hand, would they really have made these allegations just for the hell of it?

The sums are undeniably huge. Even allowing for racy reporting, cricket betting is a multi-million-pound business. But from now on it wasn't gambling that fed the grapevine: it was tactics. Having lost a match, Pakistan could no longer come top of the group. If they wanted to stay in Pakistan for the quarter-final, they'd have to come fourth; the second and third teams would go to Bangalore and Madras. Pakistan's manager, Intikhab Alam, was quoted at length in the newspapers saying that it would be within the rules to lose, and might even be sensible. 'I don't see any harm in such a proposition.' Afterwards he claimed he'd been misquoted, which is possible – he might have said, 'I don't see any charm in such a proposition.' The head of his cricket board, Arif Abbasi, leapt to his defence and pointed out that it was probably a linguistic mistake – English could be damned tricky. This might well have been the reason but, as it happened, the interview had been conducted in Urdu.

Not that Urdu isn't confusing enough. If you listen to the Urdu commentaries on the television you could hear the bizarre array of borrowed words. Most of the cricket vocabulary is English, so it tends to go: 'Mike Atherton Urdu Urdu Urdu deep mid-off Urdu Urdu Urdu caught behind Urdu Urdu Urdu the county grind Urdu Urdu Urdu complete mental fatigue . . .'

Anyway, there was a widespread feeling that the match against England could be dodgy. And when it got going it certainly looked that way. Wasim and Waqar jogged in slowly and bowled at half pace to Atherton and Robin Smith. When Smith skied to Waqar in the deep the fielder trotted in as if there was no rush, only to see the ball land a yard or two in front of him. Mushtaq bowled to the same field that cost him so many runs against South Africa, and England, who can watch the telly as well as the next man, swept him away. The score moved – past 100 and on towards 150. You had to rub your eyes. Salim Malik stepped over a ball it seemed he could have picked up with ease, and Wasim Akram gave away overthrows so clumsily it was almost impossible to imagine he hadn't done it on purpose: he muffed the throw from the outfield, ran to retrieve the ball, then turned and flung at the stumps even though the batsmen weren't running. Weird. Some old heads in the press box shook, or rested in hands. It really did look as if they were trying to help the score along.

Atherton and Smith were batting with great conviction, though. Both scored fifty and, the way things were going, they might both score hundreds. The crowd didn't know what to think. But then England collapsed from 149 for nought to 217 for seven – not bad, even by their standards. Wickets fell to back-up bowlers. Smith chipped Malik to mid-off, and went off swinging his bat as if he knew he should have bloody clouted it. Atherton was bowled attempting to cut Sohail's slow left arm, the second time he'd walked into this well-known trap on these low wickets. Hick went down the wicket straight away and was stumped for one. Atherton had attempted to have Stewart in the side keeping wicket, which might have added something to the batting line-up; but Illingworth had put his foot down. Thorpe, with another unbeaten fifty, gave some semblance of order to the second half of the innings, but without much help from anyone else. The last six wickets fell for fifty-three runs, and England finished on 249 – not enough, by the look of things. If Smith and

Atherton could bat like that, what on earth would Sohail, Anwar and Inzaman do?

Plenty. After fifteen overs – the point at which the fielders retreated – they had scored seventy-seven: more than five per over. The stands bayed for more. One row of fans had large letters on their T-shirts, and they were getting so excited that they were all jumbled up. Now the letters read: AKPITNSA. Sohail fell, flicking to midwicket, and Anwar perished when he edged a slash to the wicket-keeper. But Pakistan were always ahead of the run-rate, and in the end they reached the winning post with quite a bit in hand. Ijaz Ahmed and Inzaman seemed to be using the game for a spot of batting practice. Neil Fairbrother scrambled to pick up a ball and tore a hamstring. And Karachi finally got what it had been yelling for when Javed Miandad stalked out to the wicket to see them home. He had led them on to the field to a roar so loud you had to put your hands to your ears. This would be his last appearance on home turf.

It was a relief to find that the game hadn't been rigged after all, and that the rumour-mongering had been so much hot air. But it did serve to show how meaningless cricket could become if it lost credibility with the public. It has strong aspects of theatre and spectacle, but these are nothing on their own, without the unpredictable spiciness of a genuine contest. Those post-final warnings by Mark Taylor had real substance. Cricket was in the uncomfortable position of having to prove its innocence.

As for England, trounced again. What could one say?

The *Sun* knew: PAK IT IN! But no one else had the energy to mind too much. The press conference was a muted affair. 'Yeah, I think maybe we could have got 280, 290,' said Atherton. That would have put more pressure on them to perform. But for us the main thing was the performance. We leave here more confident than we were going into the match.' He had a right to be cheerful: he had played well himself, at least. But everyone who had watched India playing Australia in Bombay knew now that England were way adrift: both teams down there had played a different game altogether. And it was ominous that Atherton should feel it was a lucky break to have drawn Sri Lanka in the quarters. 'The old days of Sri Lanka being a pushover are gone,' he said. 'They play good cricket. But we have to feel confident.'

Did they? Had they seen Sri Lanka recently? The Lankans had slaughtered India in the most spectacular style. It looked like a shoo-in for the home side when Tendulkar (who else?) put together a dizzy 137: the man never seemed to miss. He had just signed a deal with Mark Mascarenhas that guaranteed him $5 million over the next seven years. And though he was still playing with an unsponsored bat, he was certainly hitting the ball like a man with few money worries. In a final savage burst, he helped India put on ninety-nine runs in the last ten overs, and 271 seemed a more than tidy total. But Sri Lanka came out blazing like few had ever blazed before. 'Actually, we couldn't believe it,' said their coach, Dav Whatmore, later. 'When we went out to bat they had third man and fine leg up inside the circle. We thought: We're in here.' And so they were. Jayasuriya and Kaluwitharana put on forty-two in the first three overs. The third, bowled by Prabhakar, went four, six, four, four, four. It couldn't go on for ever, but it lasted long enough to make Sri Lanka's task almost straightforward. Jayasuriya eventually fell for seventy-nine, but the damage had been done. Ranatunga and Tillekeratne steered the Lankans to a comfortable win.

And Prabhakar's international career was over.

That man Jayasuriya. England had cause to remember him. At the end of their last tour of India (played three, lost three) they had gone to Sri Lanka for a confidence-booster, and lost. Jayasuriya came out to bat with only a few runs needed to win and bags of time. Guess what he did: he hit the first ball he received for six.

Right now, he was looming up in England's rear-view mirror. The Sri Lankans were a long way away, but every time they appeared on television they gave off a low booming noise, like distant thunder. They were like some creature in a horror film, crashing their teeth into whatever small prey crossed their path. Perhaps this was what Australia's confidential security report had revealed – whatever you do, avoid this lot.

The bar kept going up. Conventional wisdom demanded that you batted first if you could, but South Africa, Pakistan and Sri Lanka had overhauled decent targets with some ease. More than that, though: the idea that these Sri Lankans could be shackled by England seemed, at this point, almost ridiculous. They were turning the game upside down, and we seemed to be among the last to have noticed. The old idea, to which Imran Khan still clung gamely in his occasional interviews and columns, was for a slow start, keeping lots of wickets in hand for a huge great clatter at the end. Today's bowlers were too crafty for that. It was hard to pick off boundaries at the end, these days. The first few overs were the key. Get the acceleration out of the way first, and then go calmly through the rest of the innings.

In a hangover from the opening ceremony, the President of India's cricket board, I. S. Bindra, ran what our tabloids would have called a 'gauntlet of hate' on his way to the match. He asked for police protection at his house, and was given it, but then one of his dogs bit a policeman on the leg, so another lawsuit was pending. It was still fun at the top.

And at the bottom too. The tournament had been waiting for a shock, and it came up with a beauty. The West Indies lost to Kenya.

The *Sun* said: Kenya Believe it!

The *Mirror* said: Kenya Believe It!

Richardson won the toss and decided to field, a decision that infuriated Lara, who felt the team needed a long bat. What followed was amazing. The West Indies bowled like sulky schoolboys playing against their will, conceding thirty-seven extras, sixteen of them wides. Even then, a total of 166 didn't look very taxing, but they never came close. Lara came out and swatted away like someone who hadn't played before. His first ball went for four, the next two swishes went through to the wicket-keeper, and then another went to the boundary. Someone ran out from the pavilion with a new pair of gloves – it looked as if he was being told to stop crying and bat properly. So naturally he had a lash and was out, caught behind. The mixture of shock and joy on the face of the portly wicket-keeper, who somehow clutched the ball in the folds of his stomach, was to become one of the World Cup's sweetest images.

And down they went, skittled by Kenya for just ninety-three. 'Our only chance was to get Lara out early,' said Kenya's Indian manager, 'and you have to say he contributed to that end.' Even a fan like me had to admit that it was a churlish performance. Most of the pundits felt it would be impossible now for him to take over as captain, but this flowed from the belief that the captain needs to be a goody-goody, head-of-school type. I tended to think that rebels often made the best captains, since they were the ones who knew their own minds.

For Kenya, it was wonderful – they were, perhaps, the Sri Lankans of the future. In a single afternoon they had vindicated their presence here, and their obvious delight made a mockery of all the carping. But it was by far the worst result in the recent history of the Caribbean –

unthinkable, really, for a region that rallied to the catchphrase 'Cricket is We!' The *Trinidad Express* called it 'a surrender of West Indian manhood'. The *Barbados Nation* begged Richie Richardson to resign (they didn't have to wait long). The heads of government were meeting in Guyana: one of them, Edison James of Dominica, called for it to be treated with the utmost political seriousness.

And England weren't the only ones who couldn't handle the papers. An Indian reporter sat in the Kenyan dressing room listening to Lara slagging off his own team, his own management, everyone in sight. The journalist subsequently sparked off a small race-row by quoting Lara as saying he didn't mind losing to 'you guys' – the Kenyans. What they really hated was losing to South Africa, where 'the white thing' came into it. Not surprisingly, this set the pigeons fluttering. It was a little ironic that a bunch of white South Africans should suddenly find themselves the victim of a racial slur, but there it was. Woolmer, who should know, said that it didn't sound like the Lara he knew, but the damage was done. Lara denied saying anything of the kind, and, who knows, maybe he didn't. Richardson said he thought the story was 'malicious and sad'.

Up in cynical Pakistan, Kenya's victory set tongues wagging. Everyone was sure that Sri Lanka would deliberately lose to Kenya in order to eliminate the West Indies: the way the rules work is that if two teams are equal on points, then whichever one beat the other in their match would go through. It was quite a tasty thought: Sri Lanka would hardly mind booting out one of the countries that had boycotted their island.

Luckily it didn't happen like that. Quite the opposite. Sri Lanka took Kenya's bowlers apart, setting a new World Cup record with a total of 398. Jayasuriya smashed a hole in the Kenyan attack, and De Silva (145), Gurusinha (eighty-four) and Ranatunga (seventy-five) poured through the gap. You had to spare a thought for Martin Suji, whose nine overs went for eighty-five runs. Sri Lanka scored over 300 more than the West Indies had managed.

The truth was, England might be better off playing Australia.

It still wasn't clear who would be playing whom elsewhere. South Africa, Pakistan, New Zealand and England were the qualifiers from one group, in that order. And Sri Lanka, Australia and India had booked their places as well. But there was a crunch game coming up between the West Indies and Australia. This time there would be no second chances: if the West Indies lost (as they were expected to) then Kenya would go through at their expense (they would both have one match, so the Africans' victory over the West Indies would be the tie-breaker).

I was bound for Bangalore, whatever happened. Fingers crossed, it would be India against Pakistan. The final, I realized with a shock, was only a week away.

While we waited, the English media took on the Pakistan media in a cricket match at the Gymkhana ground (we were thrilled with the practice facilities – marvellous). England batted first, sent a pair of photographers to the crease, and made a cautious start. But the *Star* of Pakistan began with five wides, so that kept the scoreboard ticking over. And when one of the snappers was run-out (I was amazed when I saw it on the playback: if he hadn't fallen flat on his face he'd have been fine) the *Sun* went out and started blazing the ball to the boundary. One bounced on the railing in front of the commentator (the *Mirror*), and another flew into the Governor General's garden. The *Mail on Sunday* carried on the good work, and kept up the soaraway scoring rate. Then came the climax. The *Independent* (Derek Pringle) strode to the wicket in a pair of baggy green shorts, prodded a couple of singles, and then took aim at the leg-side boundary. One . . . two . . . three . . . four . . . five . . . (go on, son, you can do it!) . . . and YES – six sixes in an over. He must have been inspired by Kenya, the country in which he'd grown up and which his father had captained. And as a result we had quite a handy total.

The other half of the *Independent* (me) opened the bowling – it would have been unfair to have given Pringle the new ball: he'd made his point. But the ball kept running past the *News of the World* at gully, so the runs came freely. The man from Tetley came on and picked up three wickets, terrifying the batsmen with his impressive England gear. But he had only half a mind on his bowling. The team's beer supply was stuck in Karachi docks. The paperwork had gone wrong, and Illingworth, for one, was not impressed. 'I don't know what's going on,' he said. 'There's thirty cases down there.'

The *Times* was sidelined through injury. The *Guardian* had an urgent appointment on the golf course. But it was a resounding triumph all the same. Pringle narrowly missed being man of the match. He was, he insisted, 'not available' for the quarter-final against Sri Lanka.

Otherwise, well, Karachi was having a party. For an alcohol-free country, it was remarkably easy to get sloshed. In Rawalpindi I met Rory Bremner, who had nipped out for a quick blast of cricket (forgetting his passport, which obliged him to fill out a form claiming 'sheer ignorance'). And after an excursion to a fashion show – a black-tie dinner with models – someone said it was the right time to go and watch turtles laying their eggs. So off we went to the seaside, down the long, dark roads on which travellers were sometimes seized. And there weren't any turtles, although there were plenty of loose dogs. We were being trailed by an armed policeman, one of the staples of well-heeled life in Karachi, but the seashore still felt touchy and rabid. We hurried along, gazing at the lights of the tankers out there on the ocean. And that is how I came to be walking along a beach in Karachi at two o'clock in the morning with someone warding off a pack of fierce hounds with Geoff Boycott impressions.

Karachi felt like a dangerous place: machine-gun emplacements on every corner. But that didn't mean life stopped. My abiding memory is of the time someone sent a car to pick me up, and I opened the door to find, on the back seat, a tennis racquet and a machine gun.

Well, you never know when these things will come in handy.

No one wanted to miss Australia's game against the West Indies. And there were still a few Lara-believers like me who thought that an upset was possible. On the day of the match, the West Indies board was meeting back in the Caribbean to discuss the defeat by Kenya, and it sounded very much as if this was going to be Richie Richardson's last waltz as captain. He made the most of it. Harper struck the first, possibly crucial, blow by having Mark Waugh stumped for thirty – a duck, by his standards. And although Ricky Ponting batted his way to a crisp and emphatic century, Australia made hard work of it. Their score – 229 – was better than anything the West Indies had managed so far, but it was within range, if anything like normal form returned to the men in maroon. In a strange twist, the team that was supposed to be a byword for solid teamwork chalked up another three run-outs, making it eight in two games.

And then Richardson walked quietly into the limelight. Lara gave the innings the spark it needed, scoring a bright sixty, but it was the captain who steered the innings to safety with an undefeated ninety-three. Luck played its part: he was caught in the deep by Ponting, who fell over the advertising hoarding as he clutched the ball, turning the catch into a six. But it was mainly a triumph of will-power – quite a moving one, coming as it did from a man not in the best of form. Before the match the West Indies had had a team meeting that had lasted two and a half hours. The subject, roughly, was: If we don't win this, it's the end of the line.

So Richardson could have been forgiven a burst of indignant, told-you-so triumphalism after the match. Instead he apologized. 'This win is for all the people in the Caribbean who were so badly hurt by our performance against Kenya. I've never felt as bad as after that defeat. And if the players or the board think I'm not the man for the job, I'll stand down.'

And that is what he did. The following morning, he announced that he was retiring after the World Cup (which, of course, he still hoped to win).

It had been, to say the least, an up-and-down sort of day.

And suddenly the knock-out stages clicked into place. England would play Sri Lanka (God help them); Australia would play New Zealand, and South Africa would face the West Indies (looking forward, no doubt, to ramming Lara's reported comments down his throat). India and Pakistan would have a showdown in Bangalore.

That's where I headed. After three weeks of haphazard play, something epic was heaving into view.

The tournament was nearly finished: the competition was about to begin.

— 9 —

INDIA PLUNGES INTO EUPHORIA

India vs Pakistan, Bangalore

Have you heard the one about the Pakistani man who died, and was met at the gates of paradise by a bouncer insisting that he show some evidence of having been brave in his life?

'Well,' he began, 'I did once leap to the assistance of an old lady who looked as if she was going to be run over.'

The bouncer shook his head.

'Well, I once strangled a tiger that was terrorizing the village goat. That was pretty brave, people said.'

The bouncer shrugged. 'Heard that one,' he said. 'Go on.'

'Okay,' said the man. 'What about the time I threw myself in front of a speeding bullet to save a friend, and was hit in the shoulder? It hurt, I can tell you.'

The bouncer nodded. 'That's more like it,' he said. 'But are you sure that's the best you can do?' He turned away. 'We'll let you know,' he said.

'Wait,' said the dead man. 'There is something else. I was once the only Pakistani to go to a cricket match against India – *in India*.'

The bouncer swung round. 'That's unbelievable,' he said. 'When was that?'

The Pakistani glanced at his watch. 'About two minutes ago,' he said.

It wasn't easy to get a ticket. When the box office opened at the beginning of the week, 60,000 people broke down the crash barriers and staged a mini-riot when they began to twig that thousands of seats were being held back for last-minute VIPs. Most of them had to go away empty-handed, but many turned up on the day: the roads outside the ground heaved with people willing to brave what the papers called a 'mild *lathi* charge'.

I was fortunate: I had the magic pass. For the knock-out stages, though, even we media types had to jump through a few hoops and submit fresh applications, with photographs and everything. I had done this in Karachi, or at any rate was prompted to do it by the man from the *Express*, who was generously acting as team leader in such matters. But it didn't seem very likely that word had come through to Bangalore. I went up the stairs, along the corridor, up the stairs, along the corridor in search of room 419. Eventually I knocked on the door and apologized for disturbing the two men inside. It was a featureless room with an iron bed and a small desk – like a prison cell. One of the men fished out a fax and asked me my name. I knew it wouldn't be there, and this wasn't at all a comment on the efficiency of Indian bureaucracy, just a reflection of my own characteristic paranoia: I never expect credit cards to be accepted; I never expect to get cash out of slot machines, even when I know I've got money in there.

Sure enough, my name wasn't on the list, but this didn't seem to raise any eyebrows. The man wrote it down and gave me the priceless sticker that would get me in tomorrow.

The pitch itself looked like a cross between a rifle range and sheep-dog trials. There were machine-gunners and Alsatians wherever you looked. Labourers climbed up what the papers were calling the 'splendorous lights' while the players practised in front of thousands of policemen. One too-bold photographer stepped over the boundary rope to get a better view, and stopped when one of the guards held a gun in his chest. Everyone wanted to take a peek at the wicket ('The curator pronounced the rectangle to be batsman-friendly') but it was covered with a carpet of damp grass cuttings to keep it from getting scorched.

The next day, when Azharuddin tossed the coin there was a fabulous noise in Bangalore. It turned into a high-pitched cheer when he turned to talk to the television camera, a signal that he had won the toss. And that was nothing compared to the thunderclap that greeted the little paddling motion he made with his hand towards the pavilion. India were batting.

The cheering continued. It reached a crescendo when Tendulkar appeared, hurriedly pulling on his gloves like someone at a village match who'd been caught short in the loo (didn't he know this was *important*?). It rose another notch when Sidhu took guard and prepared to take the first ball. And it really hit the roof when Waqar Younis's first delivery was called a wide. I was going to say that it was loud enough to take the roof off, but the roof hadn't even been put on. Steel cables poked into the blue sky. It was going to be hot.

The intensity of the national rivalry was frightening. India and Pakistan were like Siamese twins that had been ripped apart: so similar, and so different. The players themselves were pally enough: some had played for the same Pilcom side in Sri Lanka, and many met regularly in English county cricket. Two years ago, in Sharjah, they had walked on to the pitch holding hands, like children on a nature trail. And at a reception the day before the match they were chatting and smiling over the chicken biryani. But so far as the papers and politicians were concerned, the historic tensions between these two countries gave the game a unique resonance. These days they only played each other in neutral venues, like the Gulf. Pakistan hadn't bowled a ball in India for nine years. In 1991, a planned tour was called off when those nice Shiv Sena zealots in Bombay (their symbol is that cheerful pictogram, the swastika) dug up the wicket at the Wankhede Stadium and poured petrol over it. Indeed, the Bangalore branch of the party had organized a protest march on the day of the game, but called it off after some of its spokesman were arrested earlier in the week. Australia's refusal to go to Sri Lanka had been greeted with narrow-eyed sneers in Karachi and Lahore, so it was a little ironic that Pakistan had themselves pulled out of games on similar grounds. 'One should not forget,' said Wasim Akram on the eve of the match, struggling to make people believe that this was not, for him and his players, a matter of ancient grudges, 'that we are great friends.' Waqar Younis insisted for the nth time that he was happy to be playing here. 'We are relaxed,' he said. 'It is India who are under pressure.'

It seems unfair, in a way, that relatively young sportsmen should have to shoulder such weighty diplomatic responsibilities. But cricket functions well as the forum for the playing out of wider antagonisms, and not just between these two great enemies. Pakistan's recent tour of Australia had been like a screen on which various national hostilities were projected. When Warne, May and Waugh accused Salim Malik of offering them that bribe, Pakistan handed the matter over to a leading judge, Fakhruddin Ebrahim, a former Governor of Sindh Province. The Australians refused to go to Pakistan to testify, although they said they would be willing to appear before a court in London. The insult to Pakistan's cricket captain was thus extended into a slur on the entire judicial system. When Malik was found not guilty, the players took the law into their own hands (cricket is supposed to be a byword for fair play, after all, almost a metaphor for natural justice). And what happened was remarkable. Pakistan had a terrible time in the first Test match in Brisbane: they dropped catch after catch (seven, in all); about the only person who clung on to one was, of course, Salim Malik. And, wouldn't you know it, he ripped the webbing between his fingers and had to have six stitches in his hand. When he didn't come out for a bat ('absent hurt'), the Australian press came to the inescapable conclusion that this proved it. The man had no bottle; he couldn't be trusted.

In the next match he did get a bat, and who should be bowling when he came in? Shane Warne. The courts had failed to lay down the law: now it was cricket's turn. Accuser and defendant faced each other over twenty-two yards of rolled earth, like gunslingers. In the Australian mythology, it was the corn-haired up-from-the-boondocks homeboy against the swarthy, worldly mafioso. Malik survived for three balls and then . . . Shane stopped play. The catch spooned to mid-on, and Malik was out for a humiliating duck. 'It showed,' said Warne afterwards, 'that there is justice in the game.' To the media it seemed to prove Warne's innocence – a guilty man, it implied, could not possibly have prevailed. Providence had weighed these two men in the scales and delivered its judgement.

Probably it was just as well that the case never came to law. Sport models itself on the legal system, with its courts and laws (unless it is the other way round); but it does not sit comfortably in a world of litigation. There had been talk of a libel action when the Australian umpire Darryl Hair kept no-balling Muralitharan on Sri Lanka's winter tour Down Under. The sum of $30 million was mentioned. It would have been neat: a legal action about an illegal action. And it wasn't so odd: if Hair's objections to Muralitharan's bowling turned out to be unfounded then he was guilty, in effect, of a serious libel – he'd accused a man of cheating, blackened his name, perhaps for ever, and jeopardized an honest career. Nothing came of it, legally. The bowler went to Hong Kong for extensive video analysis which pronounced him clean, and it would take a brave umpire to call him now.

But one day – you can bet on it – such a case will come to court.

There were several cases going through, already, the most prominent being the farcical libel action about racism and ball-tampering between Imran Khan, Allan Lamb and Ian Botham. There were going to be plenty more if the ICC didn't get a serious grip on what was and wasn't allowed. Ball-tampering, for instance, was a disastrous grey area. Some of it is permitted: bowlers are allowed to clean and shine the ball using spit and sweat, or rub their hands in the dust to dry their fingers. But they are not, as Atherton learned, allowed to put that dust in their pocket to save their backs. And they are certainly not supposed to scuff the ball deliberately. The whole ball-tampering controversy flowed from the brilliant Pakistani discovery that instead of shining one side of the ball to make it fly faster, and thus promote swing, you could achieve the same effect by roughing up the reverse side. Instead of making one side of the ball fly faster, you made the other side fly slower. Or you soaked the absorbent, non-shiny side in sweat to make it heavier. It shouldn't be hard to clarify which of these is permitted and which is banned; but the ICC cowers behind a blanket reference to 'altering the condition of the ball', which if it means anything ought to include rubbing the ball in your groin in the time-honoured manner.

It isn't really surprising that cricket is drifting into turbulent waters when it comes to the role and reach of its authorities. The ICC is only as powerful as the member nations want it to be, and they are proving reluctant to sacrifice too much of their own sovereignty to the other members, whom they do not always trust. This is a familiar political story. It is even possible to suggest that the decline in respect for the umpire exactly mirrors the modern world's declining faith in authority of all kinds – religious, legal or moral. Television has exposed the men in white coats as fallible. Perhaps cricket really was an anachronism, the product of a time when the umpire's decision (like the empire's) was final. The trouble is, this kind of conspiratorial fever leads to an equally dogmatic conviction that corruption lurks everywhere. Many of those who leapt to Muralitharan's defence did so because they assumed that this had to be one of those cases where a rich, white, developed nation was picking on a poor, dark member of the Third World. The idea that it was just an umpire making a bish got entirely lost. Perhaps it is better that such things don't get past the threat stage.

All of this was small beer beside the ramifications that seemed to bear down on this match in Bangalore. Victory for either side would vindicate their gods, their taboos, their diets, their territorial claims – the lot. Every gesture out on the pitch would carry a powerful symbolic charge. Who said cricket was only a job?

At the reception the visiting Pakistanis were all creases and smart clothes – as guests, it behoved them to make an effort. If they looked nervous, it might have been because a few of them had received phone calls saying they wouldn't get out of Bangalore alive if they won. India, the casual hosts, slouched through in T-shirts and jeans. Younis sipped orange juice. I'd seen him at a party in Karachi just before the game against England. Someone had asked Graham Thorpe how he was going to deal with his old Surrey teammate Waqar, and Thorpe joked: 'Get him castled over the next two days.' Alas, it didn't work. And he was in a serious mood now. There'd been quite a lot of talk about the wicket: we'd all watched them spreading grass cuttings over the surface and hosing them in to keep the pitch moist.

'I don't care what the wicket's like,' said Younis. 'All I know is I'm bloody well going to bowl on it.'

Wasim Akram was still hoping he'd be able to make it. 'I'll play if I'm fifty per cent,' he said. The trouble was, he could barely lift his arm.

Just then the Indians arrived.

'Hey, what's happened to Azhar?' said Akram. 'Look at the weight he's lost.'

Azharuddin came over for a handshake, and about thirty cameramen jumped out, flashing and popping. The captains ended up shaking hands for about five minutes, until everyone had the picture. It was all over the front pages the next day. In one of them I could spot myself in the background, gatecrashing a landmark moment and grinning like a game-show host.

Azharuddin was accompanied by an attentive bodyguard. There were those who didn't like having a Muslim captaining their team. Poor Azhar – he copped it from both sides. There had been trouble from Islamic sources when he was photographed signing Reeboks. His name (Mohammad) was far too sacred to be blazoned all over a sports shoe.

Everyone assumed that Tendulkar would lead the charge against Pakistan's bowling, but he took things carefully. Perhaps he felt he'd already used up his ration of good fortune for the tournament, or perhaps he was flinching at the size of the hopes riding on his shoulders. This was war by other means, and you could feel the wild urges pouring down from the steep stands – nothing could have been further from the old sense of the game as a pleasant palliative or balm. By a nice quirk of timing, Tendulkar had been born in 1972, the year televised cricket reached India, so he truly was a child of the new era. And if it was television that had carried the game into the great Indian hinterland beyond literacy, it was Tendulkar who had planted its flag out there. The tournament organizers reckoned that more than half a billion people would be watching this match on the box, enough to make it a major world event. The fact that this was merely half the population of the subcontinent was neither here nor there.

It might have been that Tendulkar was merely given a fright by Younis' first over. His run-up didn't carry quite the same demonic menace without the Karachi rebel yell to fill his sails, but it was still a rare thing: he came bounding in straight and fast, leaping and hurling himself high through the delivery. And the first ball might have been a wide, but the rest were anything but. The next three sprang high off the wicket, narrowly passing the shoulder of Sidhu's bat. The crowd made the kind of uneasy exhalations – *oooohhhhh* – you hear just before fireworks go off.

He was a strange figure, Sidhu, a Sikh, well-born, literate. He had a good record for India – a better one-day average than Tendulkar, come to that – and a year earlier had been one of the heroes of India's victory in the Asia Cup, the annual one-day tournament held in Sharjah: he scored eighty-four in the final against Sri Lanka. But he could never be sure of his place. Indeed, after the World Cup, when India toured England, he went home in a huff when he was dropped. The Benaud version was that he had 'picked up his bat and ball', but you had to sympathize with him. He had not been selected for the third one-day match against England, but no one told him. The first he knew about it was when he went into the changing room, started to put his pads on . . . and the others started laughing. Sidhu didn't see the funny side.

But that was all in the future. He has a stooping, reluctant air about him, but when he glanced Younis down through the slips for the first boundary of the match, and then added two more with similar uneasy slashes, the stadium shook. Still, no one could relax so long as Tendulkar was playing so cautiously. Eventually he punched Aquib Javed through the covers for four and the Tannoy blared out, 'Sachin's first boundary! After twenty-six balls!' It was the sort of voice used to praise someone who's done well in a school sports day. Well done, Sachin, here's a box of crayons for you.

The score rose smoothly, like the temperature. This was turning into a solid start. It was one of those games, and one of those atmospheres, where things could skid out of control fast, so a good foundation was exactly what India needed. What they didn't need was to have their concentration disturbed, so it was a bit worrying when Salim Malik ran in from the boundary complaining that he was being pelted with fruit – hardly a unique event in these parts. The umpires to'd and fro'd as oranges splatted on the grass, and up in the referee's gantry Raman Subba Row leaned down to hector the police chief. The press box was crammed with men in uniform (no wonder it was hard to get accreditation) enjoying the vantage point, which was indeed very fine, so long as you weren't behind a big pillar advertising 'high-grade pig-iron and ductile iron span pipes'. But Subba Row wasn't happy. He wanted the police to be out there crowd-controlling, not watching the cricket.

'I want them every ten yards, and get them to stay there! It's no use going and coming away again the whole time!'

The police chief nodded, murmured into his mobile phone, and sat down again.

The twelfth man ran on with a drink for Sidhu, and he shared it with Pakistan's wicket-keeper. The crowd seemed puzzled, as if the idea that the players didn't hate each other was a strange and difficult one. It was going to be a long, hot, draining day.

I had gone to the ground early and stood in a marquee watching Sri Lanka play England on television, though Faisalabad, the scene of the great Mike Gatting–Shakoor Rana stand-off, seemed awfully far away. It felt merely as if there was some minor game going on up north, involving one of the lesser nations (England). Also, no one was there. As it turned out, it hadn't been a very good idea to schedule two quarter-finals on the same day. No Pakistani in his right mind was going to go and watch England when he could stay at home and watch Waqar Younis on the telly. Even the streets fell silent for the day.

And oh dear: play *with* was more like it.

England began brightly. Atherton hit a couple of lovely cover drives, and after five overs he and Robin Smith had put on twenty-four, a nice crisp start. And then he was caught behind (cutting: the third time he'd been out to that shot in a fortnight) and the GAME OVER lights flashed. Hick, Smith and Thorpe were back in the pavilion before the hundred was up. DeFreitas was sent in early to rev things up, and it paid off: he scored sixty-seven fine attacking runs until he fell to a naughty lbw decision. But the rest flattered to deceive, except Reeve, whose enthusiastic late hitting carried England past 200. Down in Bangalore, Tony Greig was disbelieving. 'The strategy's all wrong,' he insisted. 'Look at the other teams. They're getting their best batsmen to play the shots; it's up to the others to support them. England seem to want their top batters to play the anchor role. It doesn't make sense.' This was a good point. In one-day cricket, England still had a vague feeling that you should *protect* the better batsmen, instead of sending them out up front. They still believed that it was up to the tail-enders to do the slogging. They crawled up to 235 eventually, a far better total than looked likely when the seventh wicket fell for 173. But the way Sri Lanka batted, a score like that would occupy them for only an hour or so.

The only cause for hope was that nerves might play a part. Sri Lanka didn't need to open the throttle, and that might be just as well for England. Low totals can induce paralysis in batting sides. The big question was, how would England approach the task? Gough had reportedly been practising his yorkers, which was good news. And there had been a lot of discussion in Karachi about how to bowl at these Sri Lankan opening batsmen. Atherton was wondering whether to give the new ball to Reeve, or perhaps even to the spinner, Illingworth.

That's what he plumped for. Afterwards, the press was unanimous in calling it a daft blunder, but I for one thought it was a bold and good decision. He knew, after all, how Sri Lanka were going to bat, and Jayasuriya and company were now well in the groove when it came to fast-medium seamers. It would have been criminal simply to march on in the same old way, and be mown down in the same old way. Opening with spin might just throw them off balance, for an over or two at least.

And it worked, sort of. Illingworth took a wicket in his first over, but twelve runs came from it as well – about par for these Sri Lankans. The really brilliant thing – easy to say now – would have been to remove Illingworth immediately. He'd done his job by taking the wicket, and Atherton could have withdrawn him now to attack from another flank (especially with two left-handers at the crease).

But before you knew it, Jayasuriya was, as they say, at it again, cutting and carving, driving and pulling like crazy. He showed what he thought of the spin-bowling ruse by clouting Illingworth over the leg side three times in his second over. When Gough came on to replace him he sent three more boundaries slapping into the fence. And you could call it slogging if you liked, but they looked like great shots from where I sat (over a thousand miles away). Peter Martin whistled a few between bat and pad, but the moment he gave Jayasuriya a bit of room the ball was smashed high over midwicket. It took him only twenty-eight balls to reach sixty-eight. DeFreitas came on for a bowl and was hit for twenty-two off his first over: six, four, six, two, four. 'I've run out of things to say,' said Boycott. Was anyone getting that in writing? England had taken fifty-nine from the first fifteen overs, the key phase of this new incarnation of cricket. Sri Lanka scored 121. Ten overs later, they had 193. Jayasuriya made eighty-four off just forty-three balls. By the end they weren't even trying. Tillekeratne patted back a couple of maidens, just for the hell of it. It was as bad a beating as you could hope to receive. Talk about flashing blades: from an England point of view, it was like walking into a combine harvester. Jayasuriya's was one fantastic innings. In just over an hour he hit three sixes, thirteen fours, and just three singles. Coaching-manual types might try to point out that most of those boundaries (ten of the fours, for instance) were struck to the leg-side fence, but that only emphasized how well he played. He just swung the bat at anything straight or pitched-up, and away it went. It was superb.

Afterwards, Atherton admitted that Jayasuriya's innings was something else, but was a touch sniffy as well, implying it was nothing great, just lucky. This was not a very generous reaction: it looked as though he was perversely determined not to be impressed. It recalled that comic sketch where the boys are playing cricket with the girls, and finally, reluctantly, agree to give the girls a bat. They whack the ball all over the place. 'Well,' says the bowler, a picture of vexed, crestfallen pride, 'of *course* you hit it for six if you hold the bat like *that*.' Jayasuriya had indeed been lucky, in a way. He might well have been bowled a couple of times early on. But the sheer bravura of the thing, the whole conception of the innings . . . It was wonderful.

In the build-up to the game, the main concern of the papers had been the worry over Corky's knee. It was well founded: Cork didn't play in the quarter-final. England's best bowler had crippled himself playing all those games we hadn't needed to win. Was this a calculated risk that went wrong, or a triumph of bad planning? No prizes for getting that one right. Actually, it seemed to me that you have to give Atherton credit for trying: he'd opened with a spinner, promoted DeFreitas up the order and let him bowl off-spin too. It wasn't true to say that he had no ideas. But nothing worked. The team had too little faith in itself, and they had come up against a bunch of cricketers enjoying the hottest streak of their lives.

What would the papers say? They'd been holding back during the league games, knowing that a single turn-up could make them look silly. But now they gave it both barrels:

ENGLISH CRICKET IS DYING.

NIGHT AT THE END OF THE TUNNEL.

HAPLESS, HELPLESS, HUMILIATED.

LIKE TAKING KANDY FROM A BABY.

R.I.P. ENGLISH CRICKET.

NO SPINE, NO GUTS, NO GOOD.

It had been obvious all along that England were way off the pace out here. So this defeat was bound to trigger an almighty burst of what's-wrong-with-English-cricket breastbeating. But I clung to the thought that these weren't bad players. We lacked a really vicious fast bowler, and we hadn't seen an attacking spinner for years. But I still believed that this team could, in the right atmosphere, have thrived. It was everything else that was wrong.

Would anything happen? Would anything change? There was a lot of talk about the working party that had been set up to examine the subject, but the odd thing was, nearly everyone involved – players, commentators, reporters, camp followers – agreed about what was required: major surgery on our domestic structure. Taking a first-team squad of twenty or so players out of county cricket and putting them under contract to the international board would be a good first step, but we really needed a whole new level of cricket between the counties and the national side, a high-level competition for the best players that would allow them to play more combative games, and fewer of them. Essentially – whether it was based on regions or cities – we were talking about a six-zone championship, a mouthwatering prospect, especially if it included overseas players. Consider the teams that would be created.

London (Middlesex, Essex and Surrey) could be a crack side, Alec Stewart, Alistair Brown, Nasser Hussein, Graham Thorpe, Mark Ramprakash, Stuart Law, Keith Brown, Chris Lewis, Angus Fraser, Phil Tufnell and Mark Ilott, with some useful old hands (Gooch, Gatting) waiting in the wings and some promising young guns (Mark Butcher, Alex Tudor) knocking on the door as well.

It would be fun to see this team play the North (Durham, Lancashire and Yorkshire): Mike Atherton, David Byas, Jason Gallian, John Crawley, Michael Bevan, Craig White, Richard Blakey, Darren Gough, Peter Martin, Simon Brown and Richard Stemp.

Or how about the West Midlands (Worcester, Warwick and Derbyshire)? Nick Knight, Dominic Ostler, Graeme Hick, Kim Barnett, Jimmy Adams, Keith Piper, Dominic Cork, Philip DeFreitas, Neil Smith, Richard Illingworth and Devon Malcolm.

And so on. These teams would play each other twice, home and away (making it a ten-match season, instead of seventeen) as well as a one-day competition. They could also play the touring sides, which would produce games rather more urgent than the festival-atmosphere runarounds that prevail today.

Of course it is not clear that arbitrary conglomerations like these could swiftly command the sort of allegiances that still drive county cricket. It is one thing to be a Somerset loyalist, quite another to be a diehard West Zone man. So if these new zones were to work, then they, and not the counties, would need to receive the lion's share of the TCCB's television money. They would employ fourteen or so cricketers on, probably, fairly short contracts, lasting one or two years. County cricket, as it exists today, would have its head in the noose: it would become, in effect, minor county cricket. Probably it would have to turn semi-professional.

That would undoubtedly be a sad day. A lot of fine memories would be cremated, and a lot of players would lose their jobs, which makes it a cruel thing even to suggest. Those six zones would employ only about eighty players, as against the 400-plus presently engaged on county payrolls. But the manner of this latest set of defeats meant that something along these lines perhaps needed to happen. It would bring England into line with the rest of the world, where top players are employed by the national cricket boards, and the rest fudge through with sport-friendly part-time jobs in banks, airlines, tourist boards and so on. Even in Australia there are only thirty or so full-time cricketers. The rest get by, and dream.

It sounds hysterical to suggest that it matters whether or not England win a cricket match, but the truth is that in this media-struck age a successful international team is the principal, possibly the lone guarantor of the sport's future as a popular fact of life. 'If our team keeps going the way it has,' Dennis Silk said, 'then our game will die. All you'll have left is village cricket and club cricket.' This was the former headmaster of Radley talking, not some doomy tabloid gink out to cause a sensation. It really was time for a change.

One nice thing about this Sri Lankan team, it turned out, was that it was the product of a lot of effort and planning. In England we tend to assume that Sri Lankans must by definition be 'inexperienced', since they so rarely play against us; but Jayasuriya had played 100 one-day internationals – as many as Atherton, Hick and Thorpe combined. They had come a long way since the World Cup of 1983 in England, when six of their team were still schoolboys. England didn't seem to want to play them, and it was starting to become clear why. A year and a bit ago India, Pakistan and Australia had visited Sri Lanka for a one-day tournament, the Singer Cup, and Sri Lanka beat them all. Since then they had successfully toured Pakistan, won the Champions Trophy in Sharjah, and lost in the final of the World Series down in Australia. There was a well-publicized project to make Sri Lanka the 'Best Cricket Nation' by the year 2000. They were vivacious – anyone could see that – but also battle-hardened.

Coming into the tournament their coach Dav Whatmore, the man who had once played for Australia himself, said an interesting thing. 'We've been playing a lot of cricket since late September last year,' he pointed out. 'So the standards of fitness have gone down.'

Gone down? To English ears, this was a new idea, that the more you played the less fit you became. Maybe it explained all those injuries . . . Whatmore was part of the new generation of coaches, the sort that can say the word 'nutritionist' without blushing or feeling like a wimp. He insisted that his players swim every day, especially after training. He had done an amazing job with these Sri Lankans, and he attributed all of it to what he had learned at the Victorian Institute of Sport.

So did we need one of these élite academies for the best young cricketers? There were lots of pros and cons, and in England the cons usually prevailed. But could it hurt? It certainly seemed to have done wonders for Australia: Shane Warne, Michael Slater and Co. had come bursting out of the special cricket school set up under the stewardship of Rodney Marsh. India had set up a similar academy in Madras, with a particular emphasis on the hunt for fast bowlers, and it had been a striking success. Srinath and Prasad had come to the fore, and were now the top bowlers in the country. Such institutions guarantee nothing; and the Madras Academy had actually turned down Tendulkar. But even if they are thought of merely as seed money, venture capital scattered on the quiet waters of cricket, they have some value. Every now and then, a big fish will swim into their net. And the Australian academy costs only £400,000 per year, which is a modest enough investment in the nation's emotional life. Two years ago, the English counties had voted sixteen to two in favour of such a scheme, in theory. But a year later, when a concrete proposal landed on the table, they turned round and voted against it. *Plus ça change.*

With this in mind, I had been to see the Pace Academy in Gwalior after India's match against the West Indies. The declared aim was simple: 'The preparation of world-class fast bowlers and cricketers by the year 2000. To spot potential and train scientifically to achieve excellence in cricket.' So far the school's record was good: several of the students were already playing for India Under Sixteens and Under Nineteens.

The science made you gulp. There were biochemical assessments – blood sugar, cholesterol, neutrophils, nasophils, lymphocytes, monocytes, bile, albumen and so on – as well as physiological ones. All the cricket skills were broken down into constituent parts. For bowling the focus was on grip, run-up, jump, landing, delivery and follow-through. Each of these was broken down another notch. The run-up, for instance: first five strides, last three strides. The moment of delivery itself was deconstructed as follows: hands, shoulders, head, feet, leg action, hip rotation, trunk movement, arm action, pivot, release. It was all very exact. Diet and exercise was tailored to individual needs, on the simple theory that fast bowlers and opening batsmen need different muscles.

It goes without saying that there was a big stress on general fitness: agility, endurance, speed. But there was also a painstaking attention to psychological matters. These were divided into the following headings:

positive attitude, aggressiveness, cool mind, motivation, learning, group dynamics, no fear, fighting spirit, team spirit, anxiety, interest in the game, discipline, conviction, habits, sincerity, nobleness.

'Nobleness?' I almost laughed. 'Sincerity?' These were words you did not often hear in English cricket circles. Sincerity – used to play for Jamaica, didn't he? Great big bastard, bowled like the wind. Yeah, that's him – a good 'un.

'Yes,' said the director. 'You know. Respectfulness. You should respect others. You should keep your head down, let the wind blow over you. People should accept you as a gentleman, because that's what cricket is.'

This was why the students underwent anxiety tests, with questions that you simply couldn't ask at Old Trafford or the Oval. Are your children loving and disciplined? Do you have a relative you can turn to in need? Do you feel superior to others? Can you identify protein, carbohydrate and fat? Can you communicate with your wife without malice?

This was poignant. These old values we now titter at in England remained a powerful part of cricket's appeal in India (and in the West Indies too). They sounded quaint, but represented a touching marriage between the new (biochemistry) and the old (traditional courtesies). The working day started at 5.30 a.m.

Did our much-vaunted professionals take this amount of trouble? I didn't think so. Many of our leading lights would call this sort of thing 'mumbo-jumbo'.

Here in Bangalore, I must say, the future of English cricket felt like a side issue. Even as the reporters up in Pakistan were preparing their obituaries, the tournament was coming dramatically to life. This sunny city, full of flowers and computer programmers, was where the hot heart of world cricket was beating.

Tendulkar was still setting himself for a big one: he wasn't trying anything fancy. His score moved methodically up to thirty-one, and Pakistan's fans must have been biting their nails. And then he dragged one on to his stumps and was bowled. Perhaps all-out attack suited him better. It would not, for many batsmen, have been considered a failure, but the crowd was stunned. For a few moments you could almost hear yourself think. But India kept plodding on. Sidhu, Manjrekar, and Azharuddin played some handsome shots. For their part, Pakistan kept pegging them back. Azharuddin fell to a blinding leap of a catch by Rashid Latif behind the wicket, when he tried to steer the ball fine through the slips; Kambli overreached himself against Mushtaq Ahmed and was bowled. So when Waqar Younis came back at the end of the innings, India were some way short of a really challenging score. With four overs to go they had 230, and up to this point Waqar had bowled eight overs for twenty-seven runs. He was a specialist in the closing overs. It didn't look as though India would get more than 250.

Ajay Jadeja promptly shook the bit out of his mouth. He swatted a short one away for four behind square, then stepped back and cross-batted a huge six over the bowler's head. A perfect inswinging yorker went slicing off the inside edge for four more. Waqar's last two overs went for forty runs. The ball flew high and wide and landed in the cheering masses on all sides. The innings had needed a shot in the arm, but Jadeja had given it an overdose. And if the runs were useful, the symbolic gain was even greater. The cork flew out with a pop. All that careful, inhibited batting expanded in a sunny rush. Banners waved: 'Pak it in!'

More to the point, in collaring Waqar, Jadeja was taming Pakistan's most expensive missile. It was a dynamic and decisive few minutes. Waqar, fuming, ran in harder and faster. He had missed out on Pakistan's triumph in 1992, and had made no secret of his desire for one of those nice Cup winner's villas, for the cars and jewels that seemed to shower on the victorious team – but the ball simply flew higher and further. The crowd started throwing bottles at Salim Malik, fielding on the boundary. When they threw one at Miandad, he booted it off with a testy flourish. Jadeja himself went over and knelt down, making beseeching gestures, imploring the crowd to stop.

India finished on 287 – a mountain for Pakistan to climb. 'Young Genius Sachin With a Magic Stick,' shouted the banners. 'Old Man Javed With His Walking Stick.' This sort of jingoism seems dim and unattractive, but a therapist might say that it was merely a safety valve, a licensed and harmless form of inter-nation jeering.

Not that it was over yet (another reason to wave those banners – you never know when you'll get another chance). Perhaps Pakistan would do a Sri Lanka. Sohail and Anwar certainly seemed in the mood. On what was plainly a decent wicket for batting, they climbed into the opening overs. Saeed Anwar, one of six former captains in the team, drilled Kumble for a high six over midwicket and then, when a fielder crossed over to the leg side, stepped back and scythed the ball through the depleted covers for four. After just ten overs Pakistan were eighty-four for nought, and if they could have drawn breath at that point, they might have realized that they virtually had the match won. From here on they needed 200 off forty overs with all their wickets standing, as straightforward a proposition as you could wish for: they no longer needed to go mad. But it is hard to stop when your eyes are rolling. Anwar and Sohail both died slogging, and India closed in.

Sohail's dismissal was the one. He lashed Venkatesh Prasad for four and couldn't resist wagging his finger at him – Urdu for 'Get lost'. They glared at each other. The very next ball, Sohail went for an even bigger one and was bowled – stupid, stupid, stupid. Prasad permitted himself a few choice words of farewell. Sohail stopped, and for an instant it looked as if the pair of them would be wrestling on the grass any minute. But the umpires stepped in smartly and talked them out of it. Sohail slunk back to the dressing room. Wasim Akram had failed to beat his injury – he had been given two pain-killing injections that morning, but it was no good – so Sohail was captain for the day. He, of all people, should have kept his head. It was a hint that Pakistan might be too hot under the collar to pull off this run-chase: they didn't merely want to win, they wanted to smash this total to bits.

It was not very wise. But it was very exciting. Inch by inch Pakistan fell behind the required rate. Javed Miandad couldn't find the middle of the bat, and was no longer the sharp scamperer of singles he once had been. The target slowly receded into the distance, and 55,000 fans cheered every dot ball. In Pakistan they weren't giving up. Miandad had delivered the goods before, that time in Sharjah when he hit the last ball for six and was – rumour had it – given an awful lot of nice presents by grateful, patriotic gamblers whose bacon he had saved. But that was ten years ago. This time, off the last over they needed forty-one. And it didn't matter how many prayers were winging their way from Karachi and Lahore, that wasn't on. Javed's opponents had been saying for years that he had some good friends in the Pakistani umpiring community, but in this, his farewell to cricket, the television replay was beady-eyed. The old wizard leaned on his bat while the third umpire deliberated before flashing a red light across the stadium. The crowd, it is fair to say, was not sorry to see the back of him.

Bangalore erupted in a blaze of fireworks and traffic. As in Gwalior, people lit improvised torches and let them flare into the night. The final balls were delivered in a weird orange glow – or, as the paper put it next morning, a 'celestial atmosphere . . . a mirthquake'.

Outside the ground, someone stopped and offered me a ride on their motorbike, so I climbed on and we wove through the blaring cars and trucks, all full of waving arms and splashes of colour like some raucous coral reef. During the day the roads had been empty. One group of French tourists, indifferent to the cricket, strolled the broad thoroughfares and told a reporter that they were struck by what a *peaceful* city this was. Not any more. Gaggles of people ran down the middle of busy roads, blowing whistles, letting off firecrackers and giving away sweets in scenes reproduced in cities all over India. In Patna, thousands of people gathered at the Hanuman Temple to give rowdy thanks. Bangalore, in contrast, is a city of pubs, which promptly declared the sixty minutes till midnight a happy hour. The streets filled up fast with what the papers like to call 'drunken revellers' or 'miscreants'.

There was, I discovered, a quick way to ingratiate yourself with these happy people. All you had to do, in a slightly ironic way, was raise a fist and say, 'England! England!' They all thought that was the funniest thing ever. They knew you had to be joking.

In Calcutta, the *Telegraph* didn't beat around the bush. 'India Forces Pakistan to Surrender,' declared the front page. 'India Explodes in Joy,' said the *Times*. Down below, in a box near the corner, a box said: 'The news, other than cricket.'

Up in Pakistan, they couldn't believe it. One man, according to the papers, shot his television set, then himself, missed and was admitted to a hospital in Mardan with severe wounds. This turned out to be untrue – the hospital came forward to protest that no such person had been admitted. But the dismay was real enough. 'A wave of grief,' said the newspaper *Al-Akbar*, 'has swept the country. We have lost our global honour.' People were quick to assume that their team had lost on purpose: what other reason could there be? There were questions in Parliament about the conduct of the team and captain. Wasim Akram was pilloried for not playing. One holy man put the defeat down to the fact that the country had a female prime minister (he obviously hadn't noticed that Sri Lanka did as well); another said it was all because of the 'obscene' Western music they kept playing on the television, with all those boys and girls – ugh!

– dancing. 'This,' said Qazi Hussain Ahmed, leader of the fundamentalist Jamaat-e-Islami party, 'is a Zionist–Hindu conspiracy to destroy the character of our youth.' He then issued a *fatwa* against anyone who watched the offending TV shows.

At Lahore airport, a crowd gathered to welcome the team home with jeers and eggs. The pilot, sensing trouble, diverted to Karachi, and the players slunk away unannounced. A big poster of Sohail was smeared with mud. And one furious fan, a neighbour of Akram, filed a writ claiming that the defeat was the result of criminal negligence by the non-playing captain. Accepting the writ, the Lahore High Court judge said: 'Corruption has destroyed cricket in Pakistan.'

'I do not deserve this,' said Wasim. 'I have received death threats and my family is getting abusive phone calls. I have always played my best for Pakistan. I am ready to swear on the Koran that I am not involved in betting.'

The newspapers struggled to report on the delight over the border, but words failed them. 'India,' said the sad headline in the *Muslim*, 'Plunges Into Euphoria.' For some people this was literally true. In Midnapore, a seventy-two-year-old social worker had a heart attack when Rashid Latif started hitting boundaries at the end, giving Pakistan a late flicker of hope. And in Agartala a retired clerk watched Aamir Sohail and Saeed Anwar set off like trains, said, 'We have to win at any cost,' and died.

As luck would have it, the former Test cricketer Qasim Omar chose this day to confess to his part in several bribery scams. He appeared on Australian television to explain how he had often been paid large sums to give his wicket away, usually for a large score when he was approaching a record of some sort. The bet would be that he wouldn't break it. 'It didn't take me long, after being picked for Pakistan,' he said, 'to realize that certain Test players were deliberately throwing their wickets away for big money from bookies. Bowlers were just as bad. They deliberately gave runs away with a mix of long hops and full tosses. I was the middleman, the Mr Fixit. The bookies were everywhere, and it's the same today.'

What with one thing and another, it hadn't been a very bright day for Pakistani cricket.

Certainly, some of the glee at India's victory was fuelled by winning bets. Bangalore's bookmakers made Pakistan favourites, based on the fact that they had beaten India twenty-seven times in one-day matches, and lost only twelve. And the best estimates were that something like £10 million was riding on the outcome of this match. One has to treat figures like this with at least a handful of salt, since there's nothing official about them. One newspaper report insisted excitedly that up to £80 million had been wagered. But it all added to the swirl of excitement surrounding the match. The night air carried the faint stink of big money.

The other aspect of the hysteria was the sheer rarity-value of this match. If only these two countries could play each other all the time so that they grew used to winning a few, losing a few . . . But there didn't seem to be much chance of that. The frightening thought now was: what on earth would happen if India reached the final, and had to go to Lahore?

They'd have to beat Sri Lanka first. Good luck to them.

— 10 —

OH, CALCUTTA!

India vs Sri Lanka

All roads led now to Calcutta. The game in Bangalore might have felt like a final, but there was plenty more cricket in this tournament. For a start, there were the other two quarter-finals to be resolved. I flew to Madras to see Australia take on New Zealand. We sat at trestle tables at the pavilion end, with our notebooks on white table-cloths. I had played here once, on a newspaper tour years before. That day, a dozen or so curious passers-by wandered in and watched – quite a boisterous crowd, by our standards. Today, however, there were 40,000 people crammed into this nasty-smelling crater by the sea. It was a telling tribute to the power of cricket in these parts. And they were having a party.

On the television propped in front of us we could see South Africa playing the West Indies up in Karachi. It was weird. You watched Curtly Ambrose running in to bowl, heard the low rumble of the Karachi crowd, lifted your eyes, and there was Shane Warne tweaking the ball through the humid air of Madras.

The Kiwis scored 290, which was going to take a hell of a lot of getting. Shane Warne looked a little out of sorts, but that might have been because the New Zealanders attacked him hard. For Australia the one consolation was that if a low-ranking all-rounder like Chris Harris could get a century, then the wicket must be an absolute belter. So it proved: Mark Waugh scored another faultless 100 and Australia cruised in. That makes it sound boring, which it was, in a way: almost too good to be true. Waugh seemed to know where the ball was going to be before it was bowled, and just helped it on its way. He even managed to look cool in the terrific Madras heat, although if you looked through binoculars you could see sweat dripping from the peak of his helmet. His brother came in and punched out a rapid fifty to take the side into the semi-finals. When he stroked the winning runs, he didn't even look to see where the ball had gone or pause to savour the moment. He just tapped the ball away and marched off.

On television there was more. Lara's reported remarks about hating the thought of losing to South Africa had made headlines everywhere, and though, of course, he insisted he had been misquoted, the incident had certainly put him under a painful load of extra pressure. Woolmer had been both clear and tactful about it. He could afford to be calm. South Africa had won all five group matches in fine style; they looked sharp and strong. The only problem was they had never, at any point, been really up against it. No one knew how they would do when the going got tough.

But it wasn't only South Africa that Lara had offended. According to the article in *Outlook*, Lara had slagged off his own team as well. 'Some of the guys don't even talk to each other,' he'd said (allegedly) in that fateful dressing-room scene. 'You know, if you have a good team but a bad management you can maybe get along. But if you have a bad team and a bad management you really get f****d. I think it was really stupid of our board not to go to Sri Lanka. But it's the board that makes the decision, not us.'

So what did Lara go and do? He only went out and scored the second-fastest century in the history of the World Cup, that's all. From the moment he took guard he was at his flashing, debonair best. Courtney Browne opened the batting and set a brisk tone, with twenty-six in just eighteen balls, but from then on it was all Lara. He literally cut loose: over half of his sixteen boundaries came behind square on the offside. Sometimes he seemed to be toying with the fielder down there, moving him one way, then the other, and then back again. Hansie Cronje brought Pat Symcox into the attack, a neat enough idea (off-spin turning away from the left-hander), but Lara hit him for five fours in a single over. He scored a century in eighty-four balls, one ball outside Clive Lloyd's record-breaking 100 in the first World Cup final, in 1975.

But, these days, the West Indies were a bit like England. When Lara was out for 111, there were still more than ten overs left, and with the score on 214, they were looking at a total in the region of 300. But after his heroics in the game against Australia, Richardson seemed gridlocked, unable to rotate the strike or find the gaps. Keith

Arthurton picked up a single, bringing his World Cup total to two, and that was about it until Ambrose long-handled a few at the very end. The West Indies scored only forty-eight in their last ten overs, enough to make it interesting, but nothing to write home about. South Africa had been set a similar target by Pakistan, and they cantered all the way.

Everyone had been hoping to see a left-arm spinner called Adams make a big impact on this tournament, and now he did. But it wasn't Paul, the coloured boy from the Cape. In the middle of the South African innings Jimmy Adams took the ball, shuffled in and took three top wickets – Hudson for fifty-four, Cullinan for sixty-nine and Cronje for forty. At 185 for three, with Cronje and Rhodes running hard singles, you'd have bet your shirt on South Africa, but by the time the 200 came up they were seven wickets down. A middle-order collapse! A good start thrown away! A dropped catch by Jonty Rhodes! These South Africans were human, after all. They fell nineteen runs short.

You had to feel sorry for them. They hadn't put a foot wrong in the whole tournament, until the last hour or so. And it was bad luck running into Lara in that sort of mood. The West Indies would go through to meet Australia in an all-refusenik semi-final. What a pity they couldn't switch it to Sri Lanka, for old times' sake.

It also meant that all four semi-finals had come from the same group. England had been stuffed by the second division.

I didn't stay in Madras for very long. The first quarter-finals had been on Saturday; this second pair was on Monday, and the semis were on Wednesday; so there was no hanging about. There was time, however, for me to be reminded of a familiar truth about the media. On the flight to Calcutta, each seat had a newspaper folded into the back pocket. I opened mine with curiosity, scanning the matrimonials page where suitable boys and girls offered themselves as husbands and wives. A convent-educated, beautiful, fair Punjabi Hindu girl sought an alliance with a tall, handsome, well-settled businessman with sound family background. An exceptionally beautiful, charming, well-travelled five foot five 'film-star personality', with an MA and MBA from America, and from a highly cultured, respectable and rich Bombay family, was looking for a very handsome industrialist or a highly paid professional under thirty-nine. A twenty-seven-year-old Jain boy, handicapped in both legs and working for an insurance company, wanted 'any broadminded girl, caste no bar'. I scanned the columns, desperately seeking a reference to cricket. But even in India a love of cricket is not regarded as a marital advantage.

I turned the page, and saw with a shock my own name – right in the middle of the match report. What on earth . . . ?

This is what it said:

> Now that England are out of the Cup, the English scribes were here for the quarters. It was really refreshing to talk to an English journo who is not whining or complaining. Robert Winder, cricket correspondent of the *Independent*, though critical of the 'stupid format and hectic schedule', was thoroughly impressed by the arrangements Pilcom have made for the Cup. 'The stadia have got a facelift and media facilities are far removed from the Neanderthal age communication facilities which we had to put up with not so long ago,' he says.
>
> He adds that the telecom facilities in Pakistan is better than what it is in India and stadia too are better off. 'It is ironic then not to see people in the stadium,' Winder says wryly. On the fall in the standards of English cricket he says, 'We have no talent, our cupboard is bereft of players of high calibre.' He felt heads were bound to roll after the English fiasco. Seeing two young Indians bowling and fielding with élan and efficiency at the nets against the Aussies, Winder said wistfully, 'Wish they were English.'

Honestly! Journalists! It was especially odd, since no one had even interviewed me, so far as I was aware. Of *course* – I had chatted away to several of the Indian reporters sitting near me in the press area. It must have been one of them. But what can I say about those quotations? My views on Neanderthal age telecommunications facilities and bereft cupboards need, I suppose, no introduction, but it was a surprise to see myself having such strong opinions on how they had improved over the years, since this was my first visit. I did remember saying to someone, when I saw Australia's twelfth man Michael Slater warming up, that it was a sign of how good the Aussies must be if they could leave out such a brilliant player, but that was a far cry from gazing 'wistfully' at the boys in the nets. There weren't any nets, anyway.

Oh, well. This was what it was like for the players, I guess. I'd seen it happen a thousand times, even in the context of our own scrupulous and attentive media. I'd almost certainly been guilty of similar myself – hastily stringing a few overheard phrases into something half coherent and phoning them over. At the end of the South Africa tour, for instance, when Atherton had sat down with a group of reporters to deliver his end-of-term report. Thorpe? Very important player for us, hadn't been quite at his best. Russell? A brilliant tour, gone from strength to strength, real bouncy character, etc. Cork? Amazing bowler, would walk into any side at the moment, batting has perhaps suffered from the amount of bowling he's done, but still a heroic effort. Hick? Unlucky more than once, kept nearly dominating. And so on.

When he left, the tabloids went into their little huddle to make sure they agreed what the storyline was. It makes life so much easier if everyone can have the same World Exclusive, otherwise head office will be on the phone in the middle of the night demanding their own version of whatever the other papers have got. The correspondents in the field often cut out the middleman, and save themselves a panic, by sorting out in advance what the day's news is.

They flipped through their notes. Now, what was the story? Thorpe not at his best? They thought about that, tried a few 'Pull your finger out, Thorpey!' headlines on for size. But nah, too boring.

'Here we go, here we go,' said someone, rereading the bit about Dominic Cork. 'Corky's not an all-rounder. There.' The others nodded. That sounded good. Several things clicked into place at once. The hunt for the all-rounder – the new Botham – had been on ever since the old Botham hung up his boots (or chucked them out of the window). And Atherton had already said that the difference between the two sides in South Africa was Brian McMillan, the home side's fast-bowling strokeplayer. Cork's failure to be an all-rounder would fit the bill admirably. The tabloids like to find one thing, preferably a person, to blame when things go wrong. It was a bit cute to single out England's best bowler, the man who had revitalized this team. But that's journalism for you.

I thought back, too, to the stories about Brian Lara slagging off the South Africans. It's perfectly possible that he said all that stuff. Maybe the reporter was – pardon my language – a buffoon. Wes Hall for one had called him a 'pusillanimous humbug'.

Still, who was I to complain? I was refreshing . . . wry . . . wistful. What more could anyone want?

There were a couple of TCCB marketing men on the flight to Calcutta, out here on a scouting mission. One had walked round the ground at Madras writing down the names of potential advertisers. It didn't seem a very high-profile approach. Perhaps they didn't realize that the finances of the World Cup had gone through the roof in the last few weeks. Pilcom had sold the game harder and more successfully than ever before. The first World Cup was sponsored by Prudential for £100,000, and ticket sales generated double that. By the time of the fifth World Cup in Australia in 1992, the tournament was grossing £6 million. Suddenly, that looked like peanuts. Pilcom had earned £10 million by selling the television rights to Mark Mascarenhas, £8 million from the title sponsor and masses more from subsidiary sponsors such as Coca-Cola (who chipped in £2.5 million). Then there was stadium advertising (those billboards around the boundary cost a cool £40,000 each) and, of course, the box office. The forthcoming semi-final would pull 110,000 people into Eden Gardens, netting, very roughly, another million in ticket sales.

Along with all this money-making went a straightforward drive to spread the game or, in the new parlance, to expand the market. As the final approached, word came through that Iran was seeking membership of the ICC.

'There's been a cricketing revolution,' said the head of Pakistan's cricket board, Arif Abbasi. 'And we need to adjust to a new level of income. From now on the World Cup is going to come under the jurisdiction of the ICC, but we have to understand what this means. The ICC is a company, and the World Cup is a very valuable property. The tournament will rotate from country to country, but rotation has to be accompanied by financial guarantees, by certain minimum standards. The members won't accept less. I certainly won't. In the last World Cup the title sponsorship was five million dollars. This time it was ten million. And this time there were many co-sponsors. There's been a huge jump, and there's no going back. This is the strongest force on earth. If I were England I'd be talking to Pepsi right now.'

That wasn't a bad idea. The unofficial cola might enjoy going legitimate.

* * *

At Eden Gardens Azharuddin won the toss and this time decided to bowl first. After the victory in Bangalore he had said: 'I really wanted to chase today, but everyone wanted to bat, and it turned out to be the right choice.' This seemed like good captaincy to me, although in England it might have been thought craven. Who was 'everyone'? Surely it was the captain's job to stand up and be counted, not just go with the flow. But if the bulk of the team wants to bat, hell, let them. You're not going to have much joy chasing if most of your batsmen think it was a damn fool idea in the first place. Just look at the West Indies against Kenya.

Still, deciding to field first is always fraught with risk. And you couldn't help feeling that on this of all days it was motivated by fear of what Sri Lanka's batting could do. 'One step to go,' Ranatunga had said before the match. 'We're thinking of fielding first.' Everyone knew that the Lankans loved to chase: no target seemed beyond them. Perhaps, in a way, Azharuddin was chickening out.

Eden Gardens was full, which doesn't quite describe what it was like. It is one of the great cricket grounds of the world, and the reason is simple: it is huge. It can swallow in a single gulp the entire attendance of a five-day Test match at Lord's. If you took a full-house at Headingley and dropped it in here, the place would feel empty. The sight of the 120,000 crowd filing into the cavernous terraces was remarkable. From high up in the stadium, you could see plumes of dust rising from the columns of cricket fans as they approached. Eden Gardens is set in the middle of spacious dry meadows, and the organizers had surrounded the stadium with wooden railings to channel people into the stadium. It looked like a racetrack, and the stream of people shuffling this way looked for all the world like an army on the march. Somewhere out there – I had passed it on my way in – was a cricket net with a tank in it. The stadium itself had a ceremonial feel: red and white pennants hung from the roof. It felt like a medieval tournament (except that these fluttering awnings were a giant cigarette advert, and Sir Lancelot was, so far as I know, a non-smoker). No one knew whether the stands were strong enough. Ever since the opening ceremony they had been quarrelling about safety certificates.

There were rumours that rats had chewed through the cable leading to the stump camera, which turned out not to be true. There were reports that India, banking on victory, were offering Pakistan $4 million to move the final away from Lahore, where this Indian team, it need hardly be said, would not be welcomed with open arms.

We all stood by for another whirlwind start: here came the mighty openers, Jayasuriya and Kaluwitharan. They were escorted to the pitch by two paramilitary machine-gunners with chic black bandannas. And they were as explosive as ever, though not in the way they had hoped. Within four balls, both of them were out, caught on the deep third man boundary. A hundred thousand people screamed in unison: you had to put your hands over your ears.

One of the myths about Indian cricket crowds is that they are the voice of the great unwashed millions. In fact, of course, the unwashed millions can't afford tickets. By English standards they are not expensive: £10 will get you a place in the shade. But touts had driven up prices ten-fold, and, in any case, only a tiny proportion of the box office was open to the general public. Most of the tickets were distributed through cricket associations and official channels. This was the middle class in full cry.

It was obvious that Sri Lanka had blown it. They had no option but to take a deep breath, cut their losses and start again. But Aravinda De Silva had other ideas. He drove and cut as if there was no tomorrow, always with striking elegance. It never looked as if he was forcing the pace. At one point Azharuddin reinforced the covers, and De Silva leaned out and fetched the ball high to leg, almost falling over as he did so. It was as if those first three balls hadn't happened. He didn't blink when Gurusinha was out as well, pulling Srinath straight to mid-on. He just carried on hitting silky boundaries. He scored fifty-seven out of Sri Lanka's first sixty-seven runs, in just eleven overs. It was a one-man, six-an-over fiesta, and it was keeping the islanders in the game.

Eventually he found someone to bat with. Roshan Mahanama is a Test-match opener, but he had hardly been involved in the World Cup thus far. Now, he rose to the occasion, deflecting the ball fine and giving De Silva the strike. When he nudged the off-spinner, Kapoor, off his pads, Boycott told the television audience that the bowler ought to be aiming *outside* the off stump, turning the ball in to the batsman. So Kapoor gave it a try, and Mahanama stepped back and cut him for four through gully. By the time De Silva was bowled by Kumble for sixty-seven, Sri Lanka were back on track: they could consolidate their gripping start. Where De Silva had offered dizzy freedom, Mahanama offered guts. He was dehydrated and had cramp, and no wonder: it was over a hundred degrees out there. Eventually he collapsed and was lugged off, but not before he had compiled an effective half-century of his own. With Ranatunga he added eighty-three, and then Tillekeratne stroked them to a total of 251. By Sri Lanka's exotic standards, this was a modest score. India had bowled well, though the fact that Tendulkar was the man who had slowed the run-rate, with ten overs of lobby off-breaks for just thirty-four, was significant. It boded well for Sri Lanka's spinners.

By the time India batted there was nothing to drink in the stadium. Tendulkar came out and played with typical power, flicking and gliding the ball around with ease. Kapil Dev, the next day, said that Tendulkar was in 'his usual best form' – a nice contradiction-in-terms that made perfect sense. The best, in this tournament, had also been the usual. Perhaps he didn't fancy being upstaged by De Silva. Either way, so long as he was at the crease you believed India would win; as soon as he was out you changed your mind. At ninety-eight for one (in the twenty-second over) the home side was set fair. Half an hour later it was all over bar the shouting. First, Tendulkar was brilliantly stumped for sixty-five. The ball ran off his pads down the leg side and he made as if to run, but Kaluwitharana snatched the ball like a lizard and swiped off the bails in a flash. And here came that man Jayasuriya. He might have failed with the bat, but he popped into the game as a left-arm spin bowler, taking three wickets for twelve runs. Ranatunga wisely kept giving his spinners the ball (only eleven overs were bowled by the seamers), which by now was turning sharply. When Azharuddin weakly prodded a catch back to the bowler, Kumara Dharmasena, he was booed, and only partly for the poor shot. The whole ground knew that it had been a mistake to bowl first. Batting in these conditions was almost impossible. India promoted Srinath to slog, but the gamble failed: he fell victim to a run-out that looked, even on the television replay, impossible to judge for sure.

Slowly the match trickled out of India's reach. They were 109 for three, then 110 for four, then 110 for five, then 115 for six. The ball was spinning and bouncing. 120 for seven, 120 for eight – this was ridiculous.

That's when the bottles started flying. Empties rained on to the outfield. Some of them were full, actually: they burst when they hit the ground like little water bombs. There could have been no clearer indication of how bad people felt: most of us were gasping for a drink.

The players huddled in the middle, but some of these fans had brilliant arms; the odd orange or apple slapped into the ground near the stumps. Clive Lloyd, the match referee, walked out to feel the heat, and the umpires led the players off the field. A few over-eager stewards thought it was all over, and started putting up the presentation podium, then took it away again.

Fires were starting to sprout in the stands now, a couple at first, then half a dozen, then scores of them.

After twenty minutes they seemed to have fizzled out, and the players returned, to a big cheer. But as soon as they took up their positions, another bottle, a glass one – it looked like a fifth of whisky – came wheeling over the sightscreen and just missed Dharmasena. The referee marched out, waved his arms, and called it off.

Kambli, the not-out batsman, put his gloved hand over his eyes, while the Sri Lankans leaped for joy. De Silva tried to pull out a stump, but it wouldn't come. In the end he gave it an extra hard yank, and up came all the wires connecting it to the television system. Meanwhile there were fires everywhere. You could see people bundling up mounds of paper and setting light to them. The stadium was concrete, so was unlikely to combust, but as the fires grew brighter and higher there were moments when it felt as if the whole place could go up.

Downstairs, Lloyd murmured a few polite rudenesses about what had happened. 'I asked the police to mingle with the crowd,' he said. 'I made an announcement that we should put more people out there. It was impossible to field on the boundaries. I said to the umpires, and they agreed with me, that we'd give it another try, but if anything was thrown again that would be it.' He also said that he thought the ball turned far too much for a semi-final. No doubt about it, Sri Lanka had been given the best use of the wicket.

So the feeling afterwards was unequivocal: it was all Azhar's fault.

But it didn't really matter whose fault it was. Sri Lanka were through to the final. And even in angry Calcutta it was hard to find anyone who didn't think they deserved to be.

I stayed at the ground, watching the crowd slide away. Outside, a few car windows were broken and various World Cup arches were toppled. But it didn't feel dangerous, just furious. One-day cricket provokes fiercer reactions than the longer game. It is nerve-racking, and winds its fans up tighter, which, of course, is why they like it. They chanted curses at their captain as they streamed across the fields.

We were leaving at four the following morning, so there was no point in going to bed. I shared a sandwich in the all-night café with a gloom-filled Indian reporter, then went upstairs. Some match or other was playing on the television, but I was too dazed to pay attention. For all I knew, it was Sri Babwe versus the New Indies.

I phoned home, and caught my two-year-old, Luke, just going to bed. An eager talker, he was in that anything-goes, sleepy mood – the best mood there is. 'Are there lots of cricket balls in India?' he asked. What was he *talking* about? Didn't he know what had happened out here? 'When you come back,' he continued seriously, 'you can come and sleep in bed with me whenever you like. That'd be nice, wouldn't it?'

Yes, I thought. It would.

'Can you hear the aeroplane?' he went on. 'It's very loud – no, it's *quite* loud. Can you hear the perpella? I've saved some crisps for you, Daddy.'

I needed a walk after that. I was far too jangled to sleep. I headed back out through the lobby into the broad, warm street. There was hardly anyone about, which goes against the grain, I know – in Calcutta, you're supposed to be clambering over needy bodies every time you take a step. But it really was quiet. And without wishing to over-sentimentalize the importance of cricket in Bengal, the city felt stunned. When you closed your eyes you could still see the fires, the people hurling paper into mounds and lighting them with a cheer. It was hard to believe it was over, that the players had slunk back to their rooms, the crowd to its flats. What kind of game could so entrance these people? Sport is cruel, of course: it fans the flames of dreams, and then douses them with a wet blanket. The people here would probably watch the final on telly, but it wouldn't be the same: it wouldn't be *them*. None of the clichés count for much. Sociologists say that the team is an extension of their national pride, that success on the cricket field makes them walk tall, and it's true that these things have a big bearing in the richness of the game. But in the end the game is just the game. Losing a semi-final deprives you, above all, of fun – the fun of anticipation, the fun of the day out. The final had become a party to which these people were not invited. They could look on, in a neutral, voyeuristic way, but they wouldn't be part of it.

For the second time in three days, cricket felt momentous. At Bangalore you felt yourself to be in the eye of a storm. You could only guess at the churning emotions among the 750 million people caught up in this routine event: a game of cricket. Here, too, you could sense the slump in the air. People took to the streets to celebrate in Sri Lanka, of course, but also in Lahore. When Sri Lanka went to Pakistan, they were going to be playing at home.

Somewhere in Calcutta, the newspaper presses were turning. It wasn't difficult to imagine what they would say:

A NIGHT OF DESPAIR

SHAME IN CALCUTTA

A few cars drove past as light glimmered in the east. It was nearly dawn, which meant it was time to leave.

At Calcutta airport we were met by our indefatigable travel rep, who asked for our tickets.

'Tickets?' I spread my arms. 'What tickets?' I'd been told the previous evening, at about midnight, that we'd be picking them up at the airport.

'But I dropped them off at the hotel,' he said.

'I never got one.'

'But I dropped them off at the hotel.'

I wasn't too worried. Presumably I would be logged on the computer somewhere; it was just a question of cancelling the ticket that had been issued and giving me a new one.

Or was it? I waited for a bit, then a bit longer. There wasn't much else I could do. Eventually – about ten minutes before the flight, and if I'm honest I was starting to give up hope – the travel rep ran up and thrust a ticket into my hand.

'You might have to travel under a different name,' he said. 'But here it is.'

I hardly heard, and certainly didn't really stop to wonder what he meant. I grabbed my bags and jostled my way to the check-in desk. The man tapped a few keys on his computer, tore a few pages out of my ticket, and then looked up.

'I can't read this,' he said. 'How are you spelling your name?'

My *what*?

Who was it who said that the most important skill in a journalist was the ability to read upside down? It wasn't a skill I had ever thought of practising, but as I glanced down, pretending not to understand what he wanted, I could see a few letters.

'Er, P – E – L,' I began. Christ: how did it go on from there?

'Ah, there it is,' he said.

Thank God for computer programmers. The first three letters must have triggered the name in full.

He handed me a boarding pass and looked at his watch.

'There you are, Mr Pele,' he said. 'Better hurry. Gate seven.'

When I sat down I was soaked with sweat. Mr Pele? What if he turned up? At any moment I expected his name to come booming through the airport loudspeakers. I shrank down in my seat for a closer look at the incriminating document. There, under the small print that said 'Not Transferable', was my new name: R. Pellay.

I'm sorry, Mr Pellay, whoever you are. I hope you're not still stuck in Calcutta.

In Delhi we went to the Taj hotel for a hearty breakfast and a longish wait. Then we watched the beginning of the other semi-final in Chandigarh. I very nearly went: there was a bus leaving Delhi airport. But I decided not to risk it, and was happy enough to learn, later, that the bus had taken seven hours. I would have missed most of the game anyway.

Chandigarh was up in the north, not far from Kashmir – a strange, Le Corbusier-designed freak in the foothills of the Himalayas. It was also the home town of I. S. Bindra, the president of India's cricket board. It was not, at first sight, the natural place to hold such a big match. But not many expenses had been spared to bring the stadium up to scratch. The floodlights were low, because of their proximity to the neighbouring air-force base. But the pitch, according to the groundsman, might have some life in it. 'I have left a bit of grass on the wicket,' he said. 'The edges will carry.'

Ambrose bowled the first over, and *blimey* – the ball absolutely zinged through. That groundsman knew what he was talking about: batting was going to be a nightmare. And I don't like to boast, but I did say, as we watched the first few balls hammer past the batsmen's chests: 'Australia are going to be twenty for four here.' But we could only stay long enough to see Mark Waugh be out lbw to the second ball of the match, and then watch Lara drop Mark Taylor at slip. We climbed on to a bus, drove to the airport, and when we arrived someone scooted off to find a television.

Australia were sixteen for four.

It looked as if we weren't going to get the dream grudge match between Australia and Sri Lanka in the final, after all. It was going to be Sri Lanka versus the West Indies.

Oh, well. Mustn't grumble.

— 11 —

LOTUS FLOWERS AND PRINCES

Sri Lanka vs Australia, Lahore

While we waited for the plane in Delhi, Australia dug themselves out of trouble in Chandigarh. Waugh, Taylor, Ponting and Waugh had only scored four runs between them, but Stuart Law and Michael Bevan were toughing it out. The hundred came up, slowly. After forty overs the score had risen to 143. It was hard to see how Australia could win, but they were making a game of it. We climbed into our seats, suffering for the last time the scrupulous security checks on all flights to Pakistan and nodding gravely through the chanted prayer to Allah, which for some pessimistic reason always came at the beginning of the flight, not the end.

By the time we arrived in Lahore the semi-final was nearly over. Australia had fought bravely, adding sixty-four in the final ten overs to take their score to an improbably high 207. But it wasn't going to be enough. Lara had threatened to do a De Silva before being stopped in his tracks by a beauty from Steve Waugh, who bowled the danger man for forty-five. But Chanderpaul and Richardson were taking the West Indies towards the final with impressive assurance. With ten overs remaining they needed only forty-three runs, and they had eight wickets in hand. Perhaps that quarter-final victory over New Zealand, and the long haul north to Chandigarh, had taken more out of these Australians than people thought. Or perhaps the West Indies, in the depths of their unhappiness, had suddenly uncovered some potent, long-buried will-to-win.

Whatever it was, they soon lost it. Chanderpaul, imagining perhaps that he had done enough, played an airy swish and was caught. And Harper was immediately lbw to McGrath. Taylor brought Warne into the attack for one last thrust. Later, he was praised to the skies for this astute piece of captaincy, but to be honest you didn't need to be a rocket scientist to know that you had to hand the ball to your best bowler at a time like this. But Warne certainly made it look a smart move. In a matter of moments, Gibson was caught behind, and then Adams and Bishop were both trapped leg before. Jesus Christ, this was unbelievable. All of a sudden the West Indies were 194 for eight. Anything could happen now.

They only needed ten off the last over. And Richardson was on strike. But for some (mad) reason, Ambrose attempted a quick single and was run out. Which brought Courtney Walsh to the crease. Obviously he would be aiming to tap a single to give Richardson the bowling. Or would he? He aimed a big hit at Fleming and was bowled. Australia had won.

'They were ahead for ninety-five per cent of the game,' said Taylor. 'But we won the last five per cent. It was very tense. We were behind all day.'

Taylor was not exaggerating. They were living a charmed life.

'I am finished with playing cricket,' said Richie Richardson, glad it was all over. 'For ten years it's been cricket, cricket, cricket. I do not want to be a public figure. I want to settle down in peace. I would like nothing better than to whistle away the whole day.'

It sounded as though he'd had enough.

An Australian–Sri Lanka final seemed almost too good to be true. Pakistan licked its lips. One commentator wrote, on the front page of the *News*: 'The Australians will be given a thrashing they will remember for life. They may save their lives and limbs, yet such wounds will be inflicted on their minds and souls they will find it hard to be normal again.'

The consensus was that if Australia batted first, then Mark Waugh and his satellite powers would take the game out of Sri Lanka's reach. So it was nicely cheeky of Ranatunga to win the toss and decide to bowl: every World Cup final so far had been won by the team batting first. Dav Whatmore was quietly telling people that much as he respected this Australian team, they had already been through the wringer twice this week, against New Zealand and the West Indies. They were tough guys, but their nerves had been cork-screwing around enough. It was asking a lot for them to come up with the goods again, so soon.

Down in the blacked-out television studio, the production team was warming up. Director Gary Franses was waking up his cameramen. 'In you go, four. Go right, nine, *right*, come *on*.' A hand reached up and wiped the television screen in front of Tony Greig's face as he waited to deliver his pre-match pep talk. 'Two,' said Franses, 'one . . . one . . . stand by, red, there's music here . . . take it . . .'kay, lose it . . . and cue Greigy. Chappelli, have you got anyone down there we can talk to? We need an interview.'

'There's lots of support for both sides,' said Greig, mysteriously.

'Chappelli, are you there?' said Franses. 'Is there anyone down there or not? Green next . . . We'll run two minutes on green. Track one on green. Talk to me, Chappelli.'

'I've got Michael Slater,' said Ian Chappell.

'Greigy, can you talk about the floodlights?' Franses continued. 'First match ever under lights here, all that stuff. 'Kay, we'll take Slater. Where's the map? We need the map? Ten seconds to voiceover. Five, four, three, two, one and run green, lose effects, go . . .'

'Hopefully we can post a big total,' said Michael Slater. 'We're taking it as just another game, but the adrenaline's flowing. I went into the dressing room and they told me to get out 'cause I was too pumped.'

'Come on, come on,' Franses urged. 'Jay, where was that? Right, I want shots all the way here.'

Up popped some footage of the West Indies crashing in Chandigarh. 'Greigy, I'll come back to you to say what an amazing night that was and how we hope we'll have another amazing night tonight, all that. And I need floodlights. Who's got some nice floodlights? Five seconds, Greigy . . .'

'Don't think my nerves can stand another one of those,' said Greig. 'But maybe we'll have one. And there are the lights. Never been used before. Absolutely fantastic. People have been driving around just looking at the lights.'

'Just pause here, Greigy. Pause. Let the pictures take over. And then throw straight to the commentary box, Benaud and Gavaskar.'

'Well, there we are,' said Greig, after a nice pause. 'Great scenes here. And up in the commentary box, Richie Benaud and Sunil Gavaskar.'

Cricket lovers think that covering the game for television or newspapers is a breeze. Not for these fellows it isn't. It was like working in an air-traffic control tower, shepherding planes around the sky.

Even for the newspaper reporters a game of cricket is a longish day at the (admittedly very nice) office. You need to be at the ground by about 8.30 for these nine o'clock starts, and after the close of play there are the various press conferences. Then it's a quick scoot back to the hotel to write up the day's events, which will keep you busy until nine or so, and still leave plenty of time for London to call back and ask for more. Even a day–night match like this fitted comfortably into English deadlines: ten o'clock in Lahore would only be teatime at Lord's. The old hands in the press box spoke longingly of the West Indies, where the time difference went the other way, forcing you to dash off a match report within minutes of the game ending, and granting you a long empty evening in the beachside restaurants. There hadn't been much of that on this trip, just a lot of room service chicken tikka in top-class hotels, with a laptop propped on the coffee table.

More to the point, these television workers were, in a sense, the most important people here, the conduit to the mass market which was paying for all this. One of the curious things I had discovered while traipsing around the subcontinent after the cricket was that you are, in a sense, missing the real event. The full panorama is available only on television. Actually, of course, I had the best of both worlds – there were usually TVs in the press box. But spectators at cricket games miss almost everything now thought to be essential to a proper understanding of the game: close-ups of the players' faces, details of their career so far, slow-motion replays of their best shots (and their worst ones), computer-enhanced analyses of their progress. At the ground, you cannot involve yourself in the never-ending debate about whether that one nicked the bat or just caught the pad, or whether that lbw decision was dodgy. You certainly can't judge the accuracy of run-out decisions. And of course you are deprived of the little cameo interviews with players and managers about the wicket, the opposition, and their own performances. You are there, and not there. The crowd is part of the occasion, but it is, increasingly, detached from the game. This is why apparently mad ideas, such as holding the cricket World Cup in America, might not be as batty as they sound.

Here came Taylor and Waugh. Sri Lanka were about to get what was coming to them.

For a while they learned, at last, what it was like to be on the receiving end. Taylor began brightly, cuffing the opening bowlers,

Vaas and Wickremasinghe, to the boundary, making sure that Mark Waugh had time to make himself at home. The first seven overs went for thirty-six runs, which was not exactly Jayasuriyan, but it would do.

For the spectators – some said 25,000, some said 30,000 – it was ideal. What we wanted was to see the Sri Lankans putting their backs into the pursuit of a big total. But then Mark Waugh played uppishly and there was the man of the moment, Jayasuriya, to seize the catch. Australia were not by any standards a one-trick pony: they had plenty of batsmen capable of roughing up the bowling. But the Sri Lankans sprinted across to hug the fielder. It was a big wicket: the prospect of a giant score, built on another Waugh-torn century, receded.

The future continued to look Australian for another hour, though. Taylor and Ponting were simultaneously sensible and punishing, and put on a hundred in as many balls. Sri Lankan fans had their hearts in their mouths, but Ranatunga had the wit to repeat the trick that had worked so well in the semi-final. After thirteen overs he put the fast bowlers out on the boundary and let the spinners take over. Muralitharan came toddling in at an angle and twirled the ball over his shoulder like a conker on a string, and Dharmasena did the same from the other end. They bowled straight to tight leg-side fields, and you started to notice that the ball kept ending up in the hands of short midwicket or the man by the square-leg umpire. Slowly, they throttled the scoring rate. After twenty overs Australia were surfing, at 110 for one. Ten overs later, when they were hoping to be zooming, they were only 149 for two. Frustrated by a sense that the innings was being ever so slowly reined in, Taylor played a captain's slog and was caught at deep square leg by Jayasuriya (again) for seventy-four.

Two meagre overs later, Ponting leaned back to cut one of De Silva's unassuming off-spinners and was bowled. And you could tell that Australia were feeling the hand on their shoulder, because the next man in was Warne. Against New Zealand he had come in to switch on the turbo after a sluggish beginning, and promptly whacked two sixes. This time he came down the wicket with a view to putting Muralitharan into the crowd, and was stumped. The crowd squealed and whistled with pleasure. Multi-coloured balloons flew across the ground, twisting colourfully in the floodlights. One cluster drifted into the bulbs, and burst with an emphatic pop. It sounded, even at this early stage, like the cork thudding out of the victory champagne. Warne was the top kangaroo, and he'd been nobbled. Sri Lanka were right back where they wanted to be.

So when Steve Waugh, a couple of overs later, skied Dharmasena to De Silva, it felt almost inevitable. Australia looked desperate. They had lost four top batters for twenty-odd runs and were batting, uncharacteristically, like men caught in a swarm of mosquitoes: they were swatting this way and that, but just couldn't squash the damn things. After thirty-five overs they were 170 for five, with two new batsmen at the crease, Law and Bevan. They'd come through in the semi-final, but it was asking an awful lot for them to do it again. Ranatunga brought in a silly point to stand under the batsman's nose and put him off, a very cocky thing to do at this stage of a one-day innings.

The stadium began to rumble with attentive anticipation. Ranatunga was waddling between overs with the relaxed air of a man looking for a pedal boat to hire; his fielders were jogging smartly to their appointed places, their dark faces shining with sweat. They weren't doing anything special, but they didn't need to. A murmur began to move around the ground as everybody realized that something superb was happening out there: Sri Lanka were *teasing* the Australians. Everybody knew that the way Sri Lanka batted, Australia had to get a mammoth score. Suddenly – and possibly for the first time ever – batting first was like batting second. Australia had been going along pretty well, but you could see them thinking – the way they slapped their thigh pads if they hit the ball straight to a fielder, the way they jumped down the wicket, then changed their minds – that they were terrified that it *wasn't enough*. The Sri Lankan bowlers weren't doing anything out of the ordinary, though the ball was turning a fraction. But any of these Aussies, in grade cricket back in Perth or Melbourne, would have been carting these rinky-dink little off-spinners into the upper tiers at deep midwicket and throwing in a few contemptuous four Xs while they were about it. Fielding first was turning into a magnificent feint or bluff. Go on, then, Sri Lanka seemed to be saying, feel free. Get as many as you like, because we're going to get them anyway, just see if we don't.

There was something else, too. Sri Lanka were making a wonderful virtue of something that would have panicked every other team in the competition: they were happy to rely on part-time spinners to do the bowling for them. They seemed to have calculated that in this form of cricket you simply had to stuff the side with batsmen, and could afford to rely on them to do the bowling too. If top bowlers such as Allan Donald could go for fifty in their ten-over stints, then why not pick a batsman instead, who might go for sixty, but who could make up the difference with the bat when the time came? It had worked against India in the semi-final, in very helpful conditions. And it was working again now.

Not everyone was attentive. There were scuffles up in the special enclosures – rather sweetly known here as 'the drumstick boxes'. Quite a few expensive suits were going away in a huff having found their seats already occupied. Even an hour and a half after the start of play there were long queues scowling outside the one-at-a-time security filters on the way in. Out in the car park, touts were offering 100-rupee tickets (£2) for 1500 rupees.

Down in Mission Control it was total concentration all the way.

'Two, coming to one, one, two, one, give me a big pan right, ten, nice, and four, eight, blue, run it!' said Gary Franses, as Jayasuriya took the catch to dismiss Taylor. 'Any thoughts, Richie?'

'Ranatunga has taken a risk here,' said Benaud, 'giving Australia first use of this pitch. The gambling instinct has taken over.'

'The crowd's going kasi,' said Franses. 'Fifteen, eight, three. Someone find the crowd. Listen, can we get a light here? I can't read these bloody cards at all. Right, here comes the crowd. Can someone find out what they're shouting? Can't read it, seven, find something else. Come on, fellas, concentrate.'

Pictures of the crowd waving banners and flags appeared on television screens in front of nearly a billion people. 'They're cheering what they hope will be a very good final,' said Benaud.

One of the monitors in front of Franses was linked to a hand-held camera, which was roving the ground, picking out the pretty women in sharp sunglasses. At one point its gaze lighted on the entire upper tier of the stand at the far end of the ground, which was full of people dressed in yellow T-shirts – thousands of them.

'None of that, Nawaz,' said Franses. 'I don't want any Shell at all.'

It turned out that Shell had managed to buy an entire block of seats in what they hoped was full view of the television cameras – a nice day out for the staff, and a cheap form of ground advertising into the bargain. But the television cameras weren't playing along. They had decided to eliminate them from the coverage altogether.

It would have been a fatal precedent. Before we knew it, we'd have entire grounds bought up by multi-nationals and dressed up in company gear.

'Richie,' said Franses, 'I've got the results coming up of previous World Cup finals, quite a nice graphic about how they came bottom of the group and all that.'

'It's always nice to look back,' said Richie, as the chart bounced up on the monitor in front of him. 'Sri Lanka were last in their group in 1975, last in 1983 and 1987 again. Quite a turnaround here.'

'Richie, we need a bit of a pep-up here. Something about Sunny's bad throat, you know.'

Benaud ignored him. He hadn't spent years as Test captain, and a lifetime annotating cricket with dry insights, to start cracking sore-throat jokes in a World Cup final.

When the drinks break arrived, Franses took his glasses off, wiped his face with a towel – it was bloody hot in this windowless basement hutch – and blinked a few times. Then he clamped his headphones back on and carried on.

The mosquitoes kept buzzing and whining. Law and Bevan gritted and grunted, but it was one thing slicing the fast West Indian bowlers to the fence: these guys forced you to take your life in your hands if you wanted to swing the bat. They looked petrified to play a shot in anger. Five overs went by for only eight runs. Muralitharan took his cap having bowled ten overs for just thirty-one runs (with not a single no-ball). And at this point the conventional wisdom would have been for the opening bowlers to return. But Ranatunga's nerve held. De Silva and Jayasuriya kept poddling in, and Australia kept hitting the ball to the fielders. Eventually, Law collared a big six, but almost immediately he hoisted Jayasuriya into De Silva's running hands in the deep. Healey was bowled, and with five overs to go, Australia had only 205 on the board. The statistics told the cold story of how they had been frozen out. In the first twenty-two overs of the innings they had scored 134 for one. In the second twenty-two, they had managed seventy-one for six. It was a distinctly unAustralian performance. For the last two or three years they had been the most ruthless team in the world, stony drivers home of an advantage. But here in Lahore they had been lured into quicksand. Five had been caught in the outfield, another had been stumped. And this was a game, not a fairy story, but it was tempting to think of Gulliver, baffled and trapped in his spider's web of tiny Lilliputian threads, or Goliath outwitted by tiny pebbles and a toy catapult, or the big bad wolf huffing and puffing while those cheeky-bastard little piglets tricked him out of his wits. They ended up flailing their way to 241, and everyone knew that if Sri Lanka batted with their usual vim, this would not be a problem.

The floodlights had been switched on for the closing overs of Australia's innings, and during the dinner break they flickered and dimmed. The sky was full of dark clouds, and the weather forecast was lousy. Shane Warne put his feet up behind the glass windows of the dressing room, puffed on a cigarette and stared out at the dew settling over the outfield. This wasn't going to suit leg-spinning one bit: it would make the ball greasy.

Jayasuriya walked out practising his forward defensive stroke, which didn't seem to be one he used much. And sure enough, he began by clipping McGrath for two consecutive twos to fine leg, and then tonking him high over midwicket for four in the first over. But then, dashing for an unnecessary second run, he was run out after a prolonged inspection of the television replay by the third umpire. The man of the tournament walked off shaking his head, and you could see him thinking, Why, why why – why had he taken that stupid, stupid run? And when Kaluwitharana top-edged a dolly to Michael Bevan off Fleming, Australia were back in business. There were yellow shirts bobbing and beaming all around the catcher. They were on top again. Asanka Gurusinha had very nearly been bowled first ball, an inside edge flashing past the stumps. Perhaps, in the end, the pressure was going to get to this lot.

But Aravinda De Silva was, as they say, in his usual best form as he approached his decisive duel with Warne. Off the back foot he stroked the ball mildly through a gap in the off side for four, then clobbered a half-volley to the same boundary. Eleven runs came off Warne's first over. Gurusinha got into the act too, plonking a full-toss straight back over the bowler's head, and then picking up a short one for six over square leg. Warne was having trouble gripping the wet ball. For his part, Gurusinha had something to prove in this game: on that ill-fated tour of Australia during the winter, the Sri Lankans had not been exactly sweetness and light themselves, and he had been reprimanded and fined after a fierce exchange of pleasantries with Steve Waugh. When Waugh came on to bowl and tried a bouncer Gurusinha, who with his paunch, beard and specs looks more like a restaurateur than a sportsman, hooked him for four with a flourish. He was a dangerous man to give freebies to, so when he was dropped twice – once tricky, once a sitter – it was yet another sign that everything was going Sri Lanka's way. After thirty overs the score had risen to 147. They needed less than a hundred off the last twenty.

No one thought they would blow it now, and they didn't. Gurusinha chanced his arm once too often and was bowled, but De Silva was stroking the Sri Lankans home. And then came another of those lovely little mesmerizing games-within-the-game. Before the match Ranatunga had pooh-poohed the idea that Warne was the best bowler in the world, saying he was 'overrated'. So naturally, when Ranatunga walked out to bat, Warne gave him a hostile glare. The two men stood eyeball-to-eyeball, and the crowd whistled: this was going to be fun. Warne stepped up to bowl his last over – his first mine had gone for forty-five runs, dreadful by his standards – and the game was all but up: Sri Lanka needed only another forty to win. But there was no sense in doing anything stupid at this stage. De Silva blocked the first ball, and the commentators nodded.

'These two realize that it's Warne's last over, and they're not going to take chances,' said Tony Greig.

Sunil Gavaskar was quick to agree. 'Yes, no need to take chances,' he repeated. 'There's time to play a few dot balls without feeling the pressure.'

It was good advice. Nothing could have been more childish than to relax now. De Silva seemed to feel the same way; he prodded the next ball for a gentle single. But this brought Ranatunga up to the business end, and to him this looked like one last chance to take the mickey out of Australia's golden boy, this brilliant bleached rich sissie who had tried to face him down a few minutes earlier. He thumped his first ball straight back past Warne's outstretched hands for four. The next one went rifling over square leg for six. The crowd roared and roared. Warne was being humiliated. Next ball: a high hoist over long-off.

'Warne figures, please,' said the TV director in his bunker. 'Computer? There it is, Greigy.'

Greig took the figures in his stride. He didn't seem to feel the least remorse about what he had said at the start of the over. 'And look at that,' he said. 'Shane Warne: ten overs, nought for fifty-eight. Thirteen off that last over. Sri Lanka are giving the Aussies a real hiding here.'

It was downhill all the way after that, like a victory march. And it hadn't been whack, whack all the way. As expected, the coolest, more professional team had won. The only surprise was that this turned out to be Sri Lanka. The air filled with birds, bats, moths and flies swooping into the floodlights for a closer look. The cheering grew louder and louder as the finishing line approached. And then the rain came, and victory came, and hundreds of officials swayed and teetered on the winner's podium, and the cameras flashed.

When Ranatunga got back to the dressing room he reached into his pocket to have a closer look at the winner's cheque, and bloody hell . . . oh, but you've seen that one already.

The Australians were standing around, not knowing where to look. The strange thing was, it felt inevitable, this Sri Lankan victory. It seemed that there could have been no other outcome to the tournament. Who knows? Maybe it *was* predestined. In Bangladesh, the day after the World Cup final, there were gasps of disbelief when the result came through. Before the match a magician called Jewel Aich had written down his predictions, sealed them in an envelope and placed them in a locked iron box in a bank vault. After the game, the envelope was opened before a crowd of fans at the press club in Dhaka. This is what it said:

1. Champion – Sri Lanka.
2. Sri Lanka will win by 25 runs if they decide to bat, and by 6/7 wickets if they prefer to bowl.
3. Bad luck for dear Jayasuriya.
4. Man of the match: De Silva (his chance of hitting a century is bright).

Well, that's the mysterious Orient for you. Four out of four. Sri Lanka did win by seven wickets, De Silva was indeed man of the match, and as for dear Jayasuriya – well, did you see that run-out? It was a mad decision to go for the second run, no doubt about it, and it was clearly very close. Even the third umpire, the South African Cyril Mitchley, watching on the television replays, wasn't sure. He was sitting up there with the match referee, Clive Lloyd, when the call came through to adjudicate, and there were real problems. From side-on the bowler was blocking the view, so they had to rely on the head-on camera, which is far less precise. And then Jayasuriya swerved to his right at the end of his run to avoid the umpire, so his bat was just off the left-hand edge of the television picture. It was a tense one all right. Mitchley and Lloyd leaned forward, squinted at the screen, pointed with their fingers, and asked through their microphone for another look. Here it came again. They stared at it. Here came the ball, and here came the bat, and there went the bail – THERE! See that? Mitchley looked at Lloyd, who whistled and fell back into his chair, squirming at the appalling closeness of it. 'I think that's out,' said Mitchley, looking at Lloyd. Lloyd sat forward again, pointing at the screen with his finger, looking – there it goes, see? – for the moment when the bail flew off. Mitchley didn't look too sure. He asked for another look, and they watched it all over again. Out in the press room they were watching it too, and forming the strong view that no one could possibly give that out – there was no way you could be certain. Everyone on the ground – the players, the fans – knew from the time it was taking that this was a tight one. Looking at it for the fourth time, it looked an impossible one to call, which should mean – not out. But only one man's opinion counted. 'That's out,' said Mitchley, pressing the red button. A sigh went round the ground as the light sent Jayasuriya trudging back to the pavilion, shaking his head. How could he have taken that stupid bloody run? How could he?

Does that count as bad luck? If so, it's a clean sweep for Jewel Aich. If only he had publicized his predictions before the match, so we could be sure it hadn't been a trick.

Still, the Sri Lankans weren't worried. Back at the hotel, they ran up and down the corridor outside their rooms, shrieking. They looked like they were in eighth heaven, on cloud ten. They smiled and shook hands with whoever was hanging around, and signed autographs for the fans who had figured out their room numbers. It seemed churlish not to join in, and since one of them, Hashan Tillekeratne, had been borrowing my room-service menu for the last day or so – as chance would have it, I was in the room opposite – well, why not? He cheerfully scribbled his name on the back of a photograph of my small son, and that is how I became the proud owner of the only autograph I have ever received (or asked for). Rather sweetly, fearing perhaps that his signature was illegible, or that I wouldn't know who he was, he added a bracket containing his full name in capital letters. Tillekeratne is a wonderful batsman – four Test centuries, and an average of 42.5 – but the others were in such amazing form that he only got to the crease twice during the World Cup. They were, in truth, one heck of a good side.

The coach, Dav Whatmore, hurried by, clutching faxes. About two-thirds Aussie himself – his father was Sri Lankan, but the family moved back to Australia when he was eight – he was in an unusual position. This team he had inspired to victory was, in a sense, made in Australia, and before the match he sang along to 'Advance Australia Fair'; he didn't know the words to his own team's anthem. 'The only pressure I was under,' he said, 'was to absolutely thrash Australia.' Yet he had been fielding well-wishing, hope-you-lose phone calls from Down Under for days. His wife Kathryn watched the final on television at home in Melbourne. 'We all found it hard to turn around and barrack for another country,' she said. 'Inside we were barracking for Australia.'

The hero of the hour, De Silva, sprinted along with a towel round his waist. He knew that everyone was looking at him, wondering how it must feel to have done what he had just done. Ranatunga was in his room, trying to figure out what to do about that damn cheque.

After the match, Ranatunga had followed Mark Taylor up to the press box for an interview, his big babyish face creased into a grin. 'When I play,' he smiled, with a slight ironic lift of his eyebrows, 'I don't look at eyeballs or any other balls. I look only at the ball.' He had finished (thanks to three not outs) with a batting average of 120.5 (De Silva came next, with 89.6, followed by Tendulkar on 87.2). But now he, like everyone, was wondering when they'd be able to go home. There had been talk of a special charter flight for them, but who knew? It had taken Sri Lanka three days to travel from Kandy to Faisalabad for their quarter-final match against England. Surely it wouldn't take them three days to get home again. Jayasuriya had an additional problem: he had won a snazzy car for his remarkable batting exploits during the competition. Maybe he should just drive home – it might be the quickest way. Fancy a lift, Aravinda? It's brilliant, this new Audi – look, a sun roof and everything. It's only two thousand miles. What do you reckon?

The off-spin bowler Kumara Dharmasena, one of the men who had strangled the life out of Australia's innings that afternoon, had spent the previous summer playing club cricket in England, it turned out, in the Thames Valley League. He started off playing for Reading, but when he scored 160 and took eight wickets against Wokingham, they immediately offered him better terms. I had played against Wokingham myself; I used to live a few miles away. So there I was, in a surreal moment, standing around at midnight in Lahore, a couple of hours after the World Cup final, chatting to a member of the winning team about blokes we remembered from the stockbroker belt. While he was in Wokingham (they put him up in a big house, but he asked for somewhere smaller), he tried to get a job in the NatWest bank in the town centre. But they turned him down. He ended up doing a bit of cricket coaching at Bearwood College, a public school in the woods towards the M4. He bowled well in the World Cup, though he is not much known in England. At Lords, you can bet, they wouldn't know how to spell his name. But he is big in Berkshire.

At about half past twelve someone got out of the lift, shouted a message to the team, and there was a wild whoop of excitement. The tiny wicket-keeper, Kaluwitharana, jumped in the air with a yelp, as if he was appealing. The charter flight had come through. They were leaving immediately, in half an hour. The World Cup winners dived back into their rooms to pack, and suddenly the corridor was empty. The armed guards by the lift lowered their machine guns and sat down. Serendipity broke out all over.

But the night was still young. The previous day I had made a few sympathetic noises to the people in the next-door room, a businessman from Karachi and his wife, when their iron set fire to the ironing board. Now they announced that they were off to a reception – did I want to come? Well, what else was there to do at one o'clock in the morning? I went. We drove to the house, the home of a businessman: it had been built especially for him, and it wasn't easy to tell, as we walked across the atrium and caught the lift up to the leafy mezzanine on the top floor, whether it was a house or a merchant bank. Apparently there were a couple of Van Goghs somewhere around. Two barmen in white jackets uncorked bottles of wine and twisted the tops off bottles of Scotch. And for the next couple of hours, on an opulent roof terrace in dry Pakistan, where alcohol is banned, I got – not to put too fine a point on it – drunk.

Down in Sri Lanka, all hell was breaking loose. The President, Chandrika Banderanaike Kumaratunga, rang up a television chat-show to convey her good wishes to the nation's viewers. 'We have shown that even a small country can achieve greatness,' she said. We? Oh, never mind. Outside there were fireworks and dancing on streets normally patrolled by troops. The high-security, no-parking area around the Galle Face hotel was flooded with cheering Sri Lankans leaning out of cars, trucks, motorbikes and three-wheel scooters, honking horns and waving flags. 'There is very little we can do,' said one policeman, with a shrug. The state-run Ceylon Shipping Company offered to ferry home Jayasuriya's car for free, and insurance companies rushed to offer premium-free terms to the hard-driving opening bat. The insurance company of which Ranatunga is an employee, Union Assurance, put together some newspaper adverts for the morning edition. 'Business is suspended. At every watering hole euphoria overflows,' ran the copy. 'If we take longer to answer the phone, please forgive us.' President Maumoon Abdul Gayoom of the Maldive Islands phoned to offer the team a free holiday in one of his beach resorts. Gifts from grateful cricket lovers – cars, houses, money – arrived at the sports ministry in Colombo.

It wasn't a happy time for everyone. Wasim Akram, the captain of Pakistan, was still keeping out of sight to avoid the fury of his countrymen following the defeat against India. His house was stoned, and rubbish was dumped in his front garden. Effigies of his face, daubed with make-up to make him look like a prostitute, were carried through the streets. On the eve of the final, a parade of donkeys, each named after a member of the team, was led through Lahore as a comic protest against Pakistan's defeat. The newspapers were still full of long columns with titles like: 'The End of the World'. The players had been promised a plot of land in Islamabad if they won; the cartoonists now featured them being presented with their trophies: eleven holes in a graveyard. And the High Court in Lahore received another petition demanding an inquiry into the performance of the team, and recommending that cricket, a vile Western game, be banned. Mohammad Azharuddin hardly fared better after leading India to defeat against Sri Lanka in the semi-final. It was the same thing – effigies, stones, death threats. In Lahore there were rumours that he had been shot, and it seemed more than possible.

It wasn't much of a consolation for England's cricketers that they had been beaten by the eventual winners because they hadn't just been beaten: they had been exposed. This wasn't a touching moment for the underdog, because Sri Lanka hadn't looked like underdogs from the moment they took the field. But it was an emphatic victory for positive, thoughtful and merry cricket. A country that only fifteen years earlier had been sniffily regarded by the old-timers at Lord's as too weak to be considered a first-class nation had made quite a few points about this alteration in the balance of the world cricket order. Was it a one-off? I doubted it. This whole tournament had been devised to demonstrate that there was money in them there thrills, and there was. At exactly the moment when the game, in England, was struggling for oxygen, out here it seemed to be taking big strides forward. The future wasn't going to be English, and there would be much about the game that Anglo-purists might not much care for. But that's how it was going to be. Even as we packed our bags, the convenor-secretary of Pilcom, Jagmohan Dalmiya, was busy planning his campaign to become the next head of the ICC. India was the moneybags of world cricket, which one way or another was going to make it the most influential player in the game as well. He had even been heard to murmur that the game's ruling body should move its headquarters out of London to somewhere more central – Calcutta, for instance. The 1996 World Cup had been unusual: a long, dry run-up followed by an action-packed final week, with a wonderful flourish at the end. But I was pretty sure that it would live in the memory as something more than just another tournament. It would become known as the day cricket flew the imperial coop for good.

In future, cricket would push into new fields. India and Pakistan were agreeing to play each other in an annual face-off in, of all places, Toronto. The one-day game would be the cornerstone, though tentative plans to turn international cricket into a proper competition – home and away Test matches, with a league and prize money – were beginning to crystallize. A good job, too. The historic plank on which world cricket had balanced for over a century – England versus Australia – was cracking, because England were struggling to keep their end up.

The weekend papers back in England were delivering, for the most part, a thumbs-down verdict on the World Cup, suggesting (when they weren't drawing dunces hats on top of England players) that it had been the worst, shoddiest and most vulgar tournament ever. Several noted commentators concentrated on the crazy amount of travelling imposed by the far-flung schedule, without admitting that this was annoying above all for journalists. Their other major beef was the 'riot' in Calcutta, which they dealt with in England's usual-best censorious manner. According to the *Mirror*, it was THE DAY

THE WORLD CUP DIED OF SHAME, and even the smart papers found themselves stuck on their high horses. 'Pilcom,' said the *Guardian*, 'has lost its right to be taken seriously.' I wasn't so sure. Of course it is dangerous to throw bottles, but no one had been hurt. It had looked nice and fiery on television, but in the scheme of such uprisings it had been nothing more than a skirmish. More than that, it had drawn attention to a new force in cricket, one that many people dreaded: a sedate game was becoming torrid. Was cricket really going to be so foolish as to insist that a version of the game that makes people's hearts beat faster was not truly cricket? I hoped not. And as for all this stuff about Pilcom losing its 'right' to be taken seriously . . . it didn't really seem to be a question of rights. It was a question of money.

The hotel in Lahore was awash with cricket followers: players, managers, television producers, umpires, scorers, administrators, moneymen, reporters, sponsors and fans. The lobby filled up with suitcases. It had been a great final, everyone agreed. Apart from anything else, the Sri Lankans had by far the best names. Dharmasena's first name, Handunettige, was purely ancestral, but the next three, Deepthi Priyantha Kumara, meant 'light pretty prince'. Aravinda, as in De Silva, meant 'lotus flower'. They had poetry on their side, into the bargain.

There was an end-of-term feeling. See you at Edgbaston, people said, if not before. The party was over.

Meanwhile, up in the north of Sri Lanka, a country in which the schools were closed for security reasons, forty people were being killed that weekend. On the day of the great game, at about the time the Lotus Flower was skimming cover drives over the emerald outfield in Lahore, eleven soldiers squeezed on to a tractor, drove over a landmine placed by thoughtful freedom-fighters, and were killed.

Not everyone was watching the cricket, after all.

LATER . . .

Henley, England

The World Cup had been over for a month, but the sun never sets on the cricket empire: there's always a game going on somewhere. Sri Lanka, India, Pakistan and South Africa were off playing one-day tournaments in Singapore and Sharjah. Jayasuriya carried on where he'd left off, smashing the ball half-way to Java without so much as a by-your-leave. New Zealand were out in the West Indies, finding that there was still a worrying amount of life in Caribbean cricket. Australia had gone home to lick their wounds. England's exhausted players went off on pre-season tours for their counties, in case they hadn't played enough cricket recently. A working party was set up into the national game under the chairmanship of a man who said he hoped nothing too revolutionary would come out of it. Meanwhile, it was only a few weeks until the beginning of what used to be called the cricket season.

My first game of the summer was easily the poshest I had ever played in: country-house cricket at its finest. I drove out of London to Paul Getty's house to play for Rory Bremner's team against Mike Gatting's eleven, which turned out to be Middlesex, more or less. It was partly in aid of charity – the National Playing Fields Association – partly to do with Mike Gatting's benefit, and a lot to do with Paul Getty's great and mysterious love of cricket. In the grounds of his roomy estate he had built one of the most enviable cricket fields in England, on a ledge above a valley, the immaculate grass criss-crossed by immaculate mowers, the immaculate pavilion (with matching scorebox) topped by immaculate thatch. It was a glorious folly, a perfect reproduction-Chippendale of the English cricket idyll. Getty has been good to cricket, sponsoring all kinds of good causes, including the new stand at Lord's. He also helped save Canova's *Three Graces* for the nation, perhaps imagining for a second that it was W.G. and his brothers. Anyway, it was his touching, Gatsbyish pleasure to invite top players (and ex-players) to come and play in his back garden. Every now and then, by accident, a ringer like me got included, but that's all part of cricket – you have to make up the numbers somehow.

An élite lunch was served in the marquee. The Duke of Edinburgh nibbled at his chicken and admitted that, yes, it was the wife's birthday today – he'd be meeting up with her later for dinner. Jerry Hall went slinking between the tables looking for the loo with her head tilted on one side and a knowing half-smile (yes, it really is me) on her face. I hadn't really been paying attention when I was invited, so wasn't aware quite how exalted was the company I was keeping here. But the programmes on each table told the full story. Our team included Gower, Pringle, Cowdrey, Agnew and Downton (all former England players). And theirs was, well, Middlesex.

At the last minute I was switched over to the Gatting XI. I scurried off to change and noticed with a pang the heating pipes running under the glossy white benches in the dressing room, the clean white towels neatly laid out for each player. Most club matches require you to hang your shirt over a tangle of cobwebs and rust, and shiver on one leg as you try to protect your feet from the cold, muddy floor. Here, well, you looked around for someone to tip. Luckily, the loo had a seat that wouldn't stand up on its own – a reassuring architectural blemish, or perhaps a nice in-joke of some sort.

Gatting himself is a well-known trencherman, but I had a nasty feeling that mine might be the key belly out there today. So I wore a big sweater and held my breath.

Allan Lamb came out to open the batting with a man who used to play for Holland. VIPs – there wasn't anyone else there – spilled out of the marquee to watch. After a couple of overs Lamb swatted the ball hard at my right knee, and I dropped it. A few knowing smirks were exchanged by the fielders. What can you do? they seemed to say. Amazing how the ball always seems to pick out the non-fielder. I apologized to the bowler (Angus Fraser) but he just shrugged – no big deal. It was kind of him not to mind, but I had seen him grimace when the ball went to ground. He was only bowling off half a run-up, not taking it seriously or anything, but for an instant there he had the chance to tease Lamby in the bar afterwards; and I'd gone and ruined it. Worse, his shrug seemed to say that, hell, no one *expected* you to catch it anyway – so don't worry. No! I wanted to say. You don't understand! Normally I catch those, really. Which is true, sort of. But I sure as hell had dropped that one.

Afterwards I said to Lamb, jokingly, that I was glad to have had the chance to give him a life: it would have been a shame to deprive the crowd of those big shots of his. 'Nah,' he said, 'I was trying to get out' – a charming fit, since he had no runs at the time. The top guys never play bad shots, even in jest.

As it turned out, the crowd had reason to be grateful. Lamb prodded the first few he faced, then started clouting the ball high over the bowler's head for six. He made it look easy.

Then it was the Dutchman's turn to club the ball in my direction. It was only a couple of feet off the ground, but it was carrying all the way, and if I dived forward . . . I scooped my fingers under the ball and picked it up cleanly, knowing that it had just grazed the grass. But it must have looked like a catch because the fielders looked hopeful. I did that criss-cross movement with my hands to say the ball hadn't carried, or that I hadn't managed to catch it.

'Thought you had that one,' said Gatting, at the end of the over.

'Well, you can get away with it at Lord's, maybe,' I said. 'But not at Paul Getty's house.'

In truth, it was another failure, another dropped catch. So I was a bit nervous when my big moment came, a few overs later. Mike Gatting walked sturdily down the wicket, his rolling legs-apart gait accentuated by pads, and said, as if it was something he said all the time: 'Fancy a trundle, Rob?'

I tried to imagine what a proper player would say on such an occasion. 'Fuck off, Gatt, what, on this fucking wicket? You must be fucking joking!' Or: 'Right, skip. About bloody time. Let's get into this fucking lot, shall we? Er, four slips, two gullies, bat-pad . . . ?'

What I think I said was: 'Er, well, gosh, of course I'd love to, but you know . . . I'm sure there's someone else. Really, I'm happy to have a little go later, but whatever. All right then.'

'Same field?' said Gatt.

The serious answer to that was: no way. For goodness' sake, it was Allan Lamb batting! He had already hit about five sixes. There were proper bowlers bowling. Test-standard bowlers, and he was – no other word for it – simply lambing it over the sightscreen. I wanted everyone on the boundary – about fifteen yards behind it, if possible. Everyone saving six, all right? But that wouldn't have been the done thing.

On the spur of the moment I decided to shorten my run-up, usually a stuttering affair with a couple of hiccups at the beginning and a strange deceleration at the end. Well, if it was good enough for Fraser . . . Also, it wouldn't be so embarrassing if I got carted. I took a deep breath, wondered whether to step off with my left foot or my right, tried the right, took two strides, felt for an instant that it was all wrong, that I'd have to pull up and start again, then saw the wicket approaching at roughly the right speed and fell into the run-up, arriving only a fraction before I was ready. The result wasn't too bad. A routine ball outside the off stump which the Dutchman swished at, and missed.

I bowled three overs, two of them all right. The third went for about twenty. Lamb collared a big six back over my head, and a couple more that missed being six only by a yard or so. But it wasn't a disaster: if we'd wanted to, we could have defended that boundary. And I did hit him on the pad once with a ball that slid into him a touch, and he was absolutely bloody plumb, and how I stopped myself kicking over the stumps in disgust I'll never know.

'Thanks, Rob,' said Gatt, with superb tact. 'Like that, like it. Bit of nip there, nice. Have a rest, okay?'

A few overs later, Lamb retired, and I found myself fielding at cover point for David Gower, with an alarming amount of space around and behind me. I tried to pass word to the captain to say that I would quite understand if he wanted someone else there, someone who could field, but he didn't seem worried. So I stumbled around in circles for a while as the ball flashed first to my left, then to my right. With Lamb, you felt as if the ball might break a bone in your hand; Gower wasn't so dangerous – you'd just have to do a lot of jogging down the bank to go and fetch it. And even doing this you feel self-conscious, as if all these proper players behind you are pulling giggly faces and thinking, Jesus, the poor sap can't even run.

One thing about fielding on Paul Getty's lovely grass, though: it's pretty easy. The outfield is so smooth the ball goes in a straight line. For occasional weekend players like me, used to stooping for balls that bounce up and hit you on the wrist, or squirt off a tuft and go below your groping fingers, it was a luxurious experience. At one point I noticed a small weed in the turf: I felt like notifying the umpire (David Shepherd – who else?) or calling Security.

From the other end, I was at a sort of shortish midwicket for the spinner. Gower flicked to leg, with that trademark carefree swish, and the ball flew straight at my shoulder. And this time – lo and behold! – I grabbed it. It was basically a dolly, but context is everything in cricket, and because it was Gower it felt like a blinder. I remembered a story of Graham Thorpe's, about how he found himself bowling to Gower on his début for Surrey. His third ball grazed the bat and thumped into his hero's pad. 'I was so overjoyed that he hadn't hit it for six that I gave a yelp of triumph. The umpire mistook it for an appeal and gave him out lbw.'

This wasn't quite as cruel as that, but I couldn't help apologizing to Gower afterwards as well, with more feeling, since I had long been a fervent admirer. 'Nu, nu, nu, nu, nu,' he said, waving it away. 'That's all right.' He genuinely didn't care, though at the time he had said, 'Agh!' when he saw the ball heading my way, and swung his bat in a gesture of what looked for a second like dissent. That's the trouble with cricket: however blithe you are, the moment of being out remains a horrible lurch, an awful dissolution of everything that, a few seconds before, had seemed possible. The single most common phrase in any dressing room, however lowly, is: '. . . and it was a shame, you know, 'cause I was starting to feel pretty good out there.' When you are out, you *always* feel as if you were feeling good out there – even if you weren't. Bowlers feel the same way. The Australian Arthur Mailey once joked, when the opposition's last man was run out with the score on a dizzy 1107: 'Rather a pity . . . I was just striking a length.'

And so the short afternoon wore on. Rory Bremner ran on for a quick thrash – he had to whizz up to London to give away a Bafta award, and nearly receive one – and soon ran back out again. Then John McCarthy came out. He looked edgy: it isn't easy to come in and keep the momentum going after people like Lamb and Gower have set the tone. Also he had spent five years as hostage in Beirut, five years in which – truth to tell – his game might have declined a little. After a while he scuffed one up in the air, just out of reach to my right. But buoyed by my previous success I dived and just got my fingers under the ball, an inch off the ground, ripping the skin off my elbow as I fell. It was rotten luck on the batsman. McCarthy took it well; I sensed that it might not have been the worst thing that ever happened to him. But the fielders actually laughed, knowing it was a tough break to be out to a catch like that. Most of the team jogged up, in the professional manner, for a handshake.

'Lamby'll know now you dropped him on purpose,' said Gatting.

'Wrong way round,' I said. 'McCarthy'll know I caught him by accident.'

But as moments of boyish glory go, it wasn't bad. Phil Tufnell trotted up, shook me by the hand, and said, 'Top drawer, Rob. Top drawer.'

Top drawer! Phil Tufnell! I could have died and gone to heaven. This from the man we had all jeered at a few years ago for not being able to catch a bus, let alone a ball; this from the man who'd done the elephants and done the poverty and what else was there to do in India. I'd always liked him, mainly because he smoked a lot and was transparently bad-tempered. And here he was. Top drawer, Rob. For one happy instant I felt folded into the comradely embrace of the cricketing fraternity. It didn't matter that it wasn't a proper match, or that no one ever called me 'Rob', or that no one was even trying, except me. And I didn't care that none of these blokes knew who the hell I was, or gave a hoot. For a few fleeting seconds me and cricket were on first-name terms.

Which is what, in the end, it is all about. Cricket is a fantasy, complicated and boring enough to sap the spirit and freeze the blood, but it offers the possibility of those redeeming moments when you do something right and are ringed by warm feelings. Nearly everyone hates fielding, which means that if you catch someone, or bowl someone, or throw down the stumps in a run-out, your teammates rush up to slap you on the back and they mean it, they really do. It isn't that they are admiring your skill or anything mundane like that: they are simply relieved and grateful that you reduced the amount of time left in the field. They say well done, but they mean thank you. It makes you feel, for a few minutes, like a benefactor.

The All-Stars ran out of overs shortly after that, and it was Middlesex's turn to bat. We – can I say we? – were far too strong, and knocked off the runs with ease. The Middlesex players were in the middle of a game against Oxford University, just up the road. This was their day off, and it was probably the last Sunday they'd have off for the next five months; so it was decent of them to support Gatting by turning out today. And they don't, in truth, especially like playing in games like this. I had enjoyed a great day out; for them it was just another chance for Sod's Law to come into play and hand them an injury, or be caught by someone like me. The season stretched out ahead of them like a long-distance march.

Clouds piled up over the Chilterns, and the spectators climbed back into their German cars and cruised back towards the motorway. It was eerie, everyone leaving like that; those of us still in cricket clothes wondered why we were still here. There didn't seem much point carrying on: the people had gone, the sun had gone – what was the point? It wasn't even a match, really, more like a parody of a match, a perfectly preserved specimen of fine cricket, served in a beautiful decanter, but not really meant to be drunk. Out in the middle, the fielding side had long since decided that they were going to lose, and urged every ball to the boundary, hoping to hasten the end. This, it occurred to me, must be how it feels to play county cricket.

Getty himself hung on to hand over an impromptu trophy to Mike Gatting. 'Don't be too pleased,' he said. 'I want it back.' They froze the moment for a photographer.

And that was that.

It started to rain. The new season had begun.

THE MATCHES

Group A

Hyderabad. West Indies beat Zimbabwe by six wickets. Zimbabwe 151 (Ambrose 3 for 28); West Indies 155 for 4 (in 29.3 overs, Campbell 47, Lara 43 not out)

Cuttack. India beat Kenya by seven wickets. Kenya 199 (Tikolo 65, Kumble 3 for 28); India 203 for 3 (in 41.5 overs, Tendulkar 127, Jadeja 53)

Colombo. Sri Lanka beat Zimbabwe by six wickets. Zimbabwe 228 (Campbell 75, Vaas 2 for 30); Sri Lanka 229 for 4 (in 37 overs, De Silva 91, Gurusinha 87)

Gwalior. India beat West Indies by five wickets. West Indies 173 (Richardson 47, Kumble 3 for 35); India 174 for 6 (Tendulkar 70)

Vishakhapatnam. Australia beat Kenya by 96 runs. Australia 304 (M. Waugh 130, S. Waugh 82); Kenya 207 (Otieno 85, Odumbe 50, Reiffel 2 for 18)

Patna. Zimbabwe beat Kenya by five wickets. Kenya 134 (Strang 5 for 21); Zimbabwe 137 for 5 (in 42.2 overs, Flower 45)

Bombay. Australia beat India by five wickets. Australia 258 (M. Waugh 126, Taylor 59); India 242 (in 48 overs, Tendulkar 90, Manjrekar 62, Fleming 5 for 36)

Pune. Kenya beat West Indies by 73 runs. Kenya 166; West Indies 93

Nagpur. Australia beat Zimbabwe by 8 wickets. Zimbabwe 154 (Warne 4 for 34); Australia 158 for 2 (in 36 overs, M. Waugh 76 not out)

Delhi. Sri Lanka beat India by 6 wickets. India 271 for 3 (Tendulkar 137, Azharuddin 72); Sri Lanka 272 for 4 (in 48.4 overs, Jayasuriya 79, Tillekeratne 70 not out)

Jaipur. West Indies beat Australia by four wickets. Australia 229 (Ponting 102, S. Waugh 57); West Indies 232 for 6 (in 48.5 overs, Richardson 93 not out, Lara 60)

Kanpur. India beat Zimbabwe by 40 runs. India 247 for 5 (Kambli 106, Sidhu 80); Zimbabwe 207 (Raju 3 for 30)

Kandy. Sri Lanka beat Kenya by 144 runs. Sri Lanka 398 for 5 (De Silva 145, Gurusinha 84, Ranatunga 75 not out); Kenya 254 for 7 (Tikolo 96)

Group B

Ahmedabad. New Zealand beat England by 11 runs. New Zealand 239 for 6 (Astle 101); England 228 for 9 (Hick 85)

Rawalpindi. South Africa beat UAE by 169 runs. South Africa 321 (Kirsten 188, Cronje 57); UAE 152 for 8 (Donald 3 for 21)

Vadodora. New Zealand beat Holland by 119 runs. New Zealand 307 (Spearman 68, Fleming 66, Cairns 52, Parore 55); Holland 188 for 7 (Harris 3 for 24)

Peshawar. England beat UAE by 8 wickets. UAE 136 (Smith 3 for 29); England 140 for 2 (in 35 overs, Thorpe 44 not out)

Faisalabad. South Africa beat New Zealand by five wickets. New Zealand 177 (Donald 3 for 43); South Africa 178 for 5 (in 37.3 overs, Cronje 78)

Peshawar. England beat Holland by 49 runs. England 279 (Hick 104, Thorpe 89); Holland 230 for 6 (Van Noortwijk 64, Zuiderent 54)

Gujranawala. Pakistan beat UAE by nine wickets. UAE 109 (Mushtaq Ahmed 3 for 16); Pakistan 112 for 1 (in 18 overs, Anwar 40 not out)

Rawalpindi. South Africa beat England by 78 runs. South Africa 230 (Rhodes 37, Martin 3 for 33); England 153 (Thorpe 46)

Lahore. Pakistan beat Holland by eight wickets. Holland 145 for 7 (Waqar Younis 4 for 26); Pakistan 151 for 2 (in 30.4 overs, Anwar 83 not out)

Faisalabad. New Zealand beat UAE by 109 runs. New Zealand 276 (Twose 92, Spearman 78); UAE 167 for 9 (Samerasekera 47 not out, Thomson 3 for 20)

Karachi. South Africa beat Pakistan by five wickets. Pakistan 242 for 6 (Sohail 111); South Africa 243 for 5 (Cullinan 65)

Lahore. UAE beat Holland by seven wickets. Holland 216 for 9 (Cantrell 47, Aponso 45, Dukhanwala 5 for 29); UAE 220 for 3 (in 44.2 overs, Raza 84, Mohammad 51 not out)

Karachi. Pakistan beat England by 7 wickets. England 249 (Smith 75, Atherton 66, Thorpe 52 not out); Pakistan 250 for 3 (in 47.4 overs, Anwar 71, Ijaz 70, Inzaman 53 not out)

Rawalpindi. South Africa beat Holland by 160 runs. South Africa 328 (Hudson 161, Kirsten 83); Holland 168 (Donald 2 for 21, Symcox 2 for 22)

Lahore. Pakistan beat New Zealand by 46 runs. Pakistan 281 for 5 (Anwar 62, Sohail 50); New Zealand 235

Quarter-finals

Faisalabad. Sri Lanka beat England by five wickets. England 235 for 8 (DeFreitas 67); Sri Lanka 236 for 5 (Jayasuriya 82)

Bangalore. India beat Pakistan by 39 runs. India 287 for 8 (Sidhu 93, Jadeja 45); Pakistan 248 for 9 (Sohail 55, Anwar 48, Prasad 3 for 45)

Karachi. West Indies beat South Africa by 19 runs. West Indies 264 for 8 (Lara 111); South Africa 245 (Cullinan 69, Adams 3 for 53)

Madras. Australia beat New Zealand by six wickets. New Zealand 286 (Harris 130, Germon 89); Australia 289 for 4 (M. Waugh 110, S. Waugh 59)

Semi-finals

Calcutta. Sri Lanka beat India. Sri Lanka 251 (De Silva 66, Mahanama 58); India 120 for 8 (Tendulkar 65, Jayasuriya 3 for 12). Match abandoned after 34.1 overs

Chandigarh. Australia beat West Indies by 5 runs. Australia 207 (Law 72, Bevan 69, Ambrose 2 for 26); West Indies 202 (Chanderpaul 80, Richardson 49 not out, Lara 45, Warne 4 for 36)

Final

Lahore. Sri Lanka beat Australia by seven wickets. Australia 241 (Taylor 74, De Silva 3 for 43); Sri Lanka 245 for 3 (De Silva 107 not out, Gurusinha 65)